CW00493366

The Green Man
God, Fairy, or Extraterrestrial?

By S. L. Payne

Cover Illustrated by Daniil Malkov

ISBN: 9798835339211

DEDICATION

This book is dedicated to my wonderful family and friends who supported me on this passion project and have learnt to embrace the crazy!

CONTENTS

ACKNOWLEDGMENTS

A lot of the source material for this book was collected by using a combination of books on the relevant topics as well as Podcast's, YouTube Channels, Websites and Newspaper articles. The breadth of information and the amount of detailed research found on these platforms cannot be overstated enough. Without these forms of media, I would not have had the access to the amount of information that I did, particularly people's own personal accounts of encounters which have made this book possible. I would also like to acknowledge the T.V Documentary Series 'Hellier' by Planet Weird as it was this TV show which finally gave me the nudge to investigate 'Your Green Man'.

Links to all the sources used are in the Reference section of this book.

INTRODUCTION

'During all these centuries the Celt has kept in his heart some affinity with the mighty beings ruling in the Unseen, once so evident to the heroic races who preceded him. His legends and faery tales have connected his soul with the inner lives of air and water and earth, and they in turn have kept his heart sweet with hidden influence.' ÷ A. E.

So, who is the Green Man? He seems to be everywhere and yet nowhere, his influence permeating religion, folklore, and mythology. He is 'that which lurks in the Woods', an idea, a myth, even a scary story. As children, we are taught from a young age, not to go into the woods alone, to be careful, be vigilant as bad things can happen in there. All the fairy tale stories contain warnings of witches, wolves, and all the other bad things that lurk there. Did our ancestors know something that we don't? Were these simply stories to entertain and scare children or were they meant to be something more? The Public Services Announcements of their day. A warning to be heeded.

Certainly, these types of warnings and scary stories are alive and well today, simply look at the Missing 411 phenomenon. Some of you reading this book are probably already familiar with this curiosity but if you are not, I will briefly summarize. A retired US Police Officer, David Paulides, and his team have been investigating the series of strange disappearances of hundreds, if not thousands of people from American National Forests and Parks. According to David himself, he started looking into this phenomenon after two Forest Parks employees reached out to him and told him they thought something strange was occurring. They disclosed to him that people seem to be disappearing from the National Parks under mysterious circumstances, yet no one seems to know how or why. Many people appear to disappear off very easy trails, or seemingly disappear in the blink of an eye in full view of the people that they are with. David and his team have since spent many years researching, categorizing, and documenting all of these occurrences and his findings are just astonishing. Even more astonishing is that this phenomenon isn't just limited to the US, as instances of similar disappearances are being reported all over the World.

Once I stumbled onto this subject matter I was hooked. What on earth could it be? What could be causing so many people to just disappear completely, either never to be seen again or eventually be found deceased in the most bizarre of locations? I must have listened to dozens, if not more podcasts on the subject and watched all YouTube content, and documentaries, and even watched the several films on these occurrences that David's CanAm group has made. I read the books and scoured multiple forums and websites for any details I could find on all these cases. In the midst of all of this content I just kept coming back to the same question, what is in our Woods?

As I dived deeper and deeper into the high strangeness of our woods and our forests, the mythos seemed to fray, splintering off into many separate threads. I followed each one that I could eagerly, eyes wide, mouth agape, devouring it all. So many tales and firsthand accounts of encounters with the weird from deep within the woods. There were the usual Cryptid stories of Bigfoot, Dogman, the Jersey Devil, and the Chupacabra, as well as some more unusual cryptids which I had not heard of before. Tales straight from the pages of a horror book, stories of Centaurs, Goatmen, zombie-fied Deer, and even reports of sightings of strange Tetradactyl like creature. Unfathomably large birdlike creatures which seemed to reside in the trees and nest in caves and terrorize unsuspecting humans. The list of the entities I encountered seemed endless, some much more prevalent than others but still the number of creatures I was being exposed to seemed to grow by the month.

One such fascinating encounter that I stumbled upon whilst listening to this endless stream of odd encounters was that of the 'Glimmer Man'. This one, in particular, grabbed my attention as I had a very similar experience, although mine did not occur in the woods. In David Paulides '*Missing 411 – The Hunted*'[1] book there are stories of people encountering a strange creature in the woods. At first, they cannot see it properly, appearing as more of a light anomaly until it moves, then it is described as being almost 'invisible' as if it were camouflaging itself using some kind of cloaking device (earning it the 'Predator' nickname after the creature in the 1980 Arnold Schwarzenegger Movie of the same name).

The most interesting account of such an encounter (as described in David's Book) is that of Jan Maccabee. David also discussed this one in an episode of Where Did the Road Go Radio Show whilst promoting his *Missing 411 'The Hunted'*[2] book which is where I initially heard of it. Jan Maccabee is described as a veteran hunter and proficient woodsman with many years'

---

[1] David Paulides 'Missing 411 – The Hunted' (Published 2019).

[2] Where Did the Road Go Radio Show - YouTube (David Paulides on Missing 411 Hunters Part 1).

worth of experience in the outdoors. Jan's encounter occurred whilst she was up in her tree stand early one evening (about 6:30 pm) bow hunting. She had been there for an hour or so and was beginning to get a little bored. In order to stave off the boredom she began messaging friends and also around this time decided to take a picture of herself in the tree stand. She recalls at this point, that the forest went deathly quiet. She could no longer hear the usual sounds of the forest, she couldn't hear the birds singing or animals foraging, it was like she had just walked into a sound vacuum. Slightly unnerved she messaged a friend to say that she thought something was wrong due to the lack of sounds coming from the woods *"Something is wrong. The woods just went to a dead silence. No squirrels, no birds, no crickets. Is odd! (6:23 PM EDT) "*

It was at this time that she noticed a strange light distortion moving from left to right in her line of vision about 20ft away from her. She described it as looking through saran wrap (clingfilm in the U.K). She took off her glasses to rub her eyes as she thought that maybe her eyes were tired causing the distortion, but the strange moving anomaly continued. She still had her phone in her hand from sending the text message, so she snapped a quick picture but as soon as she snapped the picture the distortion disappeared. She continued to sit in the tree stand for a further hour and a half before descending and going home for dinner. She quickly forgot about this odd occurrence and didn't think to mention it to anyone.

Later that evening Jan's nephew posted on Facebook that he and some friends had witnessed a strange light anomaly in the sky during band practice, that day after school. He described his sighting as a huge bright light that appeared over the field and then began to move sideways, in a matter of 5 seconds or so it had disappeared, getting smaller with almost every passing second. About 5 minutes later it reappeared, this time it was amber in color. Apparently, this strange light in the sky had also been witnessed by students the previous year.

At this point, Jan told her husband Bruce, who coincidentally happens to be a renowned optical physicist about the experience that she'd had earlier that day. She proceeded to show him the picture that she had snapped of this bizarre anomaly as it had disappeared. Bruce was very interested and decided to review the photo in greater detail. What he found most peculiar about this photograph was the resolution. He said that the camera on her phone took photographs at a resolution of 1024 pixels (horizontal) x 768 pixels (vertical) but this one picture was at a resolution of 528 x 400 which he says is impossible for that phone's camera. Certainly, it is most bizarre. Bruce does a thorough and interesting analysis of this photograph and the link to his findings are in the Bibliography for anyone who would like to read it.[3]

In the witness accounts of this 'Glimmer Man,' people report seeing something moving within the trees or sometimes even at ground level that they can't quite see. At first, it is hard to make out, people often assuming that it's a trick of the light or their own eyes but once it begins to move it becomes much more noticeable. People comment that it looks like it is wearing some kind of cloaking device as you can see the movement and outline of the creature but yet it appears as if you can see right through it. Many have said that it looks like you're looking through clingfilm (saran wrap), others comment it looks more fluid, like water or even mercury, others that it appears as if the light just reflects off of it so it appears to be more of a light distortion than anything else. All, however, experienced some form of intelligent entity which seemed to be aware of their presence. Some had uneventful experiences such as in Jan's case, but others have had more traumatic experiences saying that they were 'chased' by it and fled for fear of their lives. Many never returning to the woods again.

This entity seems to be being seen more frequently with stories becoming more common, it appears to now go by the name 'The Glimmer Man'. I had heard of the Glimmer man but didn't realize that it was the same Predator-like creature that now seems to have earned itself a spot as a staple on most Fringe Podcasts.

My story is slightly different from most I've heard. Firstly, I am not a Hunter and secondly, this did not take place outside in the Woods. My encounter was in my Kitchen. Interestingly, I have recently heard of more 'predator' type encounters taking place in people's homes and bizarrely even connected to people's encounters with Praying Mantis type entities. In several stories of people's encounters with these odd-looking humanoids this 'bug' will be seen either cloaked or phasing in and out of this cloaking effect and at times also accompanied by what people commonly believe to be the stereotypical 'grey' alien. Again, the commonalities between phenomena experienced by people are astounding.

---

[3] David Maccabee's investigation of his wife's photograph.

http://www.brumac.mysite.com/JANs_Phenomenon/JANs_Phenomenon.htm

In my house at the time, there were two large windows. One to the front aspect and the other to the side aspect. I was standing in front of the window to the side aspect carefully debating what type of sandwich to make for lunch when I noticed movement out of the corner of my eye. We have a cat so I assumed that she must have also noted that it was lunchtime and had followed me in for some grub. I looked down and around, but I couldn't see her, assuming she must have turned and gone back out of the kitchen I went back to the task at hand. This happened several times, and as I was starting to get more irritated by this, I stopped what I was doing and just turned around. Staring intently at the floor and trying to 'do' science in my head wondering if maybe it was light reflecting off some surface casting shadows, I saw 'it' move.

Just like other witnesses had said, it looked just like the camouflage effect from the Predator movie. Yet this creature was much smaller and not at all humanoid, it had 8 legs and was arachnid in shape. It was the size of a large domestic cat but spider-like in appearance. I was gob smacked. I didn't feel any fear, I think I was just too confused for fear, I didn't know what to do so I just stood there dumbfounded watching it scuttle about the floor. I wondered if it even knew I was there, eventually, after a minute or two my disbelief turned to bemusement, and I said aloud 'you know I can see you right?'. Evidently, it didn't as it stopped in its tracks and dissipated right in front of me. I did try to 'google' what I had seen but didn't have any success, it wasn't until The Hunters book and David's interview on *Where did the Road Go,* where he discussed this case that the penny dropped. That's what I had in seen, at least some version of it. So, what was it and why was it in my house? What did it want and why didn't it seem to notice that I was there or know that I could see it? Is it the same thing that people are seeing whilst in the Woods, are they linked and could they be connected to the high strangeness going on in our National Parks, our Woods, and our Forests? It's questions like this, that got me thinking and led me to write this book.

How did I get here?

I've had many odd experiences throughout my life and probably up until my mid to late twenties I viewed these experiences through a very narrow lens. The 'Paranormal' to me simply meant ghosts and things that go bump in the night. I never gave any thought to there being anything more than this. Everything I experienced was funneled through this one filter giving me a very blinkered view of the world. It has only been in the last decade or so that I have come to understand that there is much more to the world around me. A vast unseen world full of strange and unexplainable phenomena and my ghosts are just the tip of the iceberg. Now I see that everything that exists is so vast and so complex that even the most brilliant of minds would struggle to comprehend it in its entirety. The more I learn the more I am convinced that many of these elements are connected, or at the very least exist independently yet parallel to each other. All together creating a mammoth Spiders Web of the 'preternatural'. A Venn diagram of weirdness so vast that it is simply impossible to stand back and see the bigger picture, let alone try to understand it all. All you can do is pick one of the great web's silken strands, follow it and see where it leads you.

The road to this point has been interesting for want of a better word. The 'paranormal' has always been a significant part of my life. Ever since I was a small child the veil between dimensions has been thin. Sometimes, I could even see through it and see things that terrified me. Some might imagine this to be a gift, not me however, I hated it. As a small child, I was terrified, as soon as the lights went out and I was alone in my room the monsters would come out to play. As I got older and into my teenage years it became easier to suppress. I would simply ignore it. I would shut my eyes tight and pray for it to just go away. Saying to myself 'it's not real' over and over like a little mantra until I fell back asleep. I became very good at suppressing it, keeping it hidden, and pretending it didn't exist. So much so, that I felt, at least for a while 'normal'. Other than the odd occurrence which would impose itself on me, it was pretty good going for a while.

I chose not to involve myself in anything paranormal during these years. I didn't relish it, and I certainly didn't want to encourage it. I would sometimes tell some of my stories at sleepovers under the guise of Ghost Stories to scare and entertain but never admitted to any of them being real. When I was a teenager there wasn't the internet as we know it today, so the only information on the Paranormal I had any access to was in books or even in movies. I remember buying one book about local ghosts in my area, but it was just a collection of folk tales and people's alleged true stories, and they didn't give me any background or understanding of what I was experiencing. So, I managed to forget about it for a while, focusing on the drama of high school, teenage life, and bad haircuts. However, as with all things repressed, slowly, it makes its way back up to the surface.

I was in my early to mid-twenties when the activity started to ramp up again. At the time I was sharing a house with some friends, one of whom was my best friend who I had met several years earlier at university. I was lucky as I discovered not long into our friendship, that she too, was 'sensitive' like me and it was a delight to finally have someone to talk to about it all. I told her everything from start to finish securing in the process a lifelong friendship.

Both of us come from very similar backgrounds and held similar belief systems so neither of us had ever really investigated the paranormal too in depth. So, it was at this point in my sheltered life, I began to branch out. I bought some tarot cards, saw a medium, and for kicks, we would visit allegedly haunted locations, sneak about in the dead of night hoping to 'catch' something but mostly just scaring ourselves. Again, it never really extended further than ghosts and ghouls until we decided to do something a bit more exotic and attend a spiritual group. This group was quite broad in its appeal, a general discussion group for all things paranormal and spiritual. It sounded like a good jumping off point, and I was excited to hear other people's stories. I wasn't quite sure what to expect, but it certainly wasn't what I got.

At this point in my life, I considered myself perfectly 'normal' not like the 'kooks' that usually attend these types of things. I am ashamed to say that I was quick to judge back then and like most folk pretty narrow-minded. It was the first 'group' of this kind that I had ever attended. When I was at University I had gone to a few Mind, Body, Soul conventions with my friends but mostly to buy incense and clothing, and maybe have the odd tarot reading. This was my first more 'intimate' foray into the spiritual and it was a heck of a start. As soon as we arrived, I felt uncomfortable. We sat in a small circle, support group style, I think that there must have been about 10 people in attendance including my friend and me. Then the group leader went around the room for introductions and asked us each for a brief explanation of what had brought us to this group. I kept my introduction brief not wanting to be drawn into a conversation as I was quickly regretting my decision to attend. I don't remember much of what the other people there had to say except for one, the last lady to speak.

This small middle-aged Irish woman started to speak. As she did, she immediately locked eyes with me. This unnerved me to the point that I gave a nervous smile and looked to my friend for reassurance to which she gave me a 'what a crackpot' look right back. The woman persisted, there was something about her voice and her demeanor that frankly sent chills down my spine. She looked me dead in the eyes and said, 'I've been given a message for Sam, I've been given a message and I think it's' for you'.

She proceeded to tell us one of the most bonkers stories that I had ever heard. She told us that she knew that she was an alien, or to be precise, an alien consciousness in a human body. That she remembered how she came to be in her current human form and why. She then told us her story. She remembered being aboard a spaceship, she called it the Mother Ship. She had an awareness that she was unhappy, that she knew she was going to have to be 'born again' and was not looking forward to it, she said she could remember feeling anxiety and frustration but also a sense that she had no choice in the matter. The one thing that she did have a choice in, was the life she was to be born into. She said that they (I assume these Alien beings) showed her three clips, like movie trailers. None of these clips looked particularly appealing but nonetheless, she was asked to pick one. She eventually settled on the one where she saw two girls chatting and playing happily in the back of a car. She thought that the children appeared to be going on a road trip, they seemed happy, and she figured maybe this would be a good life.

Aliens, it would seem, would make great Spin Doctors as her life was far from happy. Her mother was distant and abusive, her father regularly assaulted her, and life was incredibly tough. The clip she had seen was a memory that she now has of a holiday that her family went on when she was a child, which, she says ironically, is one of the only happy memories of her hard life. After this woman had recounted her rather horrific story, the meeting finished, and everyone left. I was rather shell-shocked by what had happened but not wanting to let my friend see just how shaken I was by this I laughed it off. The drive home was quiet, I wasn't in the mood for much talk and we both agreed that maybe that wasn't quite for us and resolved not to go again. I don't know why this experience affected me so much, but it did, I remember it today as clearly as I did when it happened, and it has stayed with me ever since. I thought this lady to be crazy at the time but now I think her story may have some truth to it and I believe this experience to be a pivotal point in my life. The moment when the world I thought I knew started to change irreversibly and I knew if I needed answers, I was going to have to find them myself.

I believe that we have these defining moments at certain points in our lives and that they set us on the paths that we are meant to go down and shape the person that we are to become. In one afternoon, I went from believing we die, we go to heaven or maybe hell if we're unlucky to what if, when we die, we get to be born again? What if this whole reincarnation gig is for real? What if we don't get a choice, what if we are forced to live out awful traumatic lives again and again stuck in a sick Groundhog Day loop for some unknown purpose and Alien kicks?

Are we all just alien consciousnesses? Is the human experience just a theme park? Each life is a ride delicately constructed to give us a specific experience to teach us a lesson and we can only finally leave and find eternal peace when all the rides are done. These thoughts horrified me. I don't want to have multiple lives forced upon me, being tortured within each so that I can learn who knows what before the solace of dying is ripped away from me just to go through the process all over again. If I feared Death before, I feared it so much more now.

After this little drama I pretty much left well enough alone, I didn't attend any further groups and just got on with the hustle and bustle of everyday life. At this point in my life, I was now a mother to a young child and time was a precious commodity so my love for books became replaced by a love of audiobooks and podcasts. Podcasts were becoming more popular and became a wonderful source of spooky information and a constant delight for me. I could listen and learn but more importantly, get on with doing the necessary daily chores. The choice of topics was so vast I found myself devouring it all. I followed that white rabbit down so many rabbit holes! At this point, my fascination with all things 'Woodland' began.

If you go down to the Woods Today…

I just had this feeling that all this weird Woodland phenomenon was linked. Like a cop in a gritty crime show, I took all the years of podcasts, TV Shows, Books, Forums, and websites and made myself a mental 'Investigation Board'. Taking a step back from this board one thing was evident, whatever these things are, they all seem to come from the same place. So, after nearly a decade of podcasts, documentaries, YouTube videos, books, TV shows, and the internet, I was convinced that something otherworldly was behind a vast amount of this phenomenon.

What cemented my theory was a TV documentary series called Hellier[4]. Hellier is a 2-season documentary series whose premise is the investigation by a paranormal research group of reports of 'Goblins' terrorizing a small old coal mining community. The paranormal research team was initially contacted by a gentleman called 'David' who claimed that his property was being targeted by small entities that he referred to as 'extraterrestrials'. He said that they seemed to live deep within the old mining tunnel systems near his home in Kentucky and would come out periodically to cause havoc in the area and terrorize this man's family. These creatures would frequently look into his children's windows at night to scare them, they would actively try to break into the house, vandalize the property, and were even alleged to have taken the family dog.

The team, after doing some digging connected the case to the 1955

---

[4] Hellier (TV \Mini |Series) – Planet Weird (aired January 2019).

Hopkinsville Goblin case. In the Hopkinsville case, a farmhouse was reportedly besieged by small grey hairless creatures that were at the time described as 'Goblins'. Whilst I was looking into the Hopkinsville case I also came across the Shaver Mystery, which I thought tied into the same phenomenon. From what I can find, the Shaver Mystery concerns a man named Richard Shaver who alleged that whilst doing his usual job, malfunctioning radio equipment allowed him to hear "torture sessions" by evil underground entities. He subsequently left his job after these occurrences. This event was left unreported until 1943 when he sent a couple of letters to the editor of Amazing Stories magazine describing a prehistoric underground civilization who were kidnapping, torturing, and killing humans[5], which will link into topics I'll cover later in the book.

This one case in particular grabbed my attention because of the reference to the Goblins. Stories of Fae folk have always fascinated me, and so I eagerly followed the team as they uncovered more and more high strangeness in Hellier and indeed the surrounding areas. It seemed like they had hit the paranormal jackpot, it was all here, Fae Folk, Aliens, massive cave systems, underground military bases, tales of human captives, human sacrifice, and there right in amongst it all The Green Man.

It was Season 2: Episode 4 "Your Green Man" which set my path for me. Within this particular episode, lead investigator Greg Newkirk is sent an email from a lady named 'Amy'. Within the body of this email, the sender details an event that sounds truly horrific. She and her partner had decided to take their RV and go camping for a few days. They went deep into the woods of Kentucky and set up camp. They were awoken in the dead of night to screams and cries for help which sounded to them to be coming from a young woman. 'Amy' was horrified and immediately wanted to go and find this poor soul to help but her partner wisely countered that there were only two of them, they had no weapons or way to defend themselves and had no idea how many people were out there and instead of helping they would most likely find themselves enduring the same fate. So, they hid, terrified, in the RV, listening to the woman's agonizing screams and pleading for about 30 minutes when the sender says that the woman fell silent, and they suspected that she had been eventually 'dispatched'.

The next day determined to find out what had happened she followed the tracks back to what she says was a cabin in the woods. A cabin that she was aware of, being local to the area, but until now had never paid it any attention.

---

[5] Post on Reddit by Solaris716 'The Shaver Mystery'
https://www.reddit.com/r/hellier/comments/emfuro/the_shaver_mystery/

She found that it had locked military-grade gates and caged windows. Odd, considering it was just a dilapidated old cabin, what on earth there could require such security? Determined to find out more she crawled in under the fences and broke into the cabin. There she found filthy beds shackled to rafters, in the attic she saw walls stained with blood and feces, human teeth and bleeding bowls, what she thought looked like human bones, and oddly a significant amount of paperwork.

Horrified she fled the scene and immediately reported the incident to the authorities, but she said nothing was done about it as the Police didn't seem to believe her and refused to follow up without further evidence. Now after her investigation she believes the police were complicit in the cover up and knew about the cabin which is why they didn't follow it up. After this incident she said she started to dig deeper, she doesn't go into too much detail on how or what she started looking into but ended her emails (there were 2) with the statement that her digging has put her onto the radar of some very bad people, and she is now fearful for her life. She alluded to a massive cover up, to government elements, the police, and elected members of the community all being involved in some kind of Pagan Cult that worshipped The Green Man. Now, this isn't the first time I've come across references to cults, ritual sacrifice, and Pagan Gods but it was the specific reference to The Green Man which piqued my interest. As I have mentioned I've been down many 'conspiracy' rabbit holes, so I've come across multiple references to the New World Order, the Global elite wishing to orchestrate global events in order to herd people towards a totalitarian government, one society, one government, one religion all controlled by certain elite bloodlines. This is nothing new but it's the reference to the Green Man which grabbed me, as certainly there is a theory among the 'conspiracy' or 'truther' movement that this New World Religion will be a nature-based 'Green' religion based on Pagan beliefs. Could it be that the Green Man is the intended figurehead for this intended 'one' religion?

'Amy' had described all the usual markers of occultist activity that I've been hearing about across multiple conspiracy topics. References to underground cave systems, human captives, child trafficking, human torture, and sacrifice and all seemingly ritualistic in nature. In the case of Hellier and the alleged conspiracy there, it would appear that the sacrifice is being undertaken as a form of worship or as a summoning ritual for their Green Man. Religions have always required a sacrifice of some kind, be it symbolic or physical, Gods it would appear must be fed to remain appeased. Now we can only speculate on the actual existence of such a cult, this is not proven but certainly, such cults have existed elsewhere and certainly, such practices were undertaken by ancient civilizations all over the world. Could it be that this

New World Order, is not New at all but indeed an attempt to go back to the 'Old' World order? In my later chapters on Archetypes, I think there is good evidence to support this hypothesis.

Back to 'Amy's story, at one point she references a Gate Keeper, who she said was able to perform magic, she said that he held what looked to be a curved walking stick with a crystal (we'll look at this detail in more depth later in this book). She said that he was able to suffocate her simply by blowing her a kiss. There were no additional details on where she saw him or where this incident occurred but no doubt, she was fearful for her life. Magick and ceremonial rituals have long gone hand in hand with many ancient people such as the Druids commonly using Magick as part of their religious practices. As with many beliefs all over the world, Magick can be used to shapeshift, project 'glamours', and of course, as in the example above to cause physical harm to people. This 'affecting' of others whether in a healing and positive way or in a more nefarious negative way has long been suggested as being possible in many different spiritual belief systems all over the world with people still turning to witchcraft for spells to make people fall in love or to cause bad luck. The practice of using Voodoo dolls for example or the use of witches' spell bags for protection or to hex is still common to this day.

Certainly, it has been said that the Sorcerers of old such as Merlin or the Druids from the Celtic faith, who were functioning at high levels of occult knowledge were able to harness and utilize magick as a type of technology. There are many accounts of Merlin shapeshifting and of him levitating rocks and boulders. Certainly, it can be seen as a weapon of sorts, with there being no great difference between highly sophisticated technology that is unknown to us and 'Magick'. Where does one stop and the other begin? Indeed, the great Arthur C. Clarke is quoted as saying '*Any sufficiently advanced technology is indistinguishable from magic*'. There is something to be said for the passing down of cyphers, sigils, rituals, and spells from generation to generation. If indeed the origin of these rituals and this powerful knowledge is extraterrestrial or ultra-terrestrial in nature, then we can logically take the leap and suggest that they (non-human entities) use some form of magick as a tool and at times as a weapon. It could be the ritual required to call them forward, to open portals, and in some more nefarious instances control the actions of another human being. Certainly, when reading and listening to many accounts of alleged 'alien abductions' there are often reports of aircraft having symbols and hieroglyphs either on the outside of the craft or noted inside the craft. Could these markings be Magick Sigils capable of opening the portals through which they travel?

There is no shortage of mythology surrounding the old Gods, Kings, Queens, and the Heroes of Old being able to weld great supernatural powers. Some were able to harness the powers of nature. It is said that many great Kings and Queens even had spells put over their tombs so that if disturbed there would be punishment. It is said that some tomb robbers reported stories of great thunderstorms, lightning, and heavy rains occurring almost instantaneously when certain tombs had been disturbed. Now whether this is a myth and designed to keep people from grave robbing or whether there is something more scientific such as the knowledge of geometry being used to harness and utilize natural phenomena in such a way is unknown but either way, it makes for a great story [6].

Concerning this 'Gate Keeper' referenced, I am unsure specifically what the term means, I can only assume that the Gate Keeper is considered the protector of the portal, the link between this world and the 'other' world, and someone who actively keeps outside influence or interest at bay, such as in this case. It should be said that high-level magicians who have ascended to become spiritual masters possess great power. These are people who come from a great line of priests, architects, astronomers, mathematicians, and alchemists. As mentioned above, this knowledge can be welded negatively and used as a weapon, which in this case it certainly appears to have been. The threatening act was a deterrent to scare this witness out of pursuing her line of enquiry any further.

This email was very interesting, as Greg read the contents aloud for the camera, I felt my blood run a little cold, it was quite unnerving. 'This is it' I thought, and my little light bulb switched on. There were just so many synchronicities, so many leads, and threads, and all of them it seemed, at least to me, led to this 'Green Man'. In this story, he seemed to be the sun around which the planets of weirdness orbited. All the high strangeness in our National Parks and Forests, the missing people, the reports and sightings of cryptids, weird creatures, and Fae Folk, stories of Pagan Cults, and ritual sacrifice. I believe that he is somehow, part of the vast amount of it.

So, who is he, this God of Old? One of the few old Gods still recognized and worshipped today despite our modern society's preference for science over God. He is likely one of the Old Gods, one who reigned from his forested kingdom long before man existed. He, who is seen as a giver of life but also the destroyer. Worshipped under many different names by many different people the whole world over. The Son of God Archetype. Given life only to have it snatched away before his redemptive rebirth. His story repeated in many different religions and myths for thousands of years. Who was he originally and where did his story begin?

The Green Man's Origin

So how to answer the question of who is the Green Man? The truth is no one knows for certain. In my research into his origins, I have read many differing opinions. Some historians and folklorists believe that he is of early Christian origin due to his effigy being on many medieval churches scattered all over the UK and Northern Europe. Others believe his origin to predate Christianity and speculate that his roots are within the Pagan religions and mythology. Some believe him to be benevolent, derived from Nature spirits whilst others posit that he is malevolent and symbolic of Demonic intention. For the basis of my book, I shall be using information from several excellent books, which whilst their opinions differ slightly from each other, were written so well, so extensively, and with such passion that they inspired me to write this book. I will be mentioning these books below and also referencing them in my References and Sources chapter. If anyone would like to read further on the topic, please check out these books. They are more than worthy of your time.

In my experience, it has been extremely difficult to research The Green Man's origins as our history only goes back as far as there is written word or drawing to corroborate it, and even then, it is hardly like one can 'Fact' check it. It does seem though, as if his origins predate written history and I believe the original archetype to be as old as mankind itself, maybe even older. It is this 'original' archetype that truly interests me. This character, who seems to originate from a narrative handed down to us for millennia. A character in the 'Mother' religion, this ground zero from which all our known religions seem to derive. Certainly, there is good evidence to support such a universal religion existing at one time, which for reasons unknown, seemed to then splinter into the vast array of religious ideas that we have today. Could some cataclysmic event, have occurred in our past which destroyed this original civilization leaving only the remnants to blow in the wind scattering this narrative across the globe? I certainly believe so. So, who is this Green Man and how has his Archetype survived into the present day where multiple versions of him still seem to be thriving?

Here in the UK, you can see his influence everywhere, from quaint garden ornaments in everyday Garden Centers to the names of many of our country Pubs. His effigy is part of our culture, it seems in our modern times to encapsulate ideas of nature and our relationship with it, as well as more romantic Pagan religious ideologies. He seems to be everywhere and yet somehow is able to hover just below our radar so as to be almost invisible.

He reminds me of the great line from the 1995 film 'The Usual suspects' where the main antagonist comments that *"The greatest trick the Devil ever pulled was convincing the world he didn't exist."* If you asked anyone off the street in the UK and probably even into Northern Europe who he was, I'm guessing over half wouldn't have a clue, yet if you showed them a picture of one of his 'Faces' they'd immediately recognize him.

Why? - because we know him, even if we are not consciously aware that we do. He seems so intrinsic to us Northern Europeans that he is as familiar to us as the many Christian images we see all around us. So how can it be that we know so little about one of the most recognizable faces in our collective consciousness? Indeed, his face is the most prolific non-Christian Symbol to be found in Northern Europe. There are many different iterations of his form, but the most common and well-known example is the 'foliate head'

This carving of a "foliate head" type was found on the Erzsebet ter fountain in Budapest

This version has the face covered in foliage, usually, the foliage is leaves, commonly oak but also vine or Ivy like (which will be significant in the later chapters). The second is the 'Disgorging' Head

The Green Man carving at Rosslyn Chapel, Scotland

In this image, it appears that the Green Man is either devouring or 'birthing' the foliage from his mouth dependent on your interpretation of the image. I, tend to lean towards the 'devouring' imagery. The last version is the Bloodsucker head, which is the same as the Disgorging Head but with the vegetation sprouting from all orifices.

Green Man roof boss, carved in wood, Church of St Michael, Spreyton, Devon

These Carvings and Visages can be seen all over Northern Europe, mainly the Gaelic/Gallic counties (France, England, Scotland, Wales, and Ireland)

and it is this Geographical area that I concentrate my research on. These are mainly found as adornments on Churches and Cathedrals commonly found to range from the Middle Ages from about the 11th Century, gaining in popularity from about the 13th to 16th Century. However, evidence of such effigies as old as the 4th or 5th Century has been found. In his book *The Green Man, The Archetype of our Oneness with the Earth (1990)*[7], William Anderson mentions an example found at a Parish Church in Ludlow, England thought to be from this early time period. Interestingly, there is even a Mesopotamian Green Man from the 2nd century BCE which was found in the ruined city of Hatra in Iraq[8] which I'll reference again later in the chapter on the Archetype.

After the 16th Century, there appears to be a decline in the use of The Green Man foliate head as a decorative piece which seems to coincide with an architectural movement away from the more ornate detailed decoration to more standard traditional religious iconology we still see today. However, he did enjoy a revival in the 19th century during the Gothic era of architecture, giving us some beautifully chilling designs leaning into the darker aspect of the Green Man. The Green Man does seem to have his Greek and Roman counterparts which we can still see evidence of today with the Green Man symbology being seen with Dionysos, Adonis, and Atticus.

---

[7] William Anderson – The Green Man, The Archetype of our Oneness with the Earth (1990).

[8] Eric Edwards Collected Works – Wordpress website, link below
https://ericwedwards.wordpress.com/?s=green+man.

Bacchus Dionysus decorative wall plaque

The differences are subtle such as vine leaves and grapes rather than the more Celtic Oak leaf, but the similarity is striking.

Given the widespread use of this symbology in churches and places of worship many believe the Green Man to be a Christian Icon from the Middle Ages, however, I believe that he far precedes Christianity. We know from history that when one invading dominate force wishes to introduce and enforce its own religious ideology, the old religious ideas are hijacked and manipulated. This manipulation makes it easier for the invaded indigenous population to 'accept' this new religious narrative as they are able to recognize common and familiar elements of their religion within it. This blending of religious practices makes it easier to harmonize the conversion. Examples, such as Christianity using established Pagan festivals and renaming them into Saints Feasts and Christian holidays. Samhain becomes All Saints Day, Yule or Winter Solstice becomes Christmas. The fertility festival Beltane is intertwined with Easter and the resurrection of Jesus Christ and so on. I think that it is much more likely that our Green Man is a Pagan symbol that has been integrated into Christian embellishment to harmonize the old and the new ideologies. To keep the impact on the population being converted to a minimum and ensure a smooth transition. It is also likely from an architectural viewpoint; the use of the foliate head was at times purely a decorative addition given its aesthetic appeal.

The name 'The Green Man' was coined by Lady Raglan, who was a Folklore Writer at the time after she first referenced the classic Foliate Head imagery as 'The Green Man'. She used this term in her article on the widespread use of the symbol in Churches and Christian Architecture and speculated on its religious and mythological significance. Ultimately viewing the Green Man as a 'Fertility Symbol" given his obvious links to nature and the seasonal cycles. This fascinating article was published in 1939 in The Folk-Lore Journal and is titled *"The Green Man in Church Architecture"*[9].

This conclusion complements Anderson's (1990) assertions that The Green Man is rising up into our consciousness as a counterbalance to our poor attitude to Nature. Pre Christianity we were of the notion that we are one with nature, part of it, since Christianity and even more so now with the advent of science we believe that we can somehow dominate and control nature. The onset of Christianity took the elements from the Pagan religions before it such a Tree Worship or Nature worship and demonized them. In their eyes, to see the Earth as sacred in its own right was Heresy.

As the considered pagan Lord of the Forest, the Green Man with his connection to gods and goddesses, nature, and all kinds of mythical animals, also heavily represented the belief in rebirth after death. The foliate heads came to "...suggest a deeply rooted and widely recognized cult."[10] (Carter, 1967). Cults who habitually practiced tree worship as well as the belief in the afterlife were widespread. Tree worship was known to have been practiced by the Celts, the Greeks, and the early Romans. Even going back as far as Ancient Mesopotamia the people held and practiced these beliefs, including the belief in an afterlife. We can look at Enlil the Sumerian God who spent time in the underworld before finding his escape, the Greek Dionysus who died and was born again, the Egyptian Osiris, and even Jesus Christ. All of whom have this consistent narrative of the son of a God, born, died, and risen again.

---

[9] The Green Man in Church Architecture (Article by Lady Raglan in Folklore Vol.L published 1939 – pg 45).

[10] Carter ROM & HM – The Foliate Head in England – Folklore Society 1967.

Kathleen Basford in her 1978 book '*The Green Man*'[11] infers a more demonic origin to these foliate heads, which is understandable given the ominous and evil-looking appearance of many of the carvings, many resembling gargoyles. Indeed, some scholars have commented that some of the more malevolent-looking heads may have been inspired by the faces of victims who have been decapitated or hung. Specifically, those where the tongue is engorged and protruding from the mouth. In some of the older examples, this could also be a nod to the Celtic Head Cults who often decapitated or hung their sacrifices. The Celts believed that the head was the most sacred part of the human body. It was their focal point of worship given the head's function as the cradle of knowledge, consciousness, and power. Celts would typically worship the head by hanging it from their sacred place of worship, which was usually a tree, specifically the Oak. The Celts believed knowledge to be power and put more emphasis on the growing and gaining of knowledge than many other tribes. The Druids (the priests of the Celts) were very interested in knowledge and continuously invested in expanding their skill sets to include alchemy, science, astronomy, architecture, and of course Magick.

The Man with Many Names

As well as the title 'The Green Man', the foliate headed one has also been referred to historically as the 'Green One' and the 'Verdant One'. However, as previously mentioned, since Lady Raglans' article was published 'The Green Man' label has gained traction and grown in popularity, now being the most common name by which he is known. There is good evidence to link The Green Man to other well-known characters within Mythology and Folk Lore such as The Man in the Oak, The Oak King, Jack in the Green, The May King, The Wild Man of the Woods, Robin Hood (or Robin of the Green) The Burry Man, Puck, the Greek God Pan and many more.

The Man in the Oak is derivative of Celtic folklore. The oak tree being sacred to the Druids (Celtic Priests) as already stated earlier. He is a man birthed from the woods, a figure sheathed in oak leaves, green, abundant, and bountiful. Symbolic of Nature but specifically of the Oak Tree, considered to be a symbol of knowledge and life by the Celts. The wisdom of the ancient oak is reflected in the physical embodiment of this wise, old man, a father figure to the woods and everything in it. The Oak King, similarly, is a folklore character depicted as a man covered in foliage but has more of a cyclic aspect to his narrative. The Oak in mythology comes at the onset of the Winter Solstice. The King's reign during this time symbolizes the beginning of life,

---

[11] Katherine Basford - The Green Man (First published by Boydell 1978).

the onset of fertility, birth, and abundance. The sunlight strengthens, the days lengthen, and a new cycle of vegetation and animal is born. His rival is The Holly King who symbolizes the onset of Summer Solstice, the fruition and harvest of the crops, the shortening of the days, and the dying of the sun. Autumn is the dying season, the Oak King is sacrificed, dying he begins his journey into the Underworld returning to the earth from which he was birthed. His body will decay releasing his seed, which was planted back in the womb of the Mother Goddess and will be birthed again the following year. The two Kings locked in an endless battle depicted by the cycle of the changing seasons.

Interestingly, I listened to an episode (Episode 4 – Mysterious Illuminations) of The Modern Fairy Sighting Podcast presented by Folk Lore Researcher and writer Jo Hickey-Hall[12] where a gentleman (who wished to remain anonymous) recounts a very weird experience he had in the Yorkshire area of the U.K. He describes an event that took place one evening when he and a friend decided to have a leisurely stroll near their local woods. It was wintertime so whilst it was early evening, about 7 pm, it was already very dark. As they were walking and talking when their attention was drawn to the nearby woods. They could see what appeared to be small lights moving about within the tree line. Initially, the two thought it was most likely teenagers messing about in the woods and that the lights they were seeing must be torches. 'Anonymous' then said to his friend that they should check it out. His friend wasn't so keen on the idea but eventually relented and the two headed into the woods. What they came across was very bizarre. He describes the creature that he saw as similar in appearance to an Ent from the Lord of The Rings books by Tolkien. Tall but humanoid, very skinny, with long limbs and long gnarled spindly fingers. The head was round and very large, disproportionate to the rest of its body. Its face was smooth, and it appeared to have no features, its' hair seemed like it was made up of sticks and branches. The skin appeared to be bark-like in texture. What they witnessed was a literal 'tree man'. The lights that they had seen from the tree line seemed to be coming from the creatures' hands like it was 'rolling' balls of light between them. This image really brings images of the archetypal Green Man to mind.

The Wildman of the Woods is a mythological figure which originated in the Middle Ages similarly to the afore mentioned Man in the Oak. A 'wild man' who comes from the forest, he is usually depicted as a gruff grizzly naked

---

[12] The Modern Fairy Sighting Podcast – presenter Jo Hickey-Hall (Episode 4 Mysterious Illuminations).

man, covered in foliage and shrub often seen carrying a club or similar weapon. With our Wildman, we also have the connection to the 'outlaws' living within our woods and the forests. Those who choose to live outside of the law and government, who withdraw from society, leading solitary lives or in some cases forming small communities of wild men (and wild women). It is from this mythos that we have our outlaw heroes and folktale characters such as Robin Hood or Robin the Green. An outlaw and a hero, a Wildman living in the woods who takes from the rich and gives to the poor and as he deems it, the deserving.

The Wildman has also been depicted as belonging to the Fae and magic community, often depicted as half man and half animal. Usually taking the guise of a typical woodland creature such as a Satyr or a Faun. These stories of Wildmen go back as far as ancient Mesopotamia with the account of the hero Enkidu in the Epic of Gilgamesh[13]. It is said that some of the half-man, half-bull carvings and artifacts found from this era could be in reference and celebration of Enkidu, who whilst being a primitive 'wildman' was a longtime comrade and friend of the titular Gilgamesh. Although we do have other zoomorphic entities from these periods who may also be reflected within these artifacts, Enkidu is certainly a strong contender for some of the artwork.

The Celts and the Anglo Saxons have many examples of these Fae Folk 'Wildman' characters, some of which also have zoomorphic aspects. Magic shapeshifting abilities are also another integral part of Celtic Folklore which is reflected in these 'wildmen' narratives. The 9th-century Irish tale Buile Shuibhne (The Madness of Sweeney, the third book of a trilogy about the King) tells how Shuibhne or Sweeney, the pagan King of the Dál nAraidi in Ulster, is angered by Bishop Finn (later canonized to St Rónán). The source of his anger, as the story goes, is his offence at the bishop's continued attempts to spread Christianity to the local population despite the King's protestations. One night upon hearing Finn's church bell toll, Sweeney finally snaps and in a fit of anger storms out of his castle to hunt down and execute Finn. Once he reaches the bishops' church he comes upon Finn, angered he throws Finn's psalter (prayer book) into the nearby Lake but before he can do the man any physical harm he is called away by his men to the Battle of Mag Rath. Finn gives thanks to God for his salvation and places a curse upon Sweeney. At the Battle of Mag Rath, the King becomes distant and begins to act irrationally, he grows paranoid and volatile. Eventually, he begins to grow

---

[13] Ancient Literature website, Epic of Gilgamesh – Epic Poem Summary – Other Ancient Civilizations – Classical Literature
https://www.ancient-literature.com/other_gilgamesh.html

feathers and talons as the curse runs its course, he then takes off in full flight now transformed into a bird. The story continues that this now mad and broken man can shapeshift from man to bird and back and is doomed to spend the rest of his years travelling naked through the woods, composing verses among other madmen. In order to be forgiven by God, King Sweeney composes a beautiful poem of praise to God before he dies. [14]

In Katharine Briggs' book 'The Vanishing People'[15] she tells the 'Wild Hunt' folklore story of King Herla and the Pigmy King. Herla from whose name we eventually derive the 'Harlequinn' is connected in folklore to the European Wild Hunt. It is said that Herla's story is one of the first of the Wild Hunt origin Stories. The Wild Hunt in simple terms is a chase led by a mythological figure escorted by a ghostly or supernatural group of hunters, the hunters themselves either being dead spirits or supernatural entities such as Fae Folk. Seeing this Hunt was usually a bad omen, signaling some impending doom. Whilst this is one of my favourite wild Hunt stories (I'll look at this particular story in more detail in the chapter on The Wild Hunt later in the book) it's the physical description of the Pigmy King which piqued my interest.

In this folk lore story, King Herla is the King of the early Britons (pre-Saxon invasion) and is out hunting with his men when he is approached by a small humanoid being, which is described as 'the Pigmy'. As this small being comes closer, it appears to be sat upon an enormous goat and looks by description, similar to the Greek deity Pan. He has a large head, a glowing face, and a red beard so long it reaches down to his chest. He has a hairy belly, and his legs are not those of a man but rather those of a Goat. He announces himself to King Herla stating that 'He is the King of Many Kings and Chiefs and of a people too numerous to count' so I assume here that he is the 'Fairy King'.

To briefly summarize the story, the Pigmy King says he will attend Herla's wedding and in return, Herla must agree to attend the Pigmy King's wedding. Herla rather amused agrees to this, not quite comprehending what he is getting himself into. The physical description of the Pigmy King not only looking like the Greek God Pan but the added detail of him 'riding atop a Goat' is fascinating given how intrinsically linked Goats are to mythological characters such as Pan and Puck and the correlation between the Fae Folk,

---

[14] Rachel Bromwich - Trioedd Ynys Prydein: The Triads of the Island of Britain. University Of Wales Press (2006).

[15] Katharine M. Briggs – The Vanishing People – (1978 – B.T. Batsford Ltd. London).

Pan, and the Green Man narrative. As a side note, Herla's story reminds me of the similar Arthurian story of Sir Gawain and The Green Knight, a harsh warning against entering into contracts with Fae Folk.

Continuing with our list of related titles, the May King reference derives from the pagan Beltane summer festival which falls on 1 May annually. As part of the ancient practice, a May King was chosen to bed down in a celebration of unity and fertility with the May Queen. The young man was usually stripped down, covered in earth, and wearing a crown of antlers to make himself appear as a stag. The Queen herself would usually be covered in flowers and would wear a mask to hide her identity (and to spare blushes after the event!). Such acts were not considered promiscuous back then as they are today but simply a celebration of nature. Similar celebrations were held throughout Europe, such as the 'wedding of Dionysus' where a man would act as the conduit for the Greek God of fertility Dionysus and a woman would act as his Queen and the marriage act was reconstructed as a ritual. Interestingly, the symbology of the Stag, the Goat, the Ram, and the Bull appears frequently when looking at Nature worship and Pagan religions and specifically the Green Man Motif.

During the 16th and 17th centuries, the Green Man was incorporated into local pageantry, becoming a feature of many May Day festivals and community celebrations. Such an example can be found with the Jack in the Green character[16] who gained notoriety around the late 18th century in southern England. This character seems to have enjoyed a revival in the late 19th century being taken up by the Chimney Sweeps of London who had 1st May as a holiday. It is unclear why the Chimney Sweeps took up the mantle of Jack in the Green. One suggestion is that it was another way to make money during their quiet season. Chimney Sweeps would up the pomp and the spectacle in the hopes of getting extra coins from the general public as they passed through the streets with their colourful procession.

Usually the brave (and unfortunate!) chosen man was clad from head to foot in foliage. This was done by using a conical frame made from wicker or light pliable wood constructed around the man's body which was then decorated with leaves, shrubbery, and flowers. There would then be a parade through the local town or village where the Jack in The Green would be the main attraction, assisted by his helpers as the outfit would make walking and even sitting/resting very difficult. Usually, the man under the frame would not be able to take water or food as urinating in the costume was extremely difficult.

---

[16] Fran and Geoff Doel – The Green Man In Britain (2001) Ebook Edition (2013).

Instead, he was usually allowed a sup or two of whiskey to get him through the day!

Another variation of this tradition is the Garland King celebration whose costume is entirely adorned with flowers making him, in effect, a walking garland. Garland day is usually celebrated at the end of May (29th) rather than the beginning of the month but is still considered a 'May Day' style of celebration. On the Scottish border, they have the Burry Man[17] parade, whose costume is entirely made up of hedgerow and weed (also called 'the Burr'). Very similar to the Jack in the Green character The Burry Man would be central to the parade and celebrations. The origin of the Burry Man isn't clear, and the festival takes place in August not May but the Green Man visuals and ritual remain similar. All versions of this 'character' seem tied to the Spring/Summer months specifically around the Pagan Beltane festival celebrated in May. Within these festivals, we have the Oak King whose leaves symbolize the new cycle of fertility and abundance of all things in nature. We have the visual of the Jack in the Green and Garland King, men who represent nature come to life. We have ritualistic practices which are deeply rooted within their respective communities. People coming together to give thanks for the abundance of crops and the flourishing of livestock and in more modern times for food to eat and a roof over one's head. There is the sacrificial 'gifting' to the Gods to ask for the same benevolent outcome next year. The ritual is undertaken to please the Gods so that they will look favorably upon the community. It's also a time of merriment and celebration, it also must be said that such practices can bind, bond, and strengthen community ties.

The Green Man has long been associated with the creatures of mythological folk lore. Puck being one such character, in English folklore Puck is considered a nature fairy or sprite. He is often depicted as being half man and half goat (faun or satyr) or as a small chubby sprite similar to the celestial cherub (but wingless). A mischievous imp whose love of pranks and jokes earnt him the 'jester of the fairy court' title. Puck may also be referred to as 'Robin Goodfellow' who famously made an appearance in Shakespeare's 'A Midsummers Night's Dream as the Jester of the fairy King Oberon. As we'll see in the later chapter on the Green Man's archetype, his association with zoomorphic creatures is prevalent through mythology as is his own 'shapeshifting' abilities.

This connection of the various Green Man derivatives with the Goat is interesting to me on a personal level. As a teenager, I grew up in a small

---

[17] Ibid.

village in Ireland called Killorglin. Now, during the summer in the month of August, there is an annual festival held there called 'Puck Fair'. During this 3-day long festival, a Goat is named King, is placed on the top of a tall structure and for all intents and purposes 'worshipped'. I, of course, had no idea of the origin of the fair as a teenager as my only interest was in the music, the food, the party, and the craic. It's only as an adult that I can see and appreciate the symbolism and ritualistic elements, remnants of an era long since lost to time. It's as close as I can come now to the ceremonies and beliefs of my ancestors. As part of the ritual, a young girl from the local village is picked to be 'Queen Puck'. Her job will be to crown the Goat as King as well as remove the crown 'dethroning' him after the celebrations have finished. I remember it being quite the honour, not that I was ever chosen!

The origins of the fair itself aren't clear, it is one of Ireland's oldest festivals and the evidence seems to suggest that this fair existed even before written records were kept. Unfortunately, it would seem that the actual origins have long been lost to antiquity. One theory posited by *theringofkerry.com* details a story that took place during the Cromwellian invasion of Ireland during the 1600's. According to the legend, Cromwells' forces were pillaging the countryside at the foot of the Macgillycuddy Reeks Mountain range when they came across and frightened a herd of grazing goats. The animals fled but the male goat or "Puck" broke away on his own and eventually arrived in Killorglin. His arrival there in a state of semi-exhaustion alerted the locals of the approaching danger and they immediately set about protecting themselves and their stock. It is said that in recognition of the service rendered by the goat, the people decided to institute a special festival in his honor and this festival has been held ever since[18].

Another, more probable theory suggests that the origin is linked to pagan Lughnasadh celebrations of the harvest festival which falls in August. The selection of the male goat or "Puck" was in reverence to their chosen Pagan God, whose symbol was that of a Goat. It could have been a deity such as the Greek God Pan. Pan, who in Greek Mythology was a fertility deity was often associated by the Romans with Faunus the half man half goat creature of mythology. Originally an Akkadian entity, his name is a doric contraction of Paon which means 'Pasturer' but in more modern times it is used to denote 'all'. It could also be a nod to other Pagan deities who have the goat as their totem animals such as Dionysus, Bacchus, and the Celtic horned God Cernunnos. This would make sense given the 'Shepherd' aspect would tie

---

[18] The Ring of Kerry website – Puck Fair
https://www.theringofkerry.com/puck-fair

into the fairs' possible origin story and to the Celtic Lughnasadh holiday which falls halfway between the midsummer and autumn equinox and celebrates the beginning of the harvest festival.

There certainly there seems to be a link between 'Horned' animals and The Green Man and his origins. For many Neopagans including Wiccans, there is a belief that the Green Man is representative of 'ritual' transformation. He is a derivation of the Celtic Horned God Cernunnos also known as Cernowain and Cernenus. The horned God of the Hunt and the God of the Underworld who also incorporates aspects of Silvanus, Dionysus, and Pan. His sacred animals being the Stag, the Bull, The Goat, and the Bear. Indeed, I have come across examples of all these animals being used 'symbolically' in Pagan rituals. The Bear springs to mind readily, as it was used as part of the symbology within the Scandinavian Pagan fertility ritual undertaken in the 2019 film 'Midsommar'.

Going back to Anderson's correlation between the Green Man and Nature. Has his presence pushed itself back into our modern consciousness due to our treatment of the Earth, the plants, and the wildlife within? Are we now paying the price? Are the woods in return getting more aggressive in their response? In the current social and political climate, being 'green' has never been more important as we fight to reduce our impact on nature, our climate, and the world around us. The very future of our species dependent upon it, will it be more merciful with us than we have with it?

Why is the Green Man – Green?

Another aspect of the Green Man is, of course, his colour. Pretty much every variation or derivation of this archetype is either Green in skin tone or swathed in Green. What is the significance of the Colour Green and how does it tie into the Mythos?

When you think of the colour Green what springs to mind? I would hazard that most people, when asked this question would respond with 'nature'. Trees, plants, grass, and various forms of foliage are the very evidence of the life force contained within our woodlands. So, we can easily conclude that Green is synonymous with Nature and therefore nature represents the strongest element in Green Man Mythology. Green represents growth, birth, abundance, and renewal of the seasonal cycle. It conjures images of springtime, farm animals being born, the flourishing of crops, and the promise of the warmth of summer still to come.

Pre-Christianity, nature worship was the basis of most of the old religions.

This makes sense, the Sun gives life and warmth, the Earth provides food, and shelter, the rain provides libation and irrigation. In general terms, worship became split into two halves, two deities if you will, the Sun and Earth. In the old Celtic, Gallic, Teutonic, and even Wiccan religions we have the Horned God, the male aspect who is the sun god, then we have his counterpart in the Mother Goddess who is representative of the Earth. The male and the female aspect work together in harmony to create life. This partnership is mirrored in other pagan religions such as the Greeks with their God Pan and his goddess Diana, in Asia we have Cybele and Atys, in Rome Bacchus and Ariadne, in Egypt the God Osiris and his wife Isis. These male-female archetypes are seen in most polytheistic or Pantheistic religions and have been since record keeping began. The concept of opposites coming together in union seems central to the ideology of the cyclical nature of the seasons and of life itself.

Nature aside, what other associations do we make with the Colour Green? Certainly, it's the colour of myth and Folklore. Take Robin Hood, for example, modern depictions of the rogue outlaw have him clad in Green. He makes the woods his home, living off the grid before that was even a thing! He is a folk hero, protecting the innocent and the poor. Stealing from those who can readily afford it to give to those who so desperately need it. He is a figure who is seen as being just, loyal and merciful. There is something pure about the colour green here, it's a hero's colour, it's the colour of 'hope'.

In the Chakra's, Green is the colour of the Heart Chakra. This is the colour of love. Not lustful or passionate but true self-less love. The love we feel for family, friends, partners, and the world around us. It is our center for compassion, empathy, and kindness. Interestingly it is also the center of change and transformation. Given the subject matter we're looking at here I found the below extract from _https://www.bemytravelmuse.com/heart-chakra_ very interesting: -

> _The heart chakra is special because it is the fourth of the seven chakras, making it the exact halfway point of the system and the unifier of the physical and spiritual chakras. By connecting the lower three chakras — the root, sacral, and solar plexus — with the upper three chakras — the throat, third eye, and crown — the heart chakra acts as the bridge between the earth and spirit. The heart chakra of the earth is believed to be dually located at two towns in southwestern England about 30 miles apart from each other, Glastonbury and Shaftesbury. Another 25 miles beyond lies Stonehenge, which adds another layer of mystique to this earth chakra. All kinds of legends center around this location, like the tale that Glastonbury Tor has a connection to King Arthur and the ancient mythological land of Avalon'_

A little further down the article it also references the connection to the outdoors, nature, and the heart Chakra.

The heart chakra could also be aided by focusing on its element, air. Placing oneself in environments which have a strong sense of open space and fresh air could be highly beneficial — bonus points for a natural abundance of the color green!'

When we see paintings and images of the old Anglo-Saxon Arthurian figures, again green is heavily represented here. Sir Tristan's coat of arms is green with a golden dragon upon it. Elements of green are contained within the knight's armour, their cloaks, and boots. Merlin the great sorcerer himself is often seen clad in Green. There has always been a connection between the colour green and magic, it is the colour of the supernatural. Whenever I see a cauldron bubbling in a film or a book, the colour of the potion is nearly always green. As is the spooky mists we see depicted in scary films at Halloween. By association, the mythology of the Fae Folk is also intertwined with the colour green, magic, and the supernatural.

We even have our very own derivative of the Green Man mythology interwoven with Arthurian mythology in the tale of Sir Gawain and The Green Knight[19] mentioned in the previous chapter. Our tale is set on New Year's Eve, this is significant not only because it represents the end of one year (cycle) and the beginning of a new one, but our Teutonic ancestors believed that on New Year's Eve, the boundary between the worlds of the living and the dead became thin. Similar to the Halloween mythos or the Mexican Day of the Dead celebration it's a time when the dead can walk among the living, and it is said that it is not only the spirits of the dead that can find a way through.

King Arthur is sat with his Queen, presiding over his knights in his great hall. There is a great banquet in progress and all in attendance are toasting and celebrating the New Year. During the celebrations, the large wooden doors to Arthurs Great Hall blast open and a large intimidating figure rides forth on a menacing spectral steed. I've included the fantastic description of this great Green Knight from the Jessie Weston translation of the original text as my summary would do it no justice:

For he was clad all in green, with a straight coat, and a mantle above; all decked

---

[19] Robbins Library Digital Projects - Camelot Project - Sir Gawain and the Green Knight: A Middle-English Arthurian Romance - Sir Gawain and the Green Knight.

and lined with fur was the cloth and the hood that was thrown back from his locks and lay on his shoulders. Hose had he of the same green, and spurs of bright gold with silken fastenings richly worked; and all his vesture was verily green. Around his waist and his saddle were bands with fair stones set upon silken work, 'twere too long to tell of all the trifles that were embroidered thereon—birds and insects in gay gauds of green and gold. All the trappings of his steed were of metal of like enamel, even the stirrups that he stood in stained of the same, and stirrups and saddle-bow alike gleamed and shone with green stones. Even the steed on which he rode was of the same hue, a green horse, great and strong, and hard to hold, with broidered bridle, meet for the rider.

The knight was thus gaily dressed in green, his hair falling around his shoulders; on his breast hung a beard, as thick and green as a bush, and the beard and the hair of his head were clipped all round above his elbows. The lower part of his sleeves were fastened with clasps in the same wise as a king's mantle. The horse's mane was crisp and plaited with many a knot folded in with gold thread about the fair green, here a twist of the hair, here another of gold. The tail was twined in like manner, and both were bound about with a band of bright green set with many a precious stone; then they were tied aloft in a cunning knot, whereon rang many bells of burnished gold. Such a steed might no other ride, nor had such ever been looked upon in that hall ere that time; and all who saw that knight spake and said that a man might scarce abide his stroke.

The knight bore no helm nor hauberk, neither gorget nor breast-plate, neither shaft nor buckler to smite nor to shield, but in one hand he had a holly-bough, that is greenest when the groves are bare, and in his other an axe, huge and uncomely, a cruel weapon in fashion, if one would picture it. The head was an ell-yard long, the metal all of green steel and gold, the blade burnished bright, with a broad edge, as well shapen to shear as a sharp razor. The steel was set into a strong staff, all bound round with iron, even to the end, and engraved with green in cunning work. A lace was twined about it, that looped at the head, and all adown the handle it was clasped with tassels on buttons of bright green richly broidered.[19]

Interestingly in the modern 2021 film of the same name, the Green Knight is depicted as having a head and face like tree bark making him more of a classic foliate Green Man in appearance than the Green Man from the original text.

This stranger is here to 'test' the merit of Arthurs's legendary court, he challenges a Knight of the famous Round Table to prove his worth. His challenge? He asks if there is one among them who can strike a blow at his neck and then be brave enough to have that same blow returned to him one year hence. Surely a suicide mission but certainly a challenge to test one's honour. Sir Gawain steps forward to take up the challenge and with one swift blow removes the Green Knight's head from his shoulders. This, of course, does not kill the Green Knight who does not appear to be of this mortal world. He simply picks his head back up, tells Gawain to come find him at his Green Chapel in one year exactly, and rides back out of court. Interestingly, according to the story, this chapel is not a standard church as we would think but instead a green barrow or mound similar to the fairy mounds of the Fae Folk bolstering his connection to this supernatural realm. This 'mound' description also reminded me a little of the rest havens for the Hero Gods which were described in mythology as being constructed of leafy boughs.

Back to our story and exactly one year to the day later, Gawain sets forth on his quest to find the Green Man. Along his travels, he meets with Bertilak de Hautedesert who befriends him and offers him accommodation. During his stay here Gawain engages in an affair with Bertilak's wife, who enamored with him, gifts him an enchanted girdle/belt. It is here that Gawain ultimately fails his test behaving in a manner unbecoming of a Knight of the Round Table. He is inappropriate in his actions and ungracious to his host, repaying Bertilak's hospitality with betrayal. Gawain eventually leaves Bertilak's home to find the Green Knight at his Chapel. Gawain does try to fulfill his challenge and after some wavering, due to fear he eventually kneels before the Green Knight to receive his blow but is spared. The knight did what he had sought to do, he had tested Gawain and found him unworthy. He had failed in his behaviour by not being true to his Knights oath. He had been 'unknightly' in his relationship with another Man's wife and in accepting and utilizing an enchanted object in the hopes of 'cheating' the Green Knight. This test leaves Gawain defeated and disgraced.

There are other variations on the tale involving shape-shifting, magic, and curses. In one version that I read, Bertalik is the Green Knight, a wizard who can shapeshift using magic. In other versions, it is said that the sorceress Morgan Le Fay created the Green Man (similar to a tulpa or a golem) in order to destroy Arthur's Round Table but the above is the basic outline of the general story. It is thought that the Green Knight represented here is our Pagan God the Green Man, of whom we are currently learning about.

Whilst The Green Knight is an Anglo-Saxon tale, you cannot read the story without feeling the heavy Irish influence. There are many similar tales in Irish folk lore which mirror the Arthurian Myth and vice versa. Take the tale of

Bricriu's Feast taken from the Fled Bricreen story [120] (from the Ulster Cycle of Irish Mythology). In this story, Bricriu is a crafty troublemaker (later found to be the King of Munster) who decides to hold a feast and invites three of Ireland's greatest warriors to attend. These brave warriors being Conall Cernach, Lóegaire Búadach, and finally the legendary Cúchulainn.

During the feast Bricriu challenges our three heroes to a competition, the prize for winning his challenge is to receive the 'champions' portion of the feast. To win this contest, the three heroes must complete several tasks. Cúchulainn wins these challenges easily and bitter at losing, the other two opponents object and say that they do not believe this to be true, so one final challenge is given. In this challenge, the three heroes are each challenged by a giant churl to cut off his head, on the condition that they allow him to cut off their heads in return. The first two cut off the giants' head but the next day when it is their turn to receive their blow they are nowhere to be found. Only Cúchulainn keeps up his end of the deal. The giant spares his life stating that he was the only warrior brave enough to complete the challenge and is heralded as the winner and Ireland's greatest Hero. The Churl then reveals himself to be Cú Roí King of Munster. Here we have the same themes of Hero challenge, shapeshifting magic, giants, and decapitation.

The themes of magic and the fairy realm run through a lot of our folklore and in keeping with this theme of Green as the colour of magic and mythology we have the 12th-century story of the Green Children of the Woolpit. The Woolpit is a village located not too far from me here, in the county of Suffolk. The brief accounts of these children are contained in William of Newburgh's Historia Rerum Anglicarum and Ralph of Coggeshall's Chronicum Anglicanum, both written around 1200 AD[21]. Ralph reportedly states that his source was Sir Richard de Calne, they very knight who eventually adopted the Children.

The story goes that the two children were found lost and wondering the fields by the local village people who were out farming the land. The children were brought back to Woolpit village to see if the locals could find out who they were and return them home. It is said that the children had a green hue to their skin and spoke in a language that no one could understand. They refused food seemingly unable to eat the food given to them before eventually being convinced to eat some green beans.

---

[20] Fran and Geoff Doel – The Green Man in Britain (2001) Ebook Edition (2013).

[21] John Clark – "Small, Vulnerable Ets: The Green Children of Woolpit", Science Fiction Studies (2006).

As the children could not be successfully returned home and with no relatives coming forward to claim them, they were taken in by Sir Richard de Calne mentioned above. Accounts report that the boy died shortly thereafter, unable to stomach the food and growing evermore sickly, eventually he succumbed to his ailments. The girl, however, was able to survive, she remained a live-in servant girl to Sir Richard until she eventually married and had her own family. By all accounts, the girl's colour is said to have eventually lost its green hue taking on a more 'normal' pallor and she was even able to learn some English. Once she had enough of the local language to communicate well enough she told the locals that she and her brother came from a place called St Martins land. She said that everyone there was Green like she had been, seemingly they were also Christian, and it would appear life in St Martins' Land was very similar to life in the Woolpit. She said that she and her brother had been tending to their father's sheep when they heard what sounded like a bell tolling. Unfamiliar with this bell and curious to find out where this tolling could be coming from, they followed the sound through a cavern coming out the other side in the unrecognizable fields of the Woolpit.

This story endlessly fascinates me as I frequently come across references to caves and caverns being doorways or portals between worlds. In Hindu mythology, the Gods lived in mountains called Devanica (named for the Gods or 'Devas'). Hero Gods such as Atri (who corresponds to the Roman Atlas, the Celtic Idris, and the Greek Dionysus) the Gods of the Earth lived in bowers or huts within the sides of these mountains, which were given the name Parnaslas or Parnasas because they were comprised of leafy branches of trees and bowers of green branches. Atri would 'retire' to his cave as Dionysus would 'retire' to the Underworld. Caves in mythology appear to be the bridge between life and death, somewhere in between. They are also metaphorical 'graves' being cold, dark cold tombs buried beneath the earth's surface.

If this account is true and occurred as it is written, it could be that these children accidentally stumbled across some form of dimensional portal, maybe they even came from within the core of our earth. I've seen it speculated that they may have been Dutch children who had been abandoned there due to war however, I am not sure what would account for the green hue to their skin if this were the case and the children made no reference to any travel overseas. Certainly, the colour of these children and the land in which they said that they originated seems to connect them with the fairy realm.

There is an old wife's tale that I came across in my research that warns that you should never dress a baby in green until after the Christening for fear that the fairies will come and snatch them[22]. By all accounts, green is one of the most common colours that people associate with fairy encounters. Indeed, when we think of the Fae Folk, we have that association with the colour green, whether its fairies such as Tinkerbell, gnomes, elves or goblins even Shrek the Ogre. Ireland a country steeped in mythology conjures pictures of lush greenery, St Patrick's Day parades with thousands swathed in green, even their Leprechauns are dressed head to toe in the colour, and let's not forget the luck of the Irish being synonymous with the green four-leaf clover.

As referenced above, caves and caverns appear many times when talking about portals. We have the stories of strange little creatures often described as gnomes or little people coming into and out of cave systems such as the example in Hellier. We have stories straight out of the Missing 411 phenomenon from people, usually children who have disappeared but luckily were later found. In many of these stories the recovered children have given us descriptions of unknown creatures, who took them to caves to 'look after' them for some time. Feeding them berries and keeping them warm. It is unknown why in these particular cases the children appear to be 'returned' but certainly their experiences are most bizarre.

Another famous 'Green Man' is Peter Pan, he is the classic Fae Folk representation of the Green Man motif. I think we can certainly class Peter Pan as a magical entity of some kind, he can fly, he never ages, has a fairy for a friend, and is literally called Pan! In the Peter Pan narrative, Peter decides that he doesn't wish to grow up, so in order to escape this fate, he flies away from his nursery and away from his mother. To have the capability to fly away in the first place, we must posit that Peter is not a human child, he must surely have other worldly qualities. At some point, Peter regrets his decision and tries to return only to find that his mother has had another child and has put bars up on the window preventing his access. Peter is now truly lost. He is now stuck, somewhere between worlds. He eventually gains companions in the other Lost Boys whose origins as children who 'fell out of their perambulator' seems to be symbolic of early infant death, through miscarriage or still birth. Child spirits are also stuck between worlds unable to move on. Perhaps Peter himself is the spirit of a deceased child who died at a very young age, perhaps leaving his mother was not Peter's idea but how he deals with his sudden death as an infant.

---

[22] Diane Purkiss – Troublesome Things; A history of Fairies and Fairy Stories (2000 Penguin).

I am not sure what Peter Pan is supposed to be, deceased child, fairy, or sprite I guess only J.M. Barrie knew. He certainly fits the Puck and Robin Goodfellow archetype. Dressed in Green, Charming, shroud, manipulative, and a bit of a trickster. He is the pied piper of children luring them away to play with him forever, leader of the Lost Boys, the poor souls of parentless children. As a child I never thought him sinister, maybe even seeing him as the hero of the story, the good guy. Honestly now, I think he is something much darker masquerading under the illusion of innocence. In her book 'Troublesome Things', Diane Purkiss references the link between the story of Pan and the Mesopotamian Nursery demon Kubu. Certainly, he bears a striking resemblance. A child's spirit, most likely a result of miscarriage or still birth, trapped between worlds, never growing old, so envious of other children in the land of the living that he enters their nurseries late at night and steals them away[23].

Green has many positive connotations but also it has negative ones. When Christianity first came to our shores it was not the fanatical religion of the Middle Ages. It was much more liberal and lived harmoniously side by side with the Pagan religions for many centuries. However, like most man-made things, it eventually became radicalized. Its leaders decided that Christianity was to be the only religion and that all else must be stamped out, eradicated, and wiped from existence. The liberal and tolerant ideologies went out the window in favour of Man's need for dominance, power, and greed.

As a result, the colour green which previously symbolized nature worship and Pagan Gods such as the Green Man was now dangerous. The Pagan foundations of nature worship and the pantheons of the Gods were now deemed heresy. The Pagan Horned God of the Hunt, our Green Man, became associated with the Devil, the fanatics of Christianity took his proud strong antlers and perverted them. Pureness, virginity, and chastity were prized above all else by the puritan zealots. The Pagan traditions of nature worship and their fertility celebrations were demonized. They called people who continued the old practices Devil worshippers. High Priestesses who channeled the Mother Goddess and the wise women of the communities were persecuted and called witches and burnt at the stake. Green became the colour of the witches, indeed the Wicked Witch of the West is Green in colour just so you know she's the bad one! When we think of spooky movies, books, and supernatural paraphernalia we think green. Green witches and ghouls, mists from cauldrons, green slime (poor Slimer!), and creepy crawlies, Halloween just wouldn't be Halloween without them!

---

[23] Ibid.

The colour green also has associations with negative feelings, such as sickness i.e. 'I'm feeling a bit green around the gills' or jealousy with people being referred to as 'green with envy'. Green is the colour of money and the colour of greed. The hulk has even made us associate it with loss of control and pure anger with his 'Hulk Smash'. Loki from the Marvel films reminded me very much of the 'puck' archetype, the Norse version at least. Green by birth being the son of a giant Fárbauti of the Aesir tribe. He is always dressed in Green, he is charming, manipulative and cunning, not to be trusted yet you can't quite help yourself! Certainly, Loki is the Green Man Puck of Norse mythology.

Little Green Men

Speaking of 'Alien' races we even associate the colour Green with our extraterrestrial friends, historically referring to them as 'little green men'. I've tried to pin down the origin of this saying but unfortunately was unable to find anything concrete. The reference to little green people we can speculate comes from fairy mythology but when did it become associated with Extraterrestrials? It would appear from my digging that some origin lies within the military, allegedly used as a derogatory term by the Allied military with regards to foreign hostiles, most likely the Japanese, the term was coined during the World War II conflict. Referring to the enemy as 'little green men' in reference to their small stature and uniform. The term 'little green men' is still being used in the media today, as I write this chapter, the Russian Invasion of Ukraine is well underway, and this term is back in circulation. As I type, the Press is using the term "little green men" to refer to masked soldiers of the Russian Federation in unmarked green army uniforms, bringing the term back full circle to its miliary origin.

It was used by Mack Reylands in his 1951 book "*The Case of the Little Green Men*" which depicted Aliens as little green men. It was then brought into collective consciousness during the 1950s by the Newspapers of the day when reporting UFO phenomena (which was a hot topic after the Roswell incident). A Wichita, Kansas newspaper published a story in June wherein an alleged UFO witness reported a UFO sighting stating to the journalists that he saw "absolutely no little green men with egg on their whiskers"[24].

In 1955, a farming family called the Suttons reported a terrifying story of

---

[24] Wikipedia – Little Green Men
https://en.wikipedia.org/wiki/Little_green_men#cite_note-10

being attacked by 'aliens' in southwestern Kentucky. Their story quickly became one of the strangest and most chilling accounts of an alien encounter. The incident quickly became regional and even national news and is known today as 'The Kelly-Hopkinsville Encounter'. It is said that the journalist involved in taking the account took a bit of Hollywood license with the story by using the term 'little green men' in his article when the witnesses had made no reference to seeing such humanoids[25] [26].

Similar stories of flying saucers and 'little green men' sightings were published by The New York Times, The Washington Post, and The Chicago Tribune. References were made in science fiction books and even in TV shows and movies infusing our consciousness with ideas and images of Aliens as 'little Green Men'. Even today our modern media still makes that connection with Yoda from Star Wars being a literal 'little green man'. We have the cute alien squeeze toys in the popular Toy Story movie franchise, the alien Paul from the movie of the same name, Gamora from Guardians of the Galaxy, and even the Skrull race from the Marvel universe all reconfirming that strong connection between the colour green and extraterrestrials.

One episode of the *Sasquatch Chronicles* Podcast hosted by Wes Germer, which I listened to, recounted an interesting story that also happened to involve little 'green' men. In episode number 550 titled 'Little Green Man' which aired on 8th October 2019, Wes' guest 'Kevin' told his story of how when he was much younger, he had a rather peculiar encounter. He continues, that when he was younger his family lived in a small village in rural Ireland, this village was located next to some woodland that was easily accessible from his house. The local people from the village would often speak about the fairy people and it wasn't unheard of to gift them small offerings to keep them happy. One day he and his mother decided to go for a walk down to these woods and leave a little offering of an acorn of honey, which they set down at the base of a large oak tree. Kevin said that as they did this, he caught sight of a rather strange creature, the creature proceeded to step out in from of him giving him a clear field of vision for several seconds. He described it as being about 2 ½ ft to 3 ft tall. A green, grey colour with very long limbs, spindly slender fingers, and an odd, almost doll-like face which he likened to an old-fashioned porcelain doll. It had big black eyes and slits for its nose and mouth. He said it started to act strangely just racing around in circles before it just finally 'took off'. His description is very similar to the classic ET-type beings witnesses report during alien encounters but yet the history

---

[25] Terena Bell Will the Little Green Men Of Kelly, Kentucky, Return to Watch The Solar Eclipse?

[26] Volker Janssen, How the 'Little Green Men' Phenomenon Began on a Kentucky Farm.

of Fae Folk in the area would suggest that the creature was considered more fairy than alien. Certainly, there is evidence to suggest that Fae Folk sightings and Alien encounters could be a shared phenomenon.

There is clearly a link in our social consciousness between the Fairy Folk encounters and modern-day Alien abductions. I don't think it's a huge jump to say, as Diane Purkiss mentions in her book '*Troublesome Things – A History of Fairies*' that the fascination with Aliens has replaced that of Fairies in our modern consciousness. There is a definite similarity between our historical 'little people' encounters and the modern-day Alien abduction phenomenon. Why this is I am unsure, as Diane speculates in her book, humans seem to need to fill in the empty spaces even in our modern science-based culture. We see nothing in the darkness of the dense woods so convince ourselves that something must be there. Now as we look to the sky and beyond, we cannot fight the need to fill that empty space full of wonderous and terrifying things.

When exploring The Fae Folk there seem to be many different entities that make up this broad spectrum of beings. Katharine Briggs' *A Dictionary of Fairies* gives a very comprehensive breakdown of the types and names of Fairies but for the sake of this book I've narrowed it down to the more common woodland folk. This includes fairies (traditional in appearance but can also shapeshift, this classification also includes entities such as sprites, Imps, nymphs, and elementals), satyrs, elves, gnomes, pixies, goblins and hobgoblins (can also be classed as Imp or Sprite). All of these entities have ties to the Fae Folk and all seem to live in the woodlands, fairy kingdoms as well as caverns and cave systems.

Looking at the mythology of our green man, he certainly has aspects of the Fae Folk, he seems to process un-earthly powers, has magical elements, and a connection to strange zoomorphic creatures. There are several Fairy Kings such as King Herla's Pigmy King or The Green Knight who seem to fit our Green Man archetype and who are quite clearly originating from the fairy realm. Is our Green Man part of the Fae Folk? An interdimensional being able to come in and out of our reality at will? It is certainly an intriguing thought.

The possible origins of the Fae Folk are many, some speculate that fairies are just small Briton folk who were driven underground and into caves systems when Saxon invading forces landed on our shores. Some such as Lewis Spence believe that they are the spirits of the departed. Some that they are Pagan Gods reduced in statue and forced to live in a limbo land neither here nor there, a result of waning human belief. Others say that they are fallen, angels; that when the war between heaven and hell finally reached its devastating crescendo and the gates of heaven were shut and Lucifer was cast down into Hell, and in the chaos, some Angels got stuck. Those who were stuck in Hell became demons and those stuck on earth became the vast race of the Fae folk. I must say, I am a fan of this romantic and tragic origin story. Whilst Fae Folk belief predates Christianity, it is not a huge leap to assume that people of the medieval ages would associate fairies with demons and angels giving them a biblical back story to explain the phenomenon.

Fairy Encounters (Are fairies the kinsmen or progeny of the Green Man?)

It is impossible to research the Green Man topic without quickly coming across the many Fae Folk references and connotations. Whether the link is made through nature itself, their connection to the woods, rocks, and caves, or whether it be the 'interdimensional' aspect of their existence, the link is most definitely there. Indeed, there are many accounts of a 'Green man' archetype within mythology in connection to a 'Hidden Kingdom', where he rules as King (as mentioned previously). Whatever their origin story or whoever their King, the Fae Folk have been around for as long as man has been able to spin a yarn across the glow of a fire. When researching the Fae Folk for the purposes of writing this book I was astonished at the volume of 'fairy encounter' stories from everyday people and then still by the similarities between Fairy Encounters and modern-day Alien abduction stories. I am familiar with many of the more famous abduction stories such as Betty and Barney Hill and the Travis Walton story but outside of these mainstream cases, 'alien encounters' was not a topic that I had paid a lot of attention to.

As most of us are aware, the hallmarks of the classic UFO sighting/abduction appear to be, seeing bright lights, paralysis (the abductee reports being unable to move or scream), loss of time, and memory loss specific to the event. The abductee rarely remembers the full event with only a vague sense that something may have occurred during this 'missing' time. Memories are usually brought back later by the use of meditation or by regressive hypnosis. The Abductee may suffer from night terrors, bad headaches, or some kind of medical ailment after the event with no explanation for the condition. The information above is all relatively accessible on most media platforms, TV shows, Films, and Podcasts. I would posit that most people in this day and age will have a basic awareness, as I did, of these classic abduction markers. What I was not aware of was how similar these commonalities are to the Fae Folk encounters. So similar that it cannot simply be 'just coincidence'. Could it be that what we experience today under the Alien Abduction/Encounter guise is the same phenomenon that has been occurring for thousands of years to people as a Fairy Encounter?

Certainly, the markers for fairy encounters are very similar, including reports of hearing music or seeing lights (often referred to as 'fairy lights') in the distance which attract one's attention often leading that person from their intended path. In Janet Bord's book *Fairies: Real Encounters with Little People.* She tells the tale of two sisters who lived during the 20th Century near a fairy fort in Crillaun (Ireland) who reported seeing red, green, blue, and yellow lights. According to their account, these lights sailed through the air in formation to another fort on the other side of the small lake (lough), not unlike present-day reports of alien aircraft activity[27].

Another indicator of Fae Folk interference is the reported loss of time, hours, sometimes even days, and in some rare cases - years. A 'return' to the place where one was taken but with hazy memory or even no memory of what took place. Indeed, it is said that in the fairy realm time works differently to our world, such as Herla's experience of three days in the Fairy Realm equating to about two hundred human years. Interestingly, in his book *The Fairy Faith in Celtic Countries*, Walter Wenz reports that 'The mind of a Person coming out of Fairy-Land is usually blank as to what has been seen and done there'[28].

Whilst digging into Fae Folk encounters, I found an interesting story on mysterious universe (*www.mysteriousuniverse.org*) which is also mentioned in Katharine Briggs' book '*Vanishing people*' of two Welsh farm hands (Llewellyn and Rhys) one of whom went too near a fairy fort and promptly disappeared. As the story is told, the servants were walking towards the farm on which they worked one evening, when one of them stopped dead in his tracks claiming that he could hear music being played. The other could hear nothing. Rhys, who had heard the music, told his companion to continue onto the farm while he tried to find the culprit to tell him to get off the private land. When morning came and Rhys had still not returned, Llewellyn reported his friend missing, and a thorough search of the area was conducted. Rhys, however, was not found and in an unfortunate turn of events, poor Llewellyn was suspected of having done something despicable to him. About a year later, the story of the missing servant reached the ears of a local farmer who said he suspected it could be fairies. He asked Llewellyn to take him to the exact spot where Rhys had heard the music and declared that this spot, was indeed a known fairy fort. At this time Llewellyn commented, that he could

---

[27] Janet Bord – Fairies Real Encounters with Little People (1997 by Michael O'Mara Books Limited).

[28] Walter Wenz - The Fairy Faith in Celtic Countries (2001 Blackmask Online edition).

now hear the music. The farmer looked at the servants' feet and could see that Llewellyn had one foot inside the fairy fort. He also stepped into this fort and now both men could hear the music and reported seeing child-sized figures dancing and carousing. They could also see the missing man, grabbing him they thrust him out of the circle. Once all three men had stepped out of the fort the music and merriment immediately vanished. The missing man complained that he would have liked to have stayed a while longer as he had only just got there, completely unaware that he had, in fact, been missing for an entire year.[29]

Indeed, throughout history, there have been many reports of people just vanishing into thin air, some even in full view of other people with no plausible explanation for what could have happened. There are even accounts of searchers and family members being able to hear the voice of the missing person yelling for help, yet searchers cannot pinpoint the location of these cries and the person is never found. Could it be, that like poor Rhys, some have accidentally stepped into a different dimension?

In Janet Bord's book *'Fairies Real Encounters with Little People'* we find another similar experience in the tale of a young girl from County Mayo, Ireland, who got lost in 1935 near the fairy fort at Liz Ard[30]. As her story goes, this poor girl found herself unfortunate enough to stumble upon the fairy fort on top of a hill, when she tried to leave, she found herself enclosed within an invisible barrier. It appeared to her as if something was physically stopping her from stepping out of the fort to go back down the hill, something she could feel but yet could not see. She tried for many hours to leave, obviously growing more and more distressed until finally, she spotted lights approaching. The lights belonged to a search party that had to have been organized by her concerned parents to find her. She could see them clearly and hear them yelling her name, they appeared to be looking all about the hill for her but even though she could hear them, it appeared that they could neither see nor hear her. Eventually, the search party moved on and she was left alone once again. At some point during the night, she realized that the barrier appeared to have lifted and she fled back down the hill as fast as she could. Arriving safely back home she was able to recount her rather strange if not traumatizing ordeal.

I grew up in rural Ireland (Co. Kerry) and where I lived, we were made aware of the existence of fairy forts and fairy rings and were warned not to 'mess

---

[29] Katharine M. Briggs – The Vanishing People – (1978 – B.T. Batsford Ltd. London).

[30] Ibid.

about' in these areas. I'm not sure if the grown-ups really believed in the fairies or not but certainly, they were superstitious enough to not want to take the chance. Fairies were not thought of as cute and whimsical but dangerous and cunning, trespassing into Fairy territory could be severely punished. It was said that the fairy folk could be malicious if they thought that you were being disrespectful and honestly as a kid, I never questioned it, I don't think any of us did!

Another strange and almost 'alien-like' sighting took place around the 1870's when a gentleman by the name of T.C. Kermode (a member of the Manx Parliament) describes an encounter he had on the Isle of Man one evening. He tells how he and a friend were on their way to a party at the home of another MP in Cronk-a-Voddy, when his friend noticed what appeared to be a circle of light across the river. The spot where the light appeared was a flat space surrounded on both sides by low-formed hills. From out of this light Mr. Kermode witnessed a great crowd of little people, walking in twos and threes, each no bigger than the fictional character Tom Thumb. They were all dressed in what looked like red uniforms and appeared as if they were soldiers, even their movements he commented looked as if they were participating in some kind of drill exercise. Mr. Kermode, curious wanted to move towards them to get a better look however, his friend did not and said that they should just get going to this Party. His friend then proceeded to hit a nearby wall with a stick and yell, as if to scare these little people away. At this ruckus, both the light and the little people immediately vanished.[31]

In Purkin's book *'Troublesome things'* she also describes several well recorded incidents of real people's encounters with Fae Folk. Interestingly, many of these encounters came from the testimony of both men and women during the Scottish witch trials (1550-1670). During interrogation, men and women who were asked about their accusations of witchcraft and devil worship came out with some rather fantastical tales of Fae people and Fairy Kingdoms.

Our first story of a Fairy encounter comes from one Bessie Dunlop[32], a woman who was accused of sorcery and witchcraft circa 1570. In Bessie's account, she recounts meeting an older man who introduced himself to her as Thomas Reid. She describes Thom as a wise and kind elderly gentleman with a white beard and who carried upon his person, a white wand. The most bizarre element to Bessie's story is that the actual Thomas Reid had died some 29 years earlier. Bessie later confirmed that she had not known Thomas

---

[31] Ibid.

[32] Diane Purkiss – Troublesome Things; A history of Fairies and Fairy Stories (2000 Penguin).

Reid when he was alive.

In her first encounter with Thom, Bessie said that she had seen him whilst she was tending to her cattle. She said at the time of his appearance she had been in a state of some distress, her newborn child was sickly as too was her husband. She, herself, was still recovering from the strain and exhaustion of childbirth and found herself sobbing because of the heavy burdens placed upon her at this time. She said that Thomas had come upon her in this state and had approached her to ask if she was ok. She found herself quickly confessing all her troubles to the stranger and despite their only just making acquaintance, she felt strangely comfortable in his presence. They talked further about a great many topics, including her religious orientation and Bessie said that she had made it clear that she was a good Christian woman. In return, she said that he talked a great deal about the protestant reformation and seemed to be of the mindset that the reformation at the time was not a good thing. She had wondered if he might be catholic given his objections to the reformative ideas. After this first meeting, she said that she then saw Thom disappear through a hole in a wall which she described as being far too narrow for a human to squeeze through.

After this initial introduction, Bessie states that Thom would regularly visit her to teach her a great many things, he taught her about herbal remedies and how to heal sick people. She also developed a clairvoyant ability which she had not had previously. She said that she would 'just know' where lost objects were or could prophesize someone's death or illness. When she would ask him why he had picked her to be the recipient of his knowledge he responded that he had been given the order by the Queen of Elfland.

On one of his visits, she claimed that he had tried to convince her to renounce Christianity but when this failed, he left again, this time apparently quite displeased. Another time, he just showed up at her house, Bessie's husband was there at the time along with three of his friends, however, they all seemed oblivious to his presence as if they simply couldn't see him. Thom led her to one end of the house, where she was met by a small party of people comprising of eight women and four men. These strangers greeted her and asked her if she would 'go with them' but Bessie remained silent as Thom had previously instructed her not to speak a word to these strangers. She said that she could see their lips move but could not understand what it is was that they were saying. She said that they then turned to leave and as they were leaving, they let out a hideous howl which she likened to the sound of a hurricane.

After they had left, Thom told her that these strangers were fairies who had

52

come to invite her to go to Elfland with them. She told him that she would consider it but that in all good conscience she did not think that she could abandon her husband and her child. This response seemingly went down like lead balloon with good old Thomas. Still, despite this disagreement, he would regularly visit her to give her good counsel and pass on his knowledge. She said of his manner that he was very gentlemanly and never improper. He would only press her on the topic of leaving with him to go to Elfland but never anything else. She said that she had also seen him in public, walking among people and handling goods that were for sale without drawing attention to himself. She said that she never approached or greeted him in these situations but only addressed him if he approached her first.

When pressed about her knowledge of the 'Queen of Elfland' she said she knew very little. Bessie said that whilst she was confined in childbirth that a stout woman had visited her hut. This woman demanded a drink, and Bessie accommodated her request. The woman then told her that her baby who she had just birthed and was sickly would not recover and would die but her husband who was also presently ill would make a full recovery. The lady then promptly left. It is on the next day that she first met Thomas and was later told that the stout lady had in fact been the Queen of Elfland, whom Thomas served. Over a period of 4 years, Thomas visited with her regularly and would often push her to come with him to Elfland. She would refuse and he would appear sad, shake his head and say that she would repent it. Given she was later burnt at the stake for witchcraft I imagine that she did.

Another story from the witchcraft trial documents comes from Elspeth Reoch who was tried for Witchcraft in 1616[33]. In her account, Elspeth said that when was just 12 years old, she was approached by two strange men whilst she was staying with her aunt who lived by a remote Loch. On this day, she was waiting by the Loch for a boat to get back home (after a day spent in the countryside) when two strange men made her acquaintance. She describes one man as being dressed in green tartan (In Scottish fairy folklore fairies often wear green tartan) and the other, she describes as being dressed in black. Coincidentally accounts of our modern-day Men in Black were also reported during this period, reference being made to them several times during Witch Trial testimony.

Elspeth went on to further describe her encounter with these two men. She said that the man in green told her he thought that she was pretty and offered to give her knowledge of anything that her heart desired. The man in black however seemed less than pleased with the behavior of his companion

---

[33] Ibid.

advising this green man to withhold the knowledge as he did not trust Elspeth to keep this information to herself. The man in Green, however, continued unabated, he told Elspeth that she should take an egg and boil it, then take the sweat of it for three Sundays, and then with unwashed hands wash her eyes whereby she should see anything she desires. He then sends her off to her family where she discovers a secret. There she comes across a girl similar in age and circumstance to Elspeth. The man in green tells her that this girl is pregnant by another woman's husband and that no one knows. He tells her to confront the girl which Elspeth does, the origin of this secret pregnancy is then confirmed. This hidden pregnancy is knowledge Elspeth claims that she couldn't have known if it were not for the green man.

Several years later she encounters the man in black, this time however he appears enamored with her and propositions her. As with Bessie's encounter, he tells her he is from the fairy realm but was once her slain kinsman John Stewart. He claimed to be neither dead nor living but somewhere in between. Eventually, she succumbs and sleeps with him but is punished by being struck dumb immediately after the act.

In the trial of Isobel Gowdie in 1645, she also recalls an encounter with a man dressed in all black whose limbs were longer than she'd seen on any man before and who was cold to the touch[34]. From all accounts, it appears that the most common color that these 'strange men' are reported to wear is either black or Green which I found very interesting. In 1401 a woman accused of witchcraft in Geneva told a tale in which the devil would appear to her when she called him forth and he would take the form of a man dressed in a black tunic.

Men in Black have long been associated with the UFO phenomenon but before this, they also were associated with fairies, witchcraft, and magick. As we have shown from our examples, fairy folklore is also steeped in MIB mythology. Accounts of strange unknown men, dressed in black, exhibiting peculiar behavior, and being able to present humans with supernatural gifts such as the power to healing, clairvoyance, and magical knowledge in the form of spells, rituals, and incantations. Certainly, we know that, Albert. K. Bender a well-known UFO researcher and purported MIB victim describes having multiple visits from such odd individuals but what is most interesting to me is how these visits came about in the first place. Bender admits to having performed a magick ritual several nights before his first MIB encounter occurred. After he had performed the ritual, strange occurrences started to ensue, he would report strange blue lights, then seeing a stranger

[34] Ibid.

with luminous eyes on the street at night finally culminating in the first visit from the Men in Black[35].

Could it be that the MIB appeared to Bender because he had, unwittingly, summoned them? Perhaps the ritual he performed opened a doorway for them, allowing them to cross over, or perhaps they can travel between dimensions regardless but targeted Bender as his ritual caught their attention. Perhaps he inadvertently expressed a magical knowledge that they thought he shouldn't have had access to, trying to scare him out of trying such rituals again. The question is why? What is it about uninitiated humans conducting such rituals that concern them? Could it be that this was information he wasn't supposed to have, he wasn't 'gifted' this knowledge like Bessie or Isobel who had permission to use it, possibly he stumbled across it and without trusted council was not skilled enough to wield it? As Allen Greenfield comments in his book *'The Complete Secret Cipher of the Ufonauts'* - "Maybe I mused, we were dealing more with Magick than with Martians".

We have yet another similar story in the case of Alison Pearson (Alesoun Peirsoun) of Bryehill, Scotland who was tried for witchcraft in 1588[36]. As in other stories, her visitor from Elfland claimed to be a kinsman of hers. Interestingly, Alison's tale involves a literal green man (not unlike the Woolpit Children). She recounts that one day she had laid down in Grange Muir after succumbing to a bout of sickness when a man with a green hue to his complexion approached her. He told her that if she would be faithful to him that he might do her some good. She refused saying if he was a good Christian, he would offer to help with no such demand in return. He swiftly departed. However, he would later re-appear to her in the company of other such men and women (similar to Bessie's group encounter) and she was forced to go with them. She said that they were piping (smoking) and drinking and in good spirits. She was held against her will by these strange people for some hours, allegedly not being returned home until dawn.

She said that after this ordeal, they would visit her many times, sometimes they would appear in frightening forms which would terrify her, other times they would be charming and kind in a bid to convince her to be faithful to them. They threatened that should she tell of their visits to anyone that they would martyr her. Indeed, whilst confessing to all this, she advised that she felt as if she had received a blow that numbed her left side. Upon inspection

[35] Allen Greenfield – The Complete Secret Cipher of the Ufonauts (2016).

[36] Diane Purkiss – Troublesome Things; A history of Fairies and Fairy Stories (2000 Penguin).

by her inquisitors, they found that she did indeed, have an ugly mark on her side which she claimed had no feeling.

Alison also boasted of having met with the Queen of Elfland herself, she also claimed that she had been imbued with psychic powers and with previously unknown medicinal knowledge of herbs and remedies. She said that her dead kinsman was also in Elfland and would visit her from time to time. In an interesting tidbit of information, he told her that every year a portion of the folk from Elfland are taken away to Hell, I am unsure what he meant by that, but it certainly raises many more questions about fairies and their connection to Christianity! As with Bessie, Alison's confession of such things was her undoing and she too was burnt for witchcraft, martyred after all, just as the fairies had predicted. Bessie and Alison's accounts as well as many other stories related to Elfland and encounters with the fairy folk are also detailed in Sir Walter Scott's *Letters on Demonology and Witchcraft, specifically letters IV, V, VII, and IX*[37]. These letters are a fascinating read and I recommend anyone with any interest in this topic to give them a read.

Joan of Arc also notably described visions and the auditory phenomenon of what she perceived to be from a religious origin including instructions that she said came from the Virgin Mary. Upon reading her story, however, one cannot help but spot the hallmarks of Fae Folk involvement. Joan perceives fairy lights and becomes imbued with psychic abilities allowing her to predict future events. Joan herself recounts how in order to show her devotion to Our Lady of Domremy, she would gather flowers to make Garlands for her image. Most interestingly she did this near the 'Ladies' Tree or 'Fairies' tree, where the villagers gathered every year on Laetare Sunday for a traditional springtime festival where according to Joan, Maypoles[38] would be cut from the same tree. The old people from the village could still remember a time when 'fairies' were said to live at that same tree and that girls (before Joan's time) would come and hang garlands there in a tradition similar to our May Day celebrations and similar to the Garlands Joan was leaving for Our Lady. This tree was supposed to be near the site of a 'healing' spring, which it was alleged could cure the sick.[39] Could it be that the beautiful woman imagined by Joan to be Our Lady was in fact, one of the Fae Folk misidentified? Certainly, one's encounter with an 'otherworldly' entity could be viewed as a

---

[37] Sir Malcolm Scott's letters on Demonology and Witchcraft (1884).

[38] Ann W. Astell - The Virgin Mary and the "Voices" of Joan of Arc (2003).

[39] Purkiss – "Troublesome Things".

religious experience, if like Joan, one is an extremely religious person.

Interestingly, during several of the encounters we've already examined, the people who have encountered these Fae Folk, claim that the Fae know about Christianity, with some Fae Folk referring to their 'belief' in certain religious ideologies. Could this be some form of manipulation of humans, given the sociopolitical events of the times, or could these interdimensional beings indeed have religious philosophies which mirror our own? It is certainly food for thought.

Bessie and Alison's stories of otherworldly visitors reminded me somewhat of the story of Indrid Cold. This interplanetary tale is partly linked to the notorious Mothman Sightings of Point Pleasant, which took place at roughly the same time as Colds' appearance. In this tale, a strange man wearing a 'green' metal suit approached two young boys in New Jersey in 1966. The boys, terrified, fled from the man and upon returning home, exhausted and upset, described their encounter to their parents. As well as the man's unusual green metal suit, they said that the man was 'grinning' oddly in a way that they found unsettling. I can imagine someone 'not human' may have trouble trying to simulate a human smile since human social nuances are hard to replicate with the result being seen as strange and unsettling.

The second sighting of this stranger was by a man called Woodrow Derenberger. In Derenberger's' account, he was driving home on Interstate 77 when he heard a large crash. He said that a large unidentifiable craft had landed on the road in front of him causing him to have to stop his vehicle. He said at first, all he could see were the lights and thought it must be another vehicle but as he exited his car, he said that what he saw instead was an aircraft shaped like a kerosene lamp chimney. The Grinning Man then exited this strange craft and approached Derenberger. Telepathically he told Derenberger that his name was Indrid Cold and not to be afraid as he meant him no harm. He gave Derenberger some titbits of information regarding his home planet and then he turned to leave, upon departure he told Derenberger that he would visit him again. Over the months and years that followed, Derenberger claimed that Indrid visited him many times and even took him on his spaceship to his home planet. Derenberger's' wife and children also testify to having been witness to Indrid Cold and his companions[40].

---

[40] Necronomipod - Podcast Episode titled 'Mothman Part 1' aired 3 February 2019 by Cool Down Media.

The purpose of Indrids' visits, like Bessie and Alison's 'friends' appears to be the transmission of information. Derenberger was given information about Indrid Colds' home planet Lanulos, about his people and their desires for humanity. Also, as in the cases of Bessie and Alison, Derenbergers' confession to such encounters ultimately ruined his life. He was 'metaphorically' burnt at the stake and his reputation, career, and marriage were ruined as a result. It seems that contact with otherworldly entities can have more negative ramifications on one's well-being and mental health than positive ones.

Another commonality between fairy and alien encounters are the many references to wands, rods, and staffs within these accounts. Interestingly, these implements figure very strongly in mythology, religion, and of course magick, so to see them also pop up frequently within fairy lore and alien encounters is also a fascinating aspect that should not be overlooked. It is small details like this that ultimately tie these events together. In Bessies' encounter with Thom Reid, she notes that he carries with him a 'white wand'. He isn't the only Fae person to be seen with such an instrument. In Janet Bord's *'Real Encounters with Little People'* she refers to several encounters involving wands.

In 1977, in Somerset, England, Cynthia Montefiore wrote an account of her fairy encounter whilst in her mother's rose garden. She describes seeing a small figure about six inches in height, this creature held a little wand that seemed to point towards a Rose, Cynthia then noted that at the tip of the wand there looked to be a little light that shone like a star[41]. In Somerset, England, Joan Tyrrie claimed that at one time she met with one of the 'fair fairies', being a man, in the market of Taunton, having a white rod in his hand, and she came to him, thinking to make an acquaintance of him, and then her sight was clean taken away for a time, and yet hath lost the sight of one of her eyes[42]. This temporary blinding is similar in consequence to Elsbeths' experience. As well as these types of encounters, sleep paralysis victims report experiencing seeing beings standing around their bed holding rods or wands that harshly poke and pod them. These rods and wands are even evidenced in our cave drawings, historical artifacts, and even in our landscapes. The Long Man of Wilmington is the figure of a large man carved into the steep hillside in Wilmington, East Sussex, England measuring 231 feet tall and holdings two staffs or rods in his hands.

---

[41] Janet Bord – Fairies Real Encounters with Little People (1997 by Michael O'Mara Books Limited).

[42] Purkiss – "Troublesome Things".

In 1988 in Rio de Janeiro, Ludovico Granchi was drawn to the woods one evening by the appearance of little lights. Upon entering the woods, he heard sounds that he likened to grasshoppers, shortly thereafter, he was surprised to find himself surrounded by five little men wearing what he thought looked like uniforms (similar to descriptions in Alien encounters). These little men were carrying 'wands' that had lights on their tips that acted like a torch illuminating the area. They then led Ludovico to a cave, this cave led to a large chamber wherein he saw a stone bed. They laid him on the bed and proceeded to examine him with these wands. He remembers the sound that they made, like insects chirping. He describes these little men as being white-skinned, fair-haired with green eyes and thin arms[43].

In his book 'Passport to Magonia', Jacque Valleé documents a sighting which took place at Nouâtre, Indre-et-Loire in France in 1954. George Gatay was a construction worker heading up a team of eight men, when he said that he started to feel peculiarly drowsy and found himself in an almost trance-like state, just wandering away from his co-workers. He recalls that he had no idea where he was going when eventually he came across a rather odd scene. He describes a man wearing a glass helmet, and grey coveralls and holding what he perceived to be either a metal rod or possibly a very thin pistol. Gatay became aware that he was completely paralyzed and unable to move at all. As soon as the paralysis wore off, he ran back to his colleagues terrified, and asked if anyone had witnessed the same thing. They all agreed that they too had witnessed the same odd man. In the same book, Valleé reports an incident in Carazinho, Brazil in 1965, where several teenagers saw five dwarfs dressed in dark uniforms and small boots. They said that "one of them had in his right hand a brilliantly luminous object like a wand[44]."

Janet Bords' book has a great chapter on Aliens and Fairies with many great stories of 'could be Alien-could be Fairy' encounter stories which just cements the similarity between the two almost 'interchangeable' antagonists. These Fairies/Aliens are documented as varied in size ranging from 9inches to 3 feet. Their skin colour is also wide ranging from white, tanned, black, green and yellow. The ones who are reported as 'coming out' of some type of craft are often reported as wearing skin suits or uniforms whereas the ones seen 'in the wild' seem to wear normal clothes usually red or green or black.

American Folk Lore author Walter Wentz when gathering accounts from

[43] Bord, "Fairies Real Encounters".
[44] Jacque Vallee "Passport to Magonia".

people for his thesis on Celtic Folk Lore and Traditions in the very early 20th century gathered the below account: -

'My mother used to tell about seeing the "fair-folk" dancing in the fields near Cardigan; and other people have seen them around the cromlech up there on the hill. They appeared as little children in clothes like soldiers' clothes and with red caps, according to some accounts[45].

There is a large volume of accounts that have sightings involving descriptions of almost 'miliary' style clothing, which tie this type of fairy encounter to the alien phenomena. Could they be the same phenomenon or are these cases of 'misidentification' on both sides of the fence?

Interestingly and as a side note to anyone interested in Cryptozoology there are also some reports of Monkey-like little people who can change in size and seemingly 'phase' in and out of our dimension. Take this account from Ahmad Jamaludin's '*Strange Encounters in Lumut*' bulletin, also featured in Bord's book.

In June 1980:
> *a young girl in Lumut (Malaysia) witnessed tiny entities in white suits approximately two inches in height. These creatures were described by the witness as being very hairy and 'like monkeys'. One of these creatures was wearing a white hat and white boots in addition to its white suit. They carried what looked like backpacks and long weapons. She said that even weirder their feet did not seem to touch the ground. In another report from the same area another girl describes seeing a big hairy creature shrink itself to only a few inches tall. At the same time as these sightings were being reported, UFO reports were also coming in[46].*

I've listened to many Bigfoot encounters over the years and am a fan of the Sasquatch Chronicles Podcasts. There have been multiple accounts of people witnessing Bigfoot seemingly 'phase in and out' of our plain of existence. I don't think that it would be a massive leap looking at all the accounts to suggest that the Bigfoot cryptid could be a member of the Fae Family. Certainly, we know the lore of large entities such as Trolls and Ogres who are on the larger side of the Fae Folk.

---

[45] Walter Wentz - The Fairy–Faith in Celtic Countries (2001 Blackmask Online).

[46] Ahmad Jamaludin 'strange Encounters in Lumut' article published October 1981 in Malaysian UFO Bulletin, no. 3.

Bigfoot are quite often seen at the same time as reports of strange lights either in the skies or manifesting in the woods. In his *Sasquatch Chronicles* podcast host, Wes Germer tells how he has now heard so many 'encounter' stories which involve strange lights that when he is interviewing a witness, he now includes the question regarding the sighting of strange lights as standard.

There are many Bigfoot encounter stories involving Bigfoot being seen with or within a short timescale of an apparition, commonly a 'Woman in White' type specter. They have also been spotted with what people describe as the archetypal 'Grey' aliens. Short grey-green creatures about two to three feet in height. Could in these instances, these 'greys' be Fae Folk mistaken for Aliens? I think there is good evidence to support the theory of interdimensional entities manifesting in our reality. Could the Fae Folk be the same Grey's commonly associated with the alien phenomenon? Could these creatures be interdimensional in nature, able to appear and disappear at will, are cryptids just another branch of the Fae Folk tree explaining why we don't have more 'hard evidence' of their existence?

The native Alaskans have a folklore story regarding the area near the Kobuk River. In this legend, a large Rock came from the skies, landed and little people exited the 'Rock' and with them was a 'big' person. There are several reports in Ufology of 'hairy men' exiting unidentified spacecraft. Interestingly in the early 20th century (circa 1909) Walter Wentz was gathering stories on the Fae Folk for his thesis on Celtic Traditions and had many stories from Irishmen of such encounters. One, in particular, I thought interesting, and which is also detailed in Jacque Vallee's book *'Passport to Magonia'* comes from an interview that Wentz had with a local Irishman who frequently had communication with what he referred to as 'The Gentry'. I've come across multiple references to these 'Gentry' before in several folklore books and articles. From what I can deduce they seem to be a subset of the Fae Folk. From all accounts, they appear similar in appearance to regular humans. Usually comparable in height and dressing in regular (if not a little out of date) clothing. They also appear to be the ones who are responsible for the dispensing of knowledge, such as with Bessie and Isobel.

After his encounter with the Gentry, this anonymous Irishman tells' Wentz *"They are able to appear in different forms. One once appeared to me and seemed only four feet high and stoutly built. He said 'I am bigger than I appear to you now. We can make the old young, the big small and the small big'"*. If that is indeed the case then surely, these creatures manifest the ability to make themselves or others as small or large as they wish them to be? If Bigfoot is part of this Fae Community, does it have this same ability to change size, or can its size be influenced by others from its realm of existence? Interestingly, as a side note on this encounter, the gentleman also goes on to say that he was told that whilst the Gentry are a distinct class of Fae, there are other types of Fae such as ghosts, bad spirits, and even Leprauchans. *"Besides the gentry, who are a distinct class, there are bad spirits and ghosts, which are nothing like them. My mother once saw a leprechaun beside a bush hammering. He disappeared before she could get to him, but he also was unlike one of the gentry."*[47]

Another interesting commonality between Alien and Fae Encounters is the 'baby abduction' phenomenon. Fairies for centuries have been accused of stealing babies, even replacing them at times with sickly or elderly Fae Folk called 'Changelings'. In modern alien abduction reports, we have multiple stories of women and men being taken claiming to have been used for breeding purposes. Women recount stories of being 'impregnated' and then having the fetus removed from them. There are even bizarre stories of both men and women who claim to have been brought 'somewhere' unfamiliar and asked to 'hug and hold' hybrid children as their alien custodians apparently do not know how to provide love or comfort. Why would aliens need to do this, are they not capable of reproduction on their own? There are several theories, but most seem to involve a 'strengthening' of the alien DNA by introducing fresh human DNA into the mix. Some even posit that these entities from a different dimension are physically unable to stay within our dimension for extended periods. That the hybridization of the species would allow them to spend greater time in our plane of existence. The same argument has been put forth previously as to why Fairies would steal healthy human children. Simply they need to enhance and strengthen ailing bloodlines.

Do I think Aliens and Fairies are the same thing? Well, if we posit that the greys, little folk, and characters such as Thom Reid or the grinning man are Fae Folk then yes. Certainly, there seems to be a significant number of cases where the two phenomena overlap. Several 'alien' encounters could be Fae encounters and vice versa. Whilst I believe in the existence of Extraterrestrials as a separate phenomenon, I do not believe that the reports of encounters and abductions we've just discussed are being perpetrated by them. It just doesn't make a whole lot of sense to me. If extraterrestrials had even a vague interest in us as a species, I don't think that would waste their time hanging around our solar system for thousands of years playing games of peek-a-boo and probing people. The frequency of these encounters is too great, spaceships would need to be docked permanently outside our atmosphere to facilitate the high rate of comings and goings. In a large

---

[47] Vallee, "Passport to Magonia".

majority of cases what I think we're dealing with is interdimensional in nature rather than extraterrestrial.

This leads me to an interesting account described in Vallees' *Passport to Magonia*. Gary T. Wilcox was a dairy farmer from Tioga City, New York who was tending to chores in his field located about one mile from his house when he saw something quite peculiar. According to Gary, he saw something which at first, he thought to be a refrigerator. As he got closer, he could see that it was a white, egg-shaped craft. When he put his hand out to touch it, he noted that it wasn't hot and that it looked to be completely smooth with no visible door or hatch. The latter detail is why he was so shocked when two 'human-like' beings exited the craft. He said they were small in stature about 4 ft tall and wore seamless clothing. This 'all-in-one' was complete with a headdress and a full-face hood which obscured his view making it impossible for him to make out any facial features. He said that these beings spoke with him telepathically, advising him that they were from the planet Mars and expressing an interest in his fertilizer. What is of interest to me is the next bit. Gary said that their questions seemed childlike as if they didn't know anything about farming or even know what fertilizer is. They told Gary that their planet was suffering from environmental issues and wanted to know more about our agricultural techniques. They did tell him some details about their craft and space travel, but he said he couldn't quite understand what they were talking about and therefore found it hard to follow or to repeat. They then asked Gary for a bag of fertilizer, so he left them for several minutes to go and retrieve one for them, however when he returned, they had gone. Gary then decided to leave this bag in the same spot, just in case, and indeed the next day when he went to check on it, it had gone!

What gets me about this encounter is how 'unknowledgeable' these entities were. If you were a race from Mars who is so advanced that you have conquered space travel would fertilizer or the concept of agriculture be such a mystery to you? If your planet is suffering from such considerable climate issues that you are having to go off the planet to find solutions, would you really send two representatives who knew nothing about the subject, I mean how would they comprehend what they were being told or shown? What if the farmer had gone into great detail on the subject, would they have been capable of taking that information back and applying it? Wouldn't you send your best scientists and other agriculturists? Why would you send Larry and Mo? This story is so bizarre to me and reads more like a Fae Folk encounter than anything extra-terrestrial.

Caves, Caverns, and Underground Places

Whilst man may have dominion over the land, The Green Man and his minions it would appear, have dominion over the woods, the forests, and all that fall within. Did you ever walk-through dense woodland, edging ever deeper into the wild to suddenly have the sense that you shouldn't be there, that you just don't belong? In my research on the Green Man and his connection to the Fae Folk (as interdimensional beings) I come across repeated references to caves, caverns, and huge tunnel systems. Rock, boulders, and granite seem to be intrinsically linked to this strange phenomenon as well as being home to many sightings of 'little people', weird zoomorphic animals, and even reptilian humanoids. Sub terranean tunnel systems, whether man-made or natural are a doorway into another world. Whether that world already exists within our reality or whether there is a gateway here to other dimensions I am unsure, however, I suspect that it is a combination of both concepts.

Humans have long held a fascination with caves, they sheltered us and kept us warm long before we had the privilege of civilization. They are also places of mystery, empty voids of blackness, odd noises, and sounds echoing off cold wet walls. It is not hard to see how humans could create stories of monsters looming in the darkness. For as much as they provided prehistoric man with shelter and warmth, they were also at times, places of immense danger. Prehistoric man was not the only one to enjoy their hospitality and would have to share this warmth and safety with all manner of dangerous beasts such as bears, wolves, and mountain lions. These caves have a duality, they can offer safety and protection from the elements outside but pick the wrong cave and it may be the end of you. Even today, humans retain a healthy fear of dark places, it's what has kept us safe. You never know what is lurking in the shadows, there's an imposing sense of claustrophobia, and it's hard to flee when it's dark and you are disorientated. Certainly, many have met their end this way, getting themselves lost and turned about in these cold stone mazes, never able to find their way back out. Only the really brave (or the stupid!) would dare to push deeper.

So, what do these cave systems have to do with our Green Man? Well, that is what I am trying to figure out. Certainly, there is a link between the Green Man and the Fae Folk. The Green Man is clearly recognized throughout mythology as the 'King' or 'Father' archetype, take our Pigmy King or The Green Knight for example. If we also speculate that these Fae Folk are interdimensional in nature and can manifest into and out of our reality, then it would follow that our Green Man archetype is also of the same ilk. Clearly, there is most certainly a link between 'little people' and caves, caverns, and boulder fields. Could this be where and how they are able to manifest and travel between dimensions?

When I was in my late teens and early twenties, I would regularly visit my mother's house in Co. Laois in Ireland. Ireland as you may have gathered is a place steeped in mystery and Folklore. Belief in fairies and such creatures was then and I suspect may still be now, strong. When my mother and I would take her dogs for walks across the bogs and across the fields she would point out the fairy forts and the standing stones and tell me stories of strange fairy lights and other odd occurrences that regularly took place on the bogs.

One story that I recall her telling me, occurred early one evening when she was out walking her dogs. She stepped from the path onto the peat bog when she suddenly became aware that she couldn't walk, she was frozen, physically unable to move forward. As if something external to her was preventing her from moving any further forward. She said she then heard a voice in her head tell her 'What you see all around you is within you" then she said she felt that everything became alive, she could feel the rocks, the peat, the earth beneath her feet as living breathing organisms and she felt 'God like' as if she had limitless power. She had a feeling that she could just 'let go' and her soul would leave her body and that she could float up into the heavens and touch the stars. She said that as much as she wanted to do so she was scared, she felt fear at the prospect of leaving her physical being and so fought the urge to do so. After this, things slowly returned to normal, she was able to move again and quickly returned home. She said she'd lost some time as it was late afternoon, early evening when she left but now it was late and getting dark. The bogs are not somewhere you want to be at night, there is no light except for whatever the moon decides to share, and the terrain is uneven and prone to holes and ankle-breaking drops. Upon returning home she said she felt very shaken by the whole experience, and it took her several days to recover from the shock and from the residual energy that took days to dissipate.

To take this back to my commentary on rocks and boulders, quite often walking across the fields or bogs in Ireland you would just 'come across' these large standing stones. To me, they looked just like the monoliths at stone henge but mini versions. Sometimes they'd be four or five of them, spread out almost in a circle, other times one would be just on its own. They would just be left there, undisturbed. Farmers who owned the land would refuse to move them, as they were superstitious, believing that if they moved the stones bad things would happen to them. Anything or any place deemed 'fairy' land would be left untouched and left in peace. Perhaps Ireland's best known standing stone or portal tomb is Poulnabrone, located alongside the Corofin-Ballyvaughan road in County Claire. This Late Stone Age monument, though the topic of much fairy legend, once held the bones of 16 adults and children who lived in the surrounding farming community[48].

This refusal to touch fairy stones reminds me of a story of road workers in Co. Donegal in 1968 who downed tools and refused to cut down a fairy tree to make way for a new road that was being constructed. In fact, the issue was so bad with all the men refusing to fell the tree that the road had to be re-routed so that the tree could be left untouched! Such is the power of belief and superstition, and I must be honest; I wouldn't have risked cutting it down either! [49]

Back to Bessie's story, in her account, her 'friend' Thom Reid appeared to move between tiny spaces in walls, which Bessie herself said she thought impossible. In Bessie's time in rural Scotland the walls wouldn't have been made from brick as commonly as they are today but out of natural rock and stone which would be placed one on top of the other held together with tampered earth. It seems as if Thom has able to use the Stone as a method to move between dimensional realms. There are other stories of individuals who have reported seeing little people coming out of rock formations or that these little people would seem to 'suddenly' appear from behind a rock of some kind. Stranger still, in some accounts people say that they have seen little doorways and even little windows manifest in these boulders in front of their eyes.

Indeed, it was the premise of 'Goblins' being seen coming in and out of old mining caves in Kentucky that lead the TV documentary show Hellier to its investigation. In later episodes of the show, a series of synchronicities lead the team to investigate the strange 'alien visitor' Indrid Cold. The one and same Grinning Man mentioned earlier in our previous chapter. As a result of this discovery, the team, combining historical information as left by Indrid Cold (I assume via Derenberger) and some GPS coordinates which were given to them by an elusive individual called Terry Wriste, they find themselves led to a particular Cave. In this Cave, they attempt to communicate by way of paranormal investigative equipment (the Estes Method combined with the 'God's Helmet') with Indrid Cold and/or other entities. During this communication, they are told that it is possible to 'open' a doorway or portal using a series of certain musical tones. As part of this 'opening ritual,' they were required to play these certain tones, constantly on

---

[48] Faery Mounds – on Faerypool.com

[49] Bord, "Fairies Real Encounters".

a loop. This was the end of Season 2 so I'm not sure how the ritual played out but certainly it was a very creepy if not fascinating episode.

I certainly believe that deep within these cave systems it could be possible even plausible for other non-human entities to exist and that it is from these cave systems that they enter and exit our world. If we are looking for a literal Hades/Hell within the parameters of our natural world, then we can find no greater location than the caves and tunnel system running right under our feet. In our subsequent chapter focusing on the Green Man archetype, we'll delve further into the aspect of The Underworld in his narrative and take a look at his connection to Osiris, Dionysus, and Cernunnos who were all Gods of their own respective 'Underworlds'.

Interestingly, when researching the Fae Folklore, one of the origins of the Fae Folk has them as small Briton people pushed back to cave systems to survive. We also know that some Fae Folk are troglodytes such as nature Nymphs, Trolls, and Dwarves. Dwarves are intrinsically linked to cave systems given their profession as Miners! Well, besides the many accounts of 'little people', Gnomes, Dwarves, and Goblins being seen to enter and exit from Cave systems there are also other more ominous accounts of people seeing other entities within the Cave Systems beneath our feet. Stories from cavers, spelunkers, and adventurers. Abduction stories of people being held and tortured and killed by entities unknown in underground facilities.

One famous cave system in Malta has an Urban Legend regarding the loss of 30 Maltese school children and their teacher who went missing in the hidden underground tunnels accessible from the Hal Saflieni Hypogeum[50]. Now, I tried to see if this story has any truth to it, it certainly appears to have been reported upon in the press there is even an article in the National Geographic Magazine (in the 1940 August issue - no. 78) which specifically references the incident. However, there are conflicting reports with some news articles claiming that the story is a hoax, with Heritage Malta, the authority responsible for prehistoric sites in Malta, confirming that the story is just a myth. Now whether this is a hoax or story designed to stop people wandering off and getting lost in the caves or indeed whether details are being suppressed by the Maltese government who are concerned about the negative impact on tourism which Malta so greatly relies upon, we don't know. Either way, it's a very creepy story.

---

[50] Stranger things: the mystery of the lost children of Hal Saflieni Hypogeum article by Melanie Drury posted on GuideMeMalta.com April 2021.

I did come across an 'unverified' story of two tourists who themselves got a little 'off track' within the same cave system. These two ladies claim that they came to a point in the cave where it opened up into a large almost auditorium size room. The path from the tunnel that they were following ended abruptly in a sheer drop. They stopped for a moment to take in the vast beauty before them before turning around to go back the way that they had come, when one of them noticed what appeared to be movement in the dark, out of the corner of her eye. On the opposite side of this large cavern, some ledges seemed to go down the whole depth of the cave. This woman reports that she saw in the darkness, on one of these ledges, what she describes as a large reptilian humanoid figure, which she guessed stood about 8-10 feet tall and oddly wearing what looked like a robe. I am unsure whether there would have been enough light present for them to get such a good look from that distance, but it certainly paints an ominous picture[51].

Malta as a country is riddled with underground cave systems, they account for about 1/3rd of Malta itself. Malta certainly isn't the only country where reports of strange entities or reptilian-type humanoids have been made. Take the following report made by an expert and investigator of cave systems in Austria, the Czech Republic, and Poland, a man named Gregor. In this report, Gregor claimed to have witnessed a reptilian in the old salt mine caves of northern Austria in May 2011.

The following is an excerpt of the story published on the listverse.com website: -

'He estimated that he was around 50 meters (164 ft) below the surface and was taking cave chippings to be studied. That's when Gregor heard strange voices coming from close by. He stopped and listened to the sound until the voices appeared to stop. Ignoring them, he moved farther through the cave and into a chamber where he smelled a rotting odor. Suddenly, he heard the voices again. A little spooked, Gregor decided to turn back and exited the chamber as quickly as he could. As he did so, he turned his head to look behind him and saw with horror that a light appeared to be illuminating the previously dark room. One light became several, and Gregor finally got a glimpse of what was carrying them. He stated that several muscular, lizard-like creatures, standing upright, now occupied the previously empty chamber. He stated that each one seemed to wear what appeared to be a uniform, and that they had tails that swung behind them. They appeared to be talking to each other in a language that he did not know

[51] Debunking Urban Legends – The Hypogeum Myths by Warren Bugeja published on Heritage Malta.mt.

but which still sounded similar to human speech. The creatures did not seem to notice Gregor who, as quickly as he could, made his way out of the caves and to the safety of the ground above[52].

Since the opening of the 'World's largest known Cave System' Hang Son Doong in Vietnam to the Public there have been a slew of witnesses reporting seeing a reptilian-like creature. This creature has now been nicknamed The Devil Creature of Son Doong. We even have a picture of the Devil himself, captured by a visitor to the caves in 1992[53]. The creature is described as being humanoid in appearance but with the head and skin of a reptile.

Another story I recall reading was in the comment section of a YouTube video (I cannot recall the exact video). I read the story years ago, but it stuck with me, I've tried to find the video in question to link it here but unfortunately, I can't remember specifically the video and I can't seem to find it again so I cannot credit the people involved but if this is you and you posted this story, please let me know so that I can credit you.

The story is by a young woman who was solo hiking in the wilderness, forgive me but I cannot for the life of me remember where only that it was an American National Park. During her hike, the weather took a turn for the worse and she managed to find a cave to take shelter in. Whilst taking shelter she could hear noises from within the cave. Curious she went further in as she thought that it might be other people sheltering from the weather. As she got deeper into the cave system, she began to feel uncomfortable and decided to turn back at which point she was attacked by entities unknown and rendered unconscious. Upon coming to, she found herself in a large cavern, she said that there were many different types of people there, humans in medical clothing carrying clipboards and seeming to take notes, as well as what she perceived to be reptilian-like humanoids. She could also see what looked like cages containing other humans including children who all appeared distressed and were calling for help. She said that when she came to, she was tied to a medical-style gurney and then was subjected to medical procedures. After she had been poked and prodded, she said she was sexually assaulted by one of the reptilian humanoid creatures. She then thinks that they used something on her to 'knock her out' again and when she came around, she was back at the cave entrance. She immediately fled the cave and managed to get herself back to her car. She reported this to park rangers and

---

[52] 10 Modern Day Sightings of Reptilian Humanoids by Marcus Lowth published on Listverse.com May 2016.

[53] Devil Creature of Son Doong Cave (photograph) published on Cryptidz Fandom.com.

the police, but no one took her story seriously putting her experience down to concussion stating that she must have tripped or fallen and suffered a head injury. Now I've had concussions twice in my life and I have never hallucinated such a horrific event, so I cannot believe that head injury alone could account for what this poor woman experienced.

There is another similar story documented in *'Project Red Book'* by Alan Branton[54] which I discovered through Steph Young's book *'Hunted in the Woods*[55]. This 'Project Red Book' is an index that contains hundreds of reports of Underground Cave systems and possible military and or Alien activity. Branton tells of how a female doctor told him a story of how she was abducted, and taken to a cave system where she witnessed other humans who were being raped and tortured by 'cannibal beast-men'. She claimed to be held for a period of 3 months until all the captives, herself included were freed by pale-skinned beings wearing metallic uniforms.

This next story is taken from David Paulides's book, *'Missing 411 – North America and Beyond'*. I also listened to David tell the story when he appeared as a guest on the Radio Show *Where Does the Road Go* episode[56] where the host Seriah had David on as a guest, and it got my attention immediately. As the story goes in 2010, a 3-year-old boy (only referred to as John Doe) went missing during a family fishing trip to Mount Shasta. At around 6 pm in the evening, the boy's family realized that the boy was nowhere to be found and started to look for him. After several agonizing hours with no luck, the parents then alerted the Park Rangers and an immediate search of the area was begun. Five hours after the search had been initiated rescue personnel found the boy laying dazed and confused in an area of brush just off the trail which had already been thoroughly searched.

A while later when the boy had recovered from his ordeal, he had quite the story to tell. He told his parents that when he had gotten lost in the woods his grandma who he called 'Kappy' had appeared and taken him to a cave. He said that this woman looked like his Kappy, but he didn't like her, and he knew that she wasn't his real Kappy. He said that when they were in this cave, he noticed that Kappy had a weird light emanating from her head and that's when he knew for sure that she was not his real grandma. She then led the boy to a cold dark room which he said was infested with spiders. The room

---

[54] Project Red Book published on Angelfire.com.

[55] Stephen Young – Hunted in The Woods (2015).

[56] Where did the Road Go Radio

was also full of motionless humanoid 'robots' and scattered all over the floor were old dirty purses, guns, and other types of weapons. At this point the 'woman' asked him to defecate on a piece of paper, the boy, however, said that he didn't need to 'go' and this apparently made the lady very angry. She kept trying to convince him to poop but he refused and eventually after some time, the woman became frustrated, gave up, and led the boy back to where she found him. She told him to wait there, and that he would be discovered.

Oddly, 'John' said that during his time in the cavern this woman had told him that he had been planted in his mother's womb and that he was actually from outer space. Another interesting element to this story is that his real grandmother wasn't with the family on this camping trip but had been holidaying in the same area a year previous. Whilst on her own camping trip, she said that one morning she woke to find herself face down in the dirt. She had no idea how she'd got there, and she quickly became aware of an intense pain in her neck. Upon inspection, two puncture wounds could be seen and the skin around the wound was red and inflamed. Another friend of hers, also on this camping trip, experienced a similar 'bite' both women putting it down to an insect or spider bite.

Could it be that DNA was extracted from these women the year previous and it was used to 'clone' them both at a later date? Whatever happened to 'Kappy' and 'John' was certainly very unsettling, and I am very glad to hear that John was found safe and sound. There are far too many missing children's stories that do not have such a happy ending. What was 'Kappy' and what were the 'humanoid Robots' that the young child witnessed deep within that cave? I know that children can be unreliable witnesses, but I have two children myself and neither of them has ever come up with a story nearly so fantastical. However, neither of them has ever been lost deep in the woods before so who's to say what impact this trauma can have on a child's mind? Interestingly, this isn't the only 'robot-like' entity that I have come across in my research.

In *'Passport to Magonia'*, Valleé reports an incident involving a gentleman simply referred to as Mr. S. In 1964 Mr. S had been hunting in the mountains of northern California when he became lost, having somehow become separated from the rest of his hunting party. As it got darker, and he was unable to continue walking safely, he decided to climb a tree and send up some flairs in an attempt to call for help. Sometime later he became aware of lights in the sky, at first, he thought it must be a rescue helicopter out looking for him but then as it got closer, he realized it wasn't a helicopter at all but rather some strange unrecognizable craft. He said it stopped and hovered for a moment, then he saw something dark fall from it. At this point, he became aware of movement in the forest around him and saw two strange beings coming toward his location. He describes them as a little over 5ft tall wearing silver uniforms that also covered their heads. A third creature appeared shortly thereafter, behaving, he said, more mechanical than man. It was darker in colour than the other two and had reddish-orange eyes. It didn't appear to have a mouth instead it had a slit-like opening that would 'drop' open like an oven door!

These three entities stood at the bottom of his tree and stared at him for a while before trying to get him to fall out of it. He said the entity with the oven mouth would occasionally 'drop' open this mouth and a cloud of smoke would come out. It would drift up to where he was, and he would lose consciousness for a bit. Thankfully, he had the wherewithal to use his belt to strap himself to the tree so that he would not fall out during these bouts of unconsciousness. Eventually, he fell asleep, and when he awoke the beings had thankfully disappeared[57].

Coincidentally, I also found another reference to entities disguising themselves as Grandparents. David Brewster whilst writing for the Seattle Magazine in 1970 on the Bigfoot phenomenon, refers to the Native American (First Nation People) tales of a female man-eating Sasquatch who kidnaps children, sometimes by disguising herself as the victims' grandmother. She seals their eyes shut and carries them off on her back[58]. David Paulides has also recounted many stories of children, who similarly to 'John Doe' went missing only to turn up hours or days later with strange stories. Often the children are dazed and confused, with a very hazy memory of their 'time missing'. Some of them who have some memory, tell stories of animals, which they describe as wolfmen or bear men who take care of them. Sometimes taking them into caves or up into large trees for shelter, feeding them berries, and keeping them warm by nestling up next to them. In some cases, when the children are asked how they got back, they responded that they were returned because 'they were the wrong type' which is most bizarre.

In Steph Young's book *'Hunted in the Woods; True Stories of Unexplained Disappearances'* she also references two similar stories. The first, is a story recounted by Cirila Laguens, a Shop Owner in Veracruz. She told her story to FATE magazine which published the article in its November 1977 edition. According to Mrs. Laguens, her 3-year-old son wandered off from their home and was missing for 6 days. He was eventually found, safe and well by

---

[57] Young, "Hunted in The Woods".

[58] Ibid.

a search party in a cave approximately 10 miles from their house. Even though he had been missing for nearly one week he was in perfect health, he wasn't injured, hungry or dehydrated. He said that he'd got lost near a river and five 'little men' had found him, they took him to the cave and feed him and gave him milk to drink. He said that the little ones stayed in this cave and played with him. Interestingly and paralleling a lot of the Missing 411 stories, the cave where he was found was incredibly hard to get to. The entire mouth of this cave is covered in dense shrub which caused many minor scratches and scrapes to his rescuers yet the boy himself despite having bare feet and legs was completely unscathed[59].

Also published in FATE magazine is the story of Señor R. Gutierrez. Snr Gutierrez tells how in the summer of 1970 he was walking with his nephew in the forest, near Mixtequilla in Veracruz, one minute the boy was by his side, the next he had completed vanished. After spending hours searching and calling for the boy, he decided to return to the village to gather help. A search party was quickly formed and undertook an extensive search of the area with no success. Indeed, suspicion fell on the unfortunate Snr. Gutierrez who was accused of harming the boy himself. One month later whilst waiting to go on trial for his nephew's murder the boy simply turned up back at home. He was completely unharmed and in good physical condition. When asked what had happened to him and where he'd been all this time? The boy said that he had been with the 'little men' and that they played with him, fed him honey, and gave him milk to drink before finally letting him go.[60] As a side note, milk and honey are common foods left as 'gifts' to Fae Folk.

Returning to the subject of caves and the high strangeness that lurks within them, as well as reports of reptilian humanoids, I have also come across reports of large subterranean military facilities. These facilities are speculated to be Black Sites, responsible for cloning, genetic testing, and other nefarious activities. I came across a very interesting story of a woman in The Netherlands who had a sighting of a bigfoot-type creature in one of Holland's national parks. She said that the animal was white and strange looking, it was humanoid standing on two feet, and seemed to be intelligent appearing to make eye contact with her before hiding behind trees.

In an update to the story, the woman returned to this spot several times to try to find the creature again. On one visit she had taken with her a friend who was also a psychic in the hopes of communicating with this strange

[59] Ibid.

[60] Ibid.

being. The psychic was able to pick up some information through telepathic communication with the animal. The story that she tells is fantastical that's for sure! The creature told the woman that she was female and had been created by genetic modification, specifically the genetic splicing of different animal species with human DNA also. She was born and lived in an underground facility but had recently managed to escape. Life in the facility was terrible, she was kept in a small cage and had no contact or company other than another small, modified animal that she looked after and seemingly kept as a pet. She was tested on frequently and knew that she would be 'terminated' shortly. Apparently, something had occurred in the facility and as a result, she was able to take the opportunity to escape and was now trying to evade capture by living in the woods.

In a series of update videos, the woman and her psychic friend return several times to communicate with the creature and try to learn more about it. If I remember correctly, it did give them some specifics on where the facility was located and I think they went to the area to check it out and did come across what looked like a small metal door, similar to the doors found at Power Grids but I don't think that they got much further. After a few visits, they were no longer able to see or communicate with the creature with the psychic speculating that she thought it had been recaptured and terminated as she could no longer 'feel' its presence.

I came across this story on YouTube, the woman had even created her own channel publishing updates on this story. I've since tried to find the YouTube channel to credit it here, but I cannot find it. I'm not sure if they've taken it down but if anyone else is familiar with this story and has any updates, please contact me as I would be very interested to see if it was ever sighted again or indeed if the whole story was a hoax. I did find a reference to a similar story, I cannot be sure, however, if it's recounting the same story, if it is, it is much more condensed. This story was published on the YouTube channel called *Haunting Ghost Nederland*, Season 10 Episode 2, link to the video in the references[61].

Reports of large underground facilities and medical experimentation, specifically covert genetic research is nothing new. In New Mexico, there is said to be an underground Military Base called the Dulce Base. The reports of this base first surfaced when Thomas Costello, an alleged security officer at the base blew the whistle on the covert operation, its military partnership

---

[61] Haunting Ghost Nederland YouTube Channel – Episode titled S10 E 2 Finding bigfoot in the Netherlands (creature Holland).

with aliens, and the horrific genetic experimentation taking place within its confines. When researching the Dulce Base, it is very hard to find conclusive proof of its existence, not surprising if it really is a 'Black Ops' site. Indeed, most of the testimony supporting its existence comes from only a few sources and the testimony of these sources is dubious with it being near impossible to 'verify' the validity of their reports. I couldn't find many 'factual' books on the subject with most information being found online and speculative at best[62].

However, do we know that examples of such underground bases do exist. We know that there are bunkers within cave systems that have been created to house military weapons and weapon prototypes, bunkers for the U.S. President and all over the world similar for world leaders in event of an 'apocalyptic' event. There are storage warehouses deep underground containing hard copies of information files and information as well as storing items of cultural and historic significance. So, the idea that an underground facility such as Dulce exists is not at all surprising in fact, I would hazard it's to be expected. It is however the 'Alien' involvement with this base which is what makes the story of Dulce 'fantastical'.

These more shocking details surrounding the Dulce Base are concerning the involvement of the military base with Alien species. Seemingly, the base is a joint partnership between the U.S Government (no doubt a shadow version of it) and various Alien races, including the Greys and the now infamous Reptilians. Interestingly Thomas says of the Alien races that they have a hierarchy with there being different 'castes' of aliens. From all account's the Tall Greys or the Nordics (Pleiadeans) appear to be the dominant race and are extra-terrestrial in origin. Whereas the Reptilians are native to Earth and have been here even before mankind. They thoroughly dislike humans, believing us to be the 'squatters' here. The greys are said to be under the control of the Nordics behaving more like worker bees and even some reptilians seem lower down in the caste system. Although from my research there seems to even be a caste system within the reptilian species, with some holding much higher positions than others.

The story of the Dulce base came to light back in the 1970's when an alleged security officer at the base blew the whistle on the site by leaking photographic evidence that Aliens not only existed but were also working at the site. As mentioned in the earlier paragraph, the whistle-blower in question

---

[62] The Last Podcast on the Left – Episode 187 (aired 12 Aug 2015) and Episode 188 (aired 19 Aug 2015).

is Mr. Thomas Costello. Now, in my research, I've found it hard to find out if Mr. Costello is a 'real' person. On the internet, he is referred to as both Castello and Costello which makes finding him difficult and harder still is that Mr. Costello and his family appear to have 'disappeared' after the photograph was leaked so we have nothing on him since the end of the 1970's. As is often the case, the internet sleuths are divided on the existence of Mr. Costello and the veracity of his claims. Unfortunately, the photograph of the 'alleged alien' which is on the internet has been proven to be a hoax. The picture is confirmed to be a still from the sci-fi movie The 6th Day which was released in 2000. Now the interesting detail here, is that if Mr. Costello leaked the picture at the end of the 1970's then how did he manage to get hold of a movie still from a film that hadn't even been made yet? This leads me to speculate, did Mr. Costello even exist, and did he really leak a photo? If so, where is this original photograph since this first photograph cannot possibly be the same one floating around the internet? Or is this all a hoax and the originator of the hoax created the character of Costello, Dulce Base, and the infamous photograph?

According to Costello, Dulce is an underground military facility in Dulce, New Mexico. It is approximately two miles underground and is comprised of six floors. Allegedly, the first few floors contain offices, staff quarters, and the usual administrative departments. Once you get past floor 3, things get interesting. The next few floors contain laboratories dedicated to black book projects such as genetic manipulation and splicing and mind control experiments. There are prisoner-holding cell areas where humans and even some aliens are held captive awaiting a horrific fate. Costello reports that they are creating all kinds of 'mixed' species. They are splicing human, animal, and even alien DNA to produce a number of monstrous abominations. If you're anything like me then you've already pictured Dulce as being akin to the something like Umbrella Corp facility in Resident Evil! Costello continues that on the lower levels, there are alien living quarters, where various species live, sleep and eat. Humans are not meant to be around these areas as it can be dangerous as some species such as the lower-class reptilians are known to eat humans.

It was the discovery of these human captives which ultimately convinced Mr. Costello to blow the whistle on the facility. He said that whilst working there, the human staff were under strict instruction to not 'speak' to any of the captives. They were told that they were 'prisoners' the implied assumption being that these were 'bad people'. He did, however, strike up a dialogue with one man referred to only as 'George S'. This man gave Thomas his full details and said he had been abducted and was, in fact, being held there against his will. Thomas crossed checked this man's details and found that he had indeed been reported as a 'missing person' certainly not a convicted felon as Thomas had been led to believe. From this point onwards, Thomas began to suspect that the humans being held there, had most likely been abducted and were being held there against their will and he could not in all good conscious continue to say nothing.

It is said that Thomas leaked several photographs, stills that he took off several security cameras from around the base. Photographs which he said proved that aliens existed and that they were working alongside the military and shadow government. That citizens were being taken against their will and experimented on, tortured, and killed, all with the permission of the United States Government. Thomas and his family disappeared straight after he leaked the photographs and blew the whistle. Now whether this actually happened or whether it is all part of the hoax narrative we don't know. However, we do know that Thomas isn't the only person to make reference to the Dulce Base and to its strange subterranean goings on.

In 1976 a man called Paul Bennewitz was an Electronics Engineer in San Diego who had started to see strange lights in the sky. Aware of the UFO phenomenon at the time he decided to do some investigating of his own. Being electronics engineer and being fortunate to own his own Electronics Store, Paul decided to whip up his own homemade radio device that was capable of intercepting communications coming out of the nearby Kirkland Airfield Base. He would also try to use this device to see if he could pick up any transmissions, human or otherwise when these lights in the sky made their appearance. After some time spent intercepting various communications, he believed that he had hit the jackpot and that finally, he could prove Alien Contact.

After some time spent gathering this data, Paul eventually came forward to the authorities to disclose his information. As well as his intercepted communications, Paul had also been studying the various Cattle Mutilations which had been occurring in the region at the same time. He had noted the correlation between the appearance of the lights in the sky and the subsequent reports of the cattle mutilations. Unfortunately for Paul, his claims were dismissed, and his evidence was rejected. What follows is a very tragic story of a man driven mad by relentless CIA and NSI bullying and harassment. He was ultimately discredited and made an unknowing disinformation agent, disseminating incorrect information that had been purposely 'leaked' to him. The entire experience destroyed the man's career and ultimately his life. Paul's story is far too long to get into here, but it is a sad reminder of what can happen when people try to speak out about this Phenomenon.

I cannot talk about Paul Bennewitz's case without mentioning Gabe Valdez. Valdez was a New Mexico State Police Officer who co-incidentally around 1976 began to receive reports into his police station of local cattle mutilations. The initial call was made by a local rancher called Manuel Gomez. Manuel had found one of his cows dead with some very bizarre injuries. Valdez went to meet Manuel and to see the body for himself and he was quite shocked at what he saw. This was not the last report he would receive either, as over the next 18 months a further 23 reports from local ranchers experiencing the same phenomenon would come into the New Mexico State Police Station. Valdez became increasingly frustrated with the case as he was never able to find the culprit responsible. Just when he thought he'd never progress the case he received a call.

This call came from Chief Tafoya of the Hickoria Police force on the Hickoria Reservation. The Chief also owned some cattle and unfortunately had found some of them dead and mutilated. He requested Valdez's presence at his homestead immediately. He also reported in the same call that there were lights in the sky over his house and they weren't going anywhere. Valdez stepped on the gas to get to Chef Tafoya's house as soon as he could. When he arrived, the Chief was right. Valdez stopped alongside the Chief and other members of the Hickoria Police Force and stared up into the sky. The lights didn't move but just sat there, hovering above them. Eventually, they took off and Valdez jumped into his squad car ready to give chase. He would follow them for a short time only for them to 'blink' out and 'reappear' somewhere else. Valdez gave chase but felt like he was being toyed with. Eventually, he stopped his car and gave up. At this point, the lights reappeared in front of him, hovered briefly then finally disappeared. Valdez was now convinced that these lights were connected to his cattle mutilation cases.

In April 1979 he attended a local seminar on the Cattle Mutilations which had been arranged by Senator Smitt, who was under increasing pressure at the time from Ranchers to resolve this 'problem'. Smitt had asked Valdez to speak at the conference discussing aspects of his mutilation Investigation and it was at this conference that Gabe Valdez was introduced to Paul Bennewitz. The pair continued their investigation into the lights, mutilations, and Dulce Base for several years but it eventually it concluded due to Bennewitz's rapidly decreasing mental health. A lot of these health issues were brought about by the heavy disinformation campaign waged by Special Agent Richard Doty of the U.S Air Force Office of Special Investigations as instructed by Kirtland Airforce base with the assistance of Ufologist Bill Moore. Thankfully, as a small act of mercy Moore would eventually confess to his part in the campaign making the UFO world aware that Paul had been purposely fed bad information and was 'led' down the path to his eventual ruin. It's also worth mentioning that in the 1990's, US commercial airline pilot John Lear, the son of Lear Jet designer William P. Lear, also claimed he had confirmed the existence of Dulce Base, independently of Bennowitz and Costello's claims.

Another whistleblower who come to light was Philip Schneider. Phil backed up the Costello claims by stating that he knew that Dulce did exist and that he was a Geologist who had been brought in by the Government to help build the base. The base he said is a naturally formed cave system about 2 miles underground which was widened by the Reptilians and later on enlarged further and structurally secured by both RAND and the shadow Government to create the facility. Phil reports that one day in 1979 whilst working there (unaware of any alien presence) he was sent to the lower levels to review a problem that had occurred. Whilst down there he came face to face with a 'Grey' which startled him, as a result, he instinctively and in fear for his life fired upon the alien. The alien fired back with a 'ray gun' type weapon and it clipped Phil's hand cutting off several fingers. Hearing the commotion, the security officers immediately arrived on the scene and fired on the 'Grey' causing other aliens to become involved and ultimately causing a 'shoot out' which cost the lives of many security officers and some aliens. It was this incident that would become known as the 'Dulce Wars'.

Phil has spent many years on the UFO circuit telling his story but that said it is hard to verify his account of things. He says that he decided to blow the whistle on the base and his involvement after the suspicious death of his close friend author Ron Rummel. Rummel was allegedly about to publish a book giving his thoughts on the 'Star Wars' project and what he thought its' actual purpose was when he allegedly committed suicide. Schneider says his friend was murdered to keep his book from being released. As for Schneider, we do know that he did work for the government at some point, but he was a rather dubious character on the circuit. It is said that his account of what happened that day did change from time to time which makes confirming his story all the harder. There is some speculation regarding Phil's untimely death in which he was alleged to have committed suicide by choking himself with a catheter. His wife and many of his supporters believe that he was murdered to stop him from spreading his story whilst others believe that Mr. Schneider was a deeply troubled man who sadly took his own life, even if his chosen manner of suicide is slightly odd.

I have heard that after Roswell that there was an agreement made between the President-Elect at the time, Dwight D. Eisenhower, and the Grey Aliens that would give them permission to abduct and test on a certain number of humans in return for their technology. Now whether this agreement, referred to as 'The Greada Treaty' exists we don't know but certainly if reports are to be believed there has long been a relationship between Governments the world over and non-human life forms. As a side note, when listening to the 'Last Podcast on the Left' Podcast episode on the Dulce Base[63] one of the presenters made a possible connection between this 'agreement' and the comments made by one of the Aliens during the famous Whitley Streiber abduction experience. Whitley Streiber is an author and 'abductee' survivor. Streiber has written extensively about his experiences and in his book 'Communion' recounts being abducted multiple times over a period of time in the 1980's. As Whitley recalls in a hypnotic regression session, at one point during one of his abduction experiences, he was protesting, saying to his abductors that they had absolutely no right to take him and hold him against his will when the Alien responded that indeed 'they did have permission'. A tenuous link but food for thought nonetheless. What permission exactly did they have, that they felt it authorized them to kidnap, hold and torture humans against their will?

When researching the Dulce Base case, it would appear that the natural cave systems which run under Dulce run far and wide. That vast cave systems interconnect and can be accessed at various points all over the continent, indeed, all over the world. It is speculated that entrances to this cave system can be found in Death Valley, New York, Toronto, the Nahanni Valley, Mount Shasta, Brown Mountain and may even stretch as far as our Maltese Caves mentioned earlier. It is even rumoured that you can access the cave system through the infamous Denver Airport, whose own story is almost as infamous as Dulce itself! Interestingly in the Hellier docu-series, they reference the fact that local people from the Brown Mountain area report a high Army presence. Locals found this to be very strange as there is supposedly nothing there to warrant such a large Army presence.

So, there we have it, reports from the general public, civil servants, scientists, engineers, and even members of the Military of secret underground facilities. Various reported sightings of gnomes, goblins, aliens, reptilians, cryptids, giant spiders, and other giant life forms straight from the pages of Joules Verne. The possible existence of cave systems which could possibly connect and provide a whole network of travel underneath large expanses of the earth. A whole other world right beneath our feet.

---

[63] The Last Podcast on the Left – Episode 187 (aired 12 Aug 2015) and Episode 188 (aired 19 Aug 2015).

Missing 411 – A Fairy Problem?

Whilst investigating the Fae Folk it is impossible not to see the similarities between Fae encounters and the Missing 411 phenomenon, which I've referenced several times in the earlier chapters. The more I read the more convinced I have become that Fae Folk could be the cause of a number of these disappearances. That's not to say it's the answer to 'ALL' the disappearances far from it but certainly I think, a fair few. For this chapter, I'll be taking examples from David Paulides' Missing 411 book series as well as some other sources which I'll reference along the way. This subject has garnered quite the following and there is now quite a lot of information on the topic online, discussed on various podcasts and published in several books by David Paulides, as well as many other authors and researchers.

I won't bore you by repeating myself as I have already briefly explained what the Missing 411 Phenomenon is, so let's just get to why I think that the Fae Folk could be behind a number of these cases. Looking at the books and listening to David speak in many interviews there seem to be several 'commonalities' in these cases, I'll list these below: -

a) The swiftness with which a person can disappear even when with others
b) Disappearances near boulder fields

c) Dogs can't pick up the scent or there is a lack of a physical trail
d) Articles of clothing removed or clothes on inside out.
e) Major weather disruption
f) People going missing picking berries
g) People who when found say that they have no memory of what happened or that the memory is hazy.

Let's take the first Commonality, the swiftness of disappearance even when with another person or persons. Take the example of Stacey Arras, a 14-year-old girl who went missing whilst on a horse-riding trail in Yosemite National Park in July 1981. Stacey, her father, and six others were on this trip and were camping in a picturesque area called Sunrise Meadows. When the group arrived at the campground, Stacey got changed and said she wanted to take photos of the nearby lake. Her father wanted to relax so she went with a 70-year man called Gerald who was a friend in their group. The lake and trail to it are very close to the camp, and many of the people staying there clearly saw Stacey and Gerald walking along the trail. At some point, Gerald needed to take a breather and sat down for a few minutes. Stacey said she'd scout out up ahead and be right back in a few minutes. Gerald and several others at the camp, including a camp tour guide, watched Stacey walk behind some trees, and this would be the last time anyone saw her. When the girl did not come right back as she had said, others staying at the camp decided to go up along the trail and see what she was doing. Even after a lengthy search effort the other evidence ever found was the lens cap to Stacey's camera which was ominously found in the middle of the nearby meadow [64].

In the Missing 411 series, we also have the story of Carl Landers who went missing trying to reach the summit of Mount Shasta (a site of many disappearances). Carl was climbing with friends, and all appeared well, he proceeded around a bend on the cliff face and then seemingly just disappeared out of sight. His friend followed him around the bend literally a minute or two later and Carl had vanished. His friends said that there was nowhere that Carl could possibly have gone. They were climbing on a rock face, there were no caves or crevices, no shrubbery or brush to hide behind or within. There had been no cry or yell heard from Carl that would suggest a fall and no sign of disturbance in the general vicinity. Carl had simply evaporated into thin air within the space of a few minutes[65]. These 'sudden' disappearances occur relatively frequently with the people left behind commenting that they had only taken their eyes off the missing person for a matter of minutes during which time, they simply vanished into thin air.

Another story involves the Reiger family, the Riegers were vacationing in Ecuador in June 2013 when they decided to go on a family hike near their hotel. Whilst on the trail the boys decided to run ahead, not long after they had sprinted off the parents came across their youngest son who had tired and stopped running. He told them that his brother had carried on ahead of him, he joined his parents, and the family continued their hike. Ten minutes later they reached a pavilion at the summit but were surprised that their son was not there. The father said that there would only have been 'minutes' between the boys running off and the rest of them reaching the summit. They saw no one else on the trail and had heard no screams or yells. The whole trail is visible said his father. They had no explanation for his disappearance. He was reported missing, and an extensive search was

---

[64] Canam Missing Project YouTube Channel - David Paulides Presents The Stacy Arras Case from Yosemite National Park.

[65] Missing Persons Mysteries YouTube Channel - Missing Hikers who were Found Years Later! https://www.youtube.com/watch?v=X_OXsGmJREQ

undertaken but unfortunately, the boy was never found[66].

This 'Vanishing' is not a modern phenomenon and has been occurring for centuries. Here are a few famous historical accounts of people suddenly vanishing into thin air. Our first case took place on 23rd Sept 1880 in Gallatin, Tennesee. A farmer called David Lang was working in a field near his house when he simply disappeared into thin air. This was witnessed by his wife who was sitting on the veranda watching him, whilst two of their children played nearby. A local prominent Judge (Peck) and his brother-in-law who happened to be traveling the road leading up to the house, also report witnessing the sudden disappearance. They both had eyes on Lang, as only a few moments earlier, Lang had seen their approach and had waved to them. In shock, they stopped their carriage, exited, and ran to see what had happened. Everyone immediately scrambled to the spot where he was last seen but could find nothing to indicate where he had gone. The entire area was searched but Mr. Lang was never seen again. It is said that his children reported hearing his voice for months after in the vicinity of that spot but eventually the voice ceased[67].

The validity of this story has been called into question, with author Stuart Palmer being the purported perpetrator. Palmer published the story, and what he alleged was an interview with Sarah Lang, David's surviving daughter in an issue of FATE magazine some 24 years after the event. It seems though that the affidavit was a forgery and after some investigation researchers of this case found there to be no record of a family called the Langs in Gallatin at that time, nor was there a Judge Peck. Casting some heavy doubt on the varsity of the tale. What is interesting is that some version of this 'disappeared into thin air' tale existed before this, even as much as one hundred years previous, so what is the origin, who was 'ground zero', and what occurred previously to inspire Palmers' story?

The next few cases involve the sudden strange disappearance of children. Charles Ashmore, 16, disappeared one evening in November 1878 after he had been asked by his father to fetch water from the well outside. After some time had elapsed and Charles had not returned, his father came out to see what was holding him up. Charles was nowhere to be seen. It had been snowing heavily that day and his father noticed that Charles' tracks could

---

[66] David Paulides – Missing 411 Western United States and California (2012).

[67] Pseudiom YouTube Channel - The Impossible Disappearance Of David Lang | Historia Ephemera – October 2015.

clearly be seen leading up towards the well but then just abruptly stopped. No other tracks could be seen, and Charles was never found. As is often the case in these 'sudden' vanishings people claimed to be able to hear the boy calling for help from this spot for months after but yet they could never find him to assist[68].

Interestingly, the Ashmore case originally seems to have been written by horror author Ambrose Bierce, who may also, indirectly, have been the inspiration for the Lang story, based on his own story 'The Difficulty of Crossing a Field'. He is also credited with the infamous urban legend of James Burne, the man who vanished whilst running a foot race in the story 'An Unfinished Race'. Now what inspired all these similar 'vanishing' stories is unknown, but he may have gotten the idea from folklore at the time which spoke of such similar disappearances. Even more interesting, is the fact that Bierce himself disappeared under stranger circumstances. In October 1913, Bierce left Washington D.C to travel to Mexico, where he planned to write about the Mexican revolution. The then 71 yr. old Bierce left by train from Washington bound for Mexico, he made several stops en route, and his last stop was due to be Chihuahua. His whereabouts after Chihuahua are unknown, he never made it to his final destination, and he was never seen or heard from again.

A few years later in 1889, a similar incident to the Ashmore tale occurred, this time involving an 11-Year-Old boy in South Bend, Indiana. Oliver Larch was also sent to fetch water from a well when the same fate befell him. His parents reported Oliver yelling for help, exclaiming "Help! Help! They've got me! Help!". His family who was in the house immediately came to his aid, but Oliver had disappeared. Once again, this vanishing occurred in the winter and snow had fallen, the boys' tracks set out towards the well and just stopped. The boy had just vanished[69].

We've also already encountered some stories of the Vanishing of people to the Fairy Realm such as in the tale of Rhys and Llewellyn whose story we covered in an earlier chapter. These stories parallel the ones above, in that one minute, someone is there, and the next they're not. They've completely disappeared from sight, with no evidence of their final fate left behind and yet their voices can still be heard in that spot for some time after. It is as if that person is still there but cannot be seen or touched, as if some invisible barrier is between them and us preventing one from the other.

---

[68] Disappearances (Paranormal) – Article on Encyclopedia.com.

[69] Ibid.

More recently we have the odd disappearance of Dale Stehling. Dale was a 51-year-old man from Goliad, Texas who, along with his wife Denean and his parents decided to go on a day trip to the Mesa Verde National Park on 9th June 2013. Whilst there, Dale told his family that he was going to hike the Spruce Tree House ruin trail. This trail is less than a quarter of a mile long and connects to the Petroglyph Point Trail, a 2½-mile loop that takes off from the Spruce Tree Trail. He was last seen walking this trail. When Dale failed to return a few hours later, his concerned family reported him missing to Park Rangers and an extensive search was undertaken. The search lasted for two weeks before finally being called off. Unfortunately, Dale's remains were found seven years later, remarkably, in an area that had been searched several times by SAR. Had his body been there the whole time but overlooked by searchers, or had it been placed there years later, after the search had been concluded?

Another oddity is that on the day Dale went missing, writer and blogger Jodi Peterson was also on Petroglyph Point trail. She recounts that she heard a weary male voice calling for help. She called out to the person multiple times but got no response. She quickly came back down the trail and found the chief ranger. She told him what she thought she had heard. She recalled that he seemed relieved by this information, coincidentally another member of staff then commented "We thought we heard a call for help in that area yesterday." They quickly began planning to bring in dogs and more searchers. The area where the calls were heard was once again searched thoroughly but Dale was nowhere to be found[70]. Reports of these disembodied voices calling for assistance are numerous and span centuries.

Commonality two - Disappearances near boulders or rocks. There is an intrinsic link between the Fae Folk encounters and Boulders, Stone, Granite, and Rock. There are testimonies such as Bessie Dunlops' during her Witch Trial who claimed to have seen Thom Reid enter and exit a tiny hole in a wall. Stories of people seeing 'little people' peering out from behind rocks and boulders and even reports of boulders or large rocks having strange qualities to them, such as a 'glow' or even reports of hearing voices or music coming from within them.

In Steph Young's book '*Stalked in the Woods*' she references the Black Mountain which is an area covered by boulders (and underground tunnels we

---

[70] The unexplained disappearance and death of Mitchell Dale Stehling in Mesa Verde National Park – Article published on Strange Outdoors.com – March 2020.

referenced earlier!) which is said to be an area of a lot of supernatural activity with many reports of missing people. We find a lot of areas or 'clusters' of missing people seem to coincide with boulder fields or areas with a high density of rock or granite. Interestingly, Mesa Verde where Dale Sterling went missing is renowned, for its large cliff dwellings originally constructed by the Ancestral Puebloans around the 12th Century[71].

In the same book, we have references to the belief and culture of the Icelandic people who have a strong belief in the 'hidden people' or Huldufólk. So much so that they even have an online 'school' called The Elfschool' which teaches people how to make 'contact' with the hidden people by accessing other dimensions[72]. Lára Bjarnadótir recounted an experience to Magnús Skarphéðinsson (Headmaster of Elfschool) that she had as a child in the 1930's. Lara was living on a farm outside of Brjánslaekur, in the grounds, there was a large, ragged rock that was situated in a large field outside of their farmhouse. This rock was called 'The Dwarf' and had a rather sinister reputation. It was said that fishermen could see this rock glow in the evening time when they were out at sea fishing and the children were afraid of it and choose to keep clear of it. There was, however, another similar large rock in another field which had no such reputation, and the kids would play there regularly. One day Lára was there with her siblings playing and she decided to scale the large rock, once she made it to the summit, she stood tall enjoying her accomplishment when a loud angry voice told her to get down at once or be punished. She was so startled that she jumped down in one perilous leap risking broken bones and ran all the way home. Lara said it sounded as if the voice had come from inside the rock itself.

In the town of Hafnarfjörður, just outside Reykjavik, there's a rock that protrudes so dangerously into the street that passing cars are forced to swerve around it. Indeed, the belief in the Rocks being Huldufólk homes is so strong today that like in Ireland, the roads are built around the large standing stones and boulders so as not to disturb them! Such an example is Ófeigskirkja – a 'hidden people church' located by the West Iceland Road out of Reykjavik. This elfchurch has been at the center of an eight-year battle to stop a road being built through this 8,000-year-old landscape and disturbing this sacred rock. In the 1980's a rock known locally as 'Elfhill' was due to be demolished to make way for a road that was supposed to go directly through its location, but the construction crew began to suffer sickness, accidents, and machinery

---

[71] A Civilization's Home in the Cliffs – Article published on Visit MesaVerde.com.

[72] Steph Young – Stalked in The Woods: True Stories of Unexplained Disappearances and Strange Encounters in the Woods (2016).

failure. The road crew began to complain that it was the Huldufólk and they were getting so scared to work that they refused to touch the Rock. The disruption caused was so bad that the Icelandic Road Administration in an act of desperation, contacted a local psychic who could commune with the Hidden People and managed to broker an agreement between the Road Administration and the Huldufólk. The Rock rather than be demolished was gently moved intact 15 meters back. The accidents and delays that had plagued the planned Road up to this point ceased and they were able to move on with the construction successfully[73].

Magnús Skarphéðinsson (Headmaster of the Elfschool) claims that via the use of another psychic medium who can also speak to the Hidden People, he had asked them why they live within the rock formations. He said he was told that the energy there is more stable than anywhere else. That the larger the rock the more stable. They need this stability as they live on another frequency to us[74]. Granite often contains a high density of quartz which can be used to channel and even transmute energy so it stands to reason that it could be used to channel enough energy to 'create' a portal from one dimension to another.

Certainly, we know that Granite is exceptionally good at transmitting sound waves, especially low-frequency infrasound. It has been proven that big cats use infrasound (sounds below the threshold of human hearing at 20 Hz) to stun their prey just before attacking[75]. This reminds me of an interesting story I heard on an episode of Sasquatch Chronicles, episode 57 titled *'Missing people and bigfoot encounters'* during which the host describes such an occurrence in Southeast Asia. A group of people were walking through a forest, the gentleman in front was about 25 to 30 ft ahead when the rest of the group heard a tiger growl. The group stopped but the man out in front continued onwards, towards the sound of the growl. His friends of course sprang into action and grabbed him and pulled him back, when they asked him 'why did you do that?' he claimed that he never heard a growl, instead he suddenly felt really hot and as he describes it 'euphoric' and in an almost trance like state

---

[73] Just Icelandic YouTube Channel – Episode title - True Stories of Elves and Hidden People in Iceland·

[74] In Iceland, 'respect the elves – or else' – Article by Oliver Wainwright published on The Guardian.com

[75] American Institute of Physics -- Inside Science News Service. "The secret of a tiger's roar." ScienceDaily. ScienceDaily, 29 December 2000.

had felt drawn towards the danger.[76] Could it be that these rocks especially in large volumes are emitting infrasound causing people to become confused and discombobulated? A natural phenomenon that has the adverse effect of making people become more cloudy or hazy around them, effecting their sense of direction and decision-making abilities?

With respect to the third commonality, search dogs being unable to pick up a scent, it should be said that scent dogs are only, on average effective approximately 80% of the time. Now, should I go missing I'd certainly like that 80% on my case but this does, of course, mean, that there are some cases where a scent isn't picked up? There are many different reasons for this. Environmental influences and weather will have an impact on results, hot dry air, lack of wind, or too much wind. Factors such as whether the person was on medication such as steroids or whether they were suffering from a disease can muddy the scent and make it harder to track. Even someone who usually wears perfume but isn't wearing it the day they go missing can affect the hit. The scent item provided, if the scent isn't strong enough or is mixed with another smell such as aftershave, perfume or medication can confuse a dog.

In the research, older dogs, experienced, and have had more 'training' time scored much higher in field tests than younger newer dogs. Certain breeds have better success rates than others, German shepherds, for example, score higher than their Belgian Counterparts in field tests. The fitness of the dog can impact a positive scent retrieval, if a dog is hot and tired panting decreases the ability to pick up scent particles in the air. The dog's handler is just as important as the dog is led by its handler, if the handler is inexperienced or doesn't know what they're looking for then the dog will have less chance of success[77]. Of course, in the event of someone being airlifted out, put into a vehicle, and transported or indeed, stepping into another dimension or plane of existence, it does stand to reason that a successful scent dog would have no scent to follow.

Commonality 4 – Items of clothing removed or inside out. As we've mentioned previously, in fairy folklore it is said that if you are being 'pixie led' it means that you've found yourself turned around and disorientated and have no idea where you are. It is said that if you suspect this is the direct result of paranormal influences then you should turn your pockets inside out

---

[76] Sasquatch Chronicles YouTube Channel – Episode 57 - Missing people and bigfoot encounters.

[77] Marchal S, Bregeras O, Puaux D, Gervais R, Ferry B (2016) Rigorous Training of Dogs Leads to High Accuracy in Human Scent Matching-To-Sample Performance. PLoS ONE 11(2): e0146963. https://doi.org/10.1371/journal.pone.0146963.

or remove an article of clothing such as a jacket or jumper, turn it inside out and place it back on and within a short time you should find your situation correct and once again be able to find your way home. As we've become more logical and analytical in our thought process we have dumped much of our folklore and old-world knowledge into the bin. Believing it to be superstitious hocus pocus and no longer necessary in our modern civilized world. Unfortunately, this is throwing the proverbial baby out with this dishwater. Fairytale stories, whilst today are fantasy and romance, were once upon a time warnings, a PSA (Public Safety Announcement) for our ancestors. There was useful information in them, information that could be used if one found themselves in such a predicament. I am not sure if any of the people who went missing and whose clothes/shoes were later found knew enough about Fairy Lore to try this trick, I doubt it, but I thought it an interesting connection regardless. Where the origin of the old wife's tale regarding the removal and turning inside out of clothing came from, we cannot be sure but maybe our forefathers knew something that we no longer do.

Some years back, I came across a story (as I often do) in the YouTube comments thread on a 'Missing 411' content video. I have desperately tried to find the video again for the purposes of writing this book but unfortunately been unable to do so. I do remember it was people relaying their 'near miss' experiences, describing how close they came to being one of the Missing 411 cases. This close-call experience is that of a young woman on a day hike with friends in a National Park somewhere in North America. As she describes it, the day was nice, not too hot not too cold, she was wearing a t-shirt, a long sleeve zip-up hoodie/sweater, long trousers, and walking boots.

At some point on this hike, all three ladies were walking side by side chatting when she became aware of a shimmering out of the corner of her eye. She took her eyes off her friends for mere seconds to stop and look but when she turned back around, her friends had completely vanished. She was puzzled given she believed she'd only taken her eyes off them for a few seconds, so she yelled out for them. They did not respond. She wondered if they had gone ahead so she ran to catch up but still couldn't see them. It's worth noting that she also commented that the landscape seemed off, it was at the same time familiar yet different. She spent quite some time calling out and running to catch up to them but with no luck. She was somewhere between anger and panic at this point when she said that she noticed it had gotten hot. Not just a few degrees hotter, like the sun, had peaked out from behind a cloud but more like someone had turned an oven on. She said every few minutes the heat was cranked up another notch to the point where she could no longer bear it. She removed her long sleeve top and then her boots and her socks in an effort to cool herself down. She was debating stripping down to her underwear as the heat became unbearable when she noticed the shimmering again. She stepped off the path and walked towards it only to find herself in front of a beautiful blue lake. She was surprised, as to her knowledge there was no lake there, but she was delighted and started to strip off to take a dip, relieved to have some way to cool herself down. Before she could take a step into this Oasis, she said she heard a voice in her head (not sure if it was hers or not as she didn't specify) say 'No!' loudly and aggressively. This stopped her in her tracks and gave her quite the fright. Whatever this short sharp shock was it seemed to be enough to break whatever enchantment she was under and suddenly the heat ceased, the sky darkened, and the lake disappeared.

Terrified she hurriedly redressed and headed back to the path, a short time later she saw lights in the woods and heard voices and yells. I can't remember whether it was the search party or her friends who finally found her, but thankfully she was found safe and sound. She had been 'missing' for hours causing quite the concern but to her mind, she feels that she had only been gone for maybe 30-45 minutes. If this is a true account, then it does appear as if this woman did indeed have a close call. The description of the 'heat' and needing to remove her clothing could shed some light on why clothing is found but the person is not, or vice versa the person is found but they are missing articles of clothing usually their shoes. This kind of nefarious manipulation lends credence to the argument that there is something in the woods actively 'hunting' humans.

David Paulides, when being interviewed as a guest on 'Where did the Road Go' makes references to the number of cases where people are found missing their shoes and other items of clothing[78]. Take the strange disappearance of Charles McCullar in Crater Lake National Park in 1975. Charles 'Chuck' McCullar was a keen photographer and had undertaken a trip to Crater Lake to take some winter photographs. He had only planned on taking a short hike and was unprepared to camp in the hard Oregon cold. He told friends that if he did not return within a few days that they should report this to the authorities. Unfortunately, this request was put into action and Chuck was reported missing when he failed to return after two days.

An extensive Search and Rescue effort took place, but Chuck was not found,

[78] Where Did The Road Go Radio YouTube Channel - David Paulides - Missing 411: Hunters Parts 1 and 2 (Repost) August 2016.

that is until nearly two years later. Quite by chance, two hikers had gotten themselves lost and found themselves off their intended trail. Whilst trying to get their bearings and taking stock of their surroundings they found a backpack. Feeling like this backpack was an omen of something bad they called it into Rangers who promptly came to search the area. This is where bone fragments were found and later identified to be Chucks'. What is strange is that Chuck's boots, coat, and shirt were never found. All that was left were some foot bones left in the socks and his jeans, but the jeans were empty except for a bit of shin bone. Chuck's remains were found in a canyon about 12 miles from the trailhead. How did he manage to get that far in bad weather and deep snow with next to no equipment and where were his clothes and boots? [78]

Another experience very similar to both the female hiker experience and the East Asia 'tiger' story mentioned earlier, involves a Mountain Biker called 'Gord'. This story was featured on episode 57 of *Sasquatch Chronicles* entitled *'Missing People and Bigfoot Encounters*[79]. Gord is a mountain biker at a competitive level, he does a lot of high-elevation and cross-country training. On this particular day, Gord and some friends were planning a high-elevation ride. He describes the day as being cold, about 5 degrees Celsius (45 degrees Fahrenheit), it had snowed the week before, so it was very wet and muddy and there was still some snow at the higher elevation. They got out their bikes and started up the 'Misty Creek' Trail. Gord was some way ahead and summited first. He said when he got to the top, it was so beautiful that he got out his camera and started snapping pictures. He said he didn't see or smell anything out of the ordinary, as far as he was concerned there was nothing there with him. He said when the last guy 'Dave' summited, Dave commented that he thought that he could smell a bear, so being cautious, they all got back on their bikes and quickly descended.

Once again, being the fittest and most experienced Gord was quite some distance in front of the others, when he reached a creek about halfway down the trail and stopped. He says he has no idea why he stopped here, it is unlike him to just stop, and he had no reason to do so. At this point, he hears something to his left and as he turns to investigate, he hears growling. Most peculiarly, he said that he kept saying to himself that it was water, so instead of registering a growl and the danger which accompanies it, all he could think about was water. It sounded relaxing and comforting, soft like it was a fountain or small waterfall. He said that he suddenly started to overheat, and

[79] Sasquatch Chronicles YouTube channel - SC EP:57 Missing people and bigfoot encounters – 2 December 2018.

desperate to cool down he started to undress. Now he is almost completely undressed at this point when his friends catch up to him and understandably ask him 'what the hell are you doing?'. At this point, Gord snaps out of it and instantly remembers that he had heard a growl. He tells the others what he heard, one of them believes him, and the other thinks he's pulling his leg but they both could see Gord was obviously shaken up. He said that he was now freezing cold having come to his senses and immediately started to redress and then they all got out of there pretty darn quickly. Who knows what would have become of him, had his friends not been there to snap him out of it. As a side note, he said he'd listened to the sasquatch chronicles episode on infrasound (episode 7) and the growl of a Bengal Tiger featured is the exact sound that he heard. But what would a Bengal Tiger be doing in North America?

Another oddity is the case of Dr. James McGrogan, a Doctor from Indiana. James and three friends had decided to hike a trail to Iceman's Hut in Vail Colorado[80]. Several hours into this hike the group wanted to take a short break, James who was incredibly fit and used to such arduous activity being a marathon runner, said he wanted to continue. So, the group agreed to meet up at the next stop on the trail. After a short rest, the friends continued their hike but when they got to the next stop James wasn't there. The friends weren't concerned at this point, figuring he had just continued on ahead and that they'd catch up with him at some point on the trail. That point never came. After the friends had finished the trail and realized James wasn't waiting for them, they undertook a quick search of the trail themselves. When they still couldn't locate him one of the group went back down the trail to find the Rangers and to report James as missing.

The entire area was searched over the next five days, but no sign of James was found. James had come fully prepared, he had with him a Split Snowboard (which can double as skis), a cellphone, a GPS Unit, a Shovel, medical supplies, and all manner of protective equipment. He would have been perfectly able to survive for the duration of time it would have taken for the search and rescue teams to find him. Unfortunately, James' body was found 20 days later, 4.5 miles from the trail. To get to the location where he was finally found, James would have had to travel through 2 gulleys and over a 12,000 ft mountain. He was found wearing only black leggings, a shirt, an undershirt, and grey socks. His boots were nowhere to be found. Shockingly his coat was found still in his backpack, along with his GPS which was fully functional and would have told him where he was and his cell phone which

---

again was working. The coroner later checked the cell phone at the site James' body was found and could see that he would have had at least 2 bars of signal. Certainly, if he did travel over that mountain, he would have had a good signal the higher up he was, so theoretically he would have had enough signal to call for help at any point during his 'missing time'. James' was also wearing a helmet at the time that his body was recovered. The coroner noted that James had suffered a severe head injury, trauma to the left-hand side of his chest, and a broken femur. We can only wonder what on earth happened to this poor man. Why he ended up where he did and why he never stopped to call for help at any point? There definitely seems to be some external intelligent force that is almost 'bewitching' people, causing them to act irrationally, make decisions that they would never normally make, and to ignore obvious signs of danger.

A very interesting video link was posted on Reddit under the Missing 411 sub-reddit which I came across whilst researching Missing 411 cases. This video titled '*How To Survive A Plane Crash*' was published by the LADBible and aired on their YouTube channel on 9th August 2020. The video contains an astonishing interview with an extraordinary man who managed to not only survive a plane crash but also survive being on fire. 8.39 minutes into the video he describes how upon thinking that he was going to die he removed his socks and shoes and placed them neatly to one side. He said that he doesn't even know why he did it, he can only think now that he knew he was going on a trip that he wouldn't need them for and was almost 'getting things in order' before he left[81]. Its food for thought isn't it, that even we don't know why we do the things that we do when we are staring Death in the face.

Whilst for the purposes of the chapter I am focusing on the Fae Folk, I would like to clarify that I am not dismissing or ignoring other explanations. I am, of course, aware of Paradoxical undressing due to Hypothermia which may be a factor in some of the cases mentioned. Or naturally occurring infrasound, causing people to get confused and disorientated. There are even more deeply rooted psychological factors that affect our decision-making process at times of high stress and trauma which could account for some of the oddities. I choose to remain open-minded to all possible explanations.

Commonality 5 – Severe weather disruption. Paulides states that in a number of these cases severe weather will often come on suddenly after someone has gone missing and will usually hamper the search or indeed be the reason for a search being called off all together. Certainly, you'll be aware of weather

---

[81] LADBible – How to survive a Plan Crash https://www.youtube.com/watch?v=Z5lcOMvAvlc

fairies, Jack Frost is a good example or the Snow Queen from The Lion, The Witch, and The Wardrobe. Elementals who control the wind, the earth, and the water. Imbued with the power to cause all kinds of havoc should they so wish. In folklore, we have the Tiddy Mun of the East Anglian Fens who control the water and mists and fogs that come off the Fen[82]. Should the waters rise too high the locals would call to the Tiddy Mun and offer gifts and tributes if he would drain the water and spare their homes, crops, and animals. Should such tributes be forgotten, the punishment was swift and harsh. Fairies are intrinsic to nature, they live in it and are part of it, so it should be no surprise that they have a degree of control over it.

The following is an excerpt from an article on the British Fairies website regarding Fae Folk and their propensity for meddling with the weather: -

> *"The pixies are known for their ability to control the weather and this can be used as a way of trapping victims. Men travelling across Dartmoor from Crediton to Exeter were advised that, if a cloud descended, they should strip and sit on their clothes for half an hour or so. The pixies would in due course raise the fog thrown around them. Patience is evidently important in such cases. A woman on the Quantocks became demented with terror when the pixies caused an evening mist to rise suddenly around her, so that she was lost in a field minutes away from her home".[83]*

Commonality 6 – Berry Picking. It is a strict rule within Fairy Lore that you must not harm a fairy tree. Trees believed to belong to the Fae Folk include the Hawthorne, Blackthorn, Ash, and Oak but they are also precious about shrubbery and plants that grow within their territory. The price for cutting or harming a fairy tree is great and punishment swift. Any fruit taken from a fairy tree or indeed from shrubbery or bushes in their territory without permission (which can be requested by offering a gift of some libation such as milk) could result in fairy intervention. It does seem from all the 'real life' stories of fairy encounters that shrubs or trees that possess fruit or berries ripe for picking do seem to be found startling close to supposed fairy territories with boulders and large rocks often being located near to plants that produce edible berries.

Within folklore, there are several tales of people stumbling across little people

---

[82] Weather Fairies – Article published on The Circle.com
https://www.thecircle.com/uk/magazin/psychics/weather-fairies.do

[83] Up Hill and Down Dale' – Pixie Led in the West Country: A Study of Pixie Tricks – Article published on British Fairies Wordpress.com – 5 July 2022.

while they are picking berries or collecting fruit. In a YouTube Video titled *'True Stories of Elves and Hidden People in Iceland'* published on the Just Icelandic channel (18th October 2019) a man tells of how when he was a small boy about 5 or 6 years old, there was a large rock formation in a field near his home. One day he went berry picking and saw that there were berries in an area near these rocks. After a short time, he became aware of two very nicely dressed children near him. The children all played together for some time. Eventually, the young boy asked these children where they were from as he didn't recognize them. He said that they just pointed towards the rock formation, it was at this point that he could now clearly see little windows and doors within the rocks. He had never seen the windows and doors there before. He became friends with these children, often playing with them, until one day they told him that they were moving. After they left, he said he could no longer see the little windows and doors in the Rock Formation[84].

In Janet Bord's *Fairies Real Encounters with Little People*, she quotes W.Y. Evans Wentz's book on fairy lore, which he was collecting personal experiences for in Ireland in the early 1900's. In one personal encounter story Mr. Neil Colton, who was at the time of telling his story 73 years of age, lived close to the Shores of Lough Derg in County Donegal, one day when he was a boy, he, his brother, and his cousin were picking Bilberries up by some rocks when all at once they heard music. They hurried around the back of the rocks and saw some 'little people' who were dancing. When they saw the children one of these little people dressed all in red ran up to them and managed to whip the cousin around the face with what appeared to be a green rush. They fled for home as quickly as they could but upon returning home the cousin dropped dead. The father grabbed his horse and rode as quick as he could for Father Ryan who I am guessing was a Catholic priest in the village. The Father upon arriving at the homestead put his stole quickly around her neck and began praying and reading psalms and striking her with his stole. Fortunately, she was revived. The Father said that had she not caught hold of the brother when this occurred, she would have been 'taken' forever[85].

A more recent berry-picking story comes from a video posted on the Top Mysteries YouTube channel titled *'Strange Berry Picker Disappearances'*[86]. Mary Byman was an 84-year-old woman from Menisino, Canada. Mary went

---

[84] Just Icelandic YouTube Channel - True Stories of Elves and Hidden People in Iceland
https://www.youtube.com/watch?v=vO7EB0xnib4

[85] Bord, "Fairies Real Encounters".

[86] Strange Berry Picker Disappearances – Top Mysteries YouTube Channel published 19/08/2020
https://www.youtube.com/watch?v=Tlz9-j4QzSM

missing whilst picking berries with a friend in southeastern Manitoba. This was something that they would do frequently, and the women had a little routine in place in order to find each other. The two women would wear a whistle when picking berries so that when they separated, one would blow the whistle when it was time to come out of the bush and the other would hear and follow suit. The friend blew her whistle and swore that she heard Mary's whistle in response, yet Mary never emerged from the bush. A search was conducted in the area but Mary wasn't found until four days later when volunteer searchers from Dauphin who were camping after helping out for the day heard a voice cry out "help me,". Mary was found in a spot about 2 kilometers from where she'd been picking berries. Oddly it took firemen two hours to clear a path to the spot where she was found which begs the question how on earth did she get in there?

Unfortunately, I couldn't find many updates to this case just an article saying she'd been found safe[87] so I am unsure if Mary ever said what had happened to her during the four days that she was lost. I've noticed that this seems to happen in a lot of cases where the information seems to stop cold once the person has been found with little to no follow up after. Consequently, we've no idea how she got into her final location which was covered in shrubbery so dense firefighters spent two hours hacking through it to get to her, and what made her 'get lost' in an area that is familiar to her especially as she had a friend in such close proximity whose attention she could get with her whistle? One more interesting detail regarding this case is that the night before she was found her son Daryl had a dream in which he saw her location, he left the following morning despite having no money to travel to this spot to find his mother. He and a small group of searchers went to the location he dreamt about, where miraculously she was found.

While Wentz was collecting his material in Ireland, he was told this story about a "leprechaun":

> *One day I was gathering berries along a hedge not far from here and something made me turn over a flat stone which I saw in the ditch where I stood. And there beneath the stone was the most beautiful little creature I have ever seen in my life, and he in a hole as smug as could be. He wasn't much larger than a doll and he was most perfectly formed with a little mouth and eyes. I turned the stone over again and ran as hard as I could to bring my mother, but when we*

---

[87] 'One tough bird': Woman, 84, asked for a cold beer and a hot tub when rescuers found her in bush – Article by Aidan Geary on CBC news.

got back we couldn't see a thing of him.[88]

In his book *The Good People: New Fairylore Essays* (1991) editor P Narváez documented those reports of people being 'Pixie Led' in the Newfoundland are characterized by places that represent boundaries between geographical areas of purity (safe and known), liminal places (places in-between, places in transition) and dangerous places (unknown). For men, these liminal places tend to be forests, and for women, berry patches[89]. Could it be that some people accidentally wander into Fairy territory unintentionally and are 'punished' by Fae Folk as result? Certainly, whilst some Berry Pickers have disappeared never to be seen again, many are found days later dazed and usually confused, miles from their original location may be the result of some otherworldly admonishment. Maybe the berries themselves are a lure, placed purposefully near such places in the hopes of tempting unsuspecting passersby?

The next story comes from Fort Knox, on 23rd June 1949 Veteran Soldier Clarence D. Lunsway (49) went berry picking in the fields around the base at Fort Knox. When he didn't return to base an immediate search of the area was initiated. The military threw all their resources into finding Clarence, with over 10,000 men and searchers combing miles of land around the base to no avail. His body was found nearly 2 years later in a training field next to the base which had been searched by thousands of people in the time since his disappearance. His skeletal remains were found and an autopsy into his death determined that he most likely died of natural causes as they could find no signs of any trauma[90].

Commonality 7 – People who, when found, say that they have no memory of what happened or that their memory is hazy. I have come across this quite a lot when looking at real-life fairy encounters, folklore tales, and Missing 411 cases. When looking more deeply into the disappearances of Berry Pickers I came across the following cases.

Theresa Hoffman was a 25-year-old woman who had gone missing on 24th August 1953 whilst picking berries on her family's farm with her mother and

---

[88] Walter Wenz - The Fairy Faith in Celtic Countries (2001 Blackmask Online edition).

[89] P Narváez Lore and Language, vol. 06, no. 01 (January 1007).

[90] Strange Berry Picker Disappearances – Top Mysteries YouTube Channel published 19/08/2020
https://www.youtube.com/watch?v=Tlz9-j4QzSM

cousin. Theresa seemingly disappeared into thin air after she became separated from her relatives and despite her father and her extended family combing their farm top to bottom, they could not find any trace of her. At this point, her family contacted the police to report Theresa missing. The local sheriff organized a search party with over 2,000 willing participants but still, Theresa could not be located. She was eventually found on 2nd October 1953 by her brother in the woodshed on the family farm, some 10 days later. She had no memory of where she had been or what had happened to her[91].

The below excerpt involving the case of a 6-year-old girl is taken from the *'The Eerie Vanishing and Reappearance of Katherine Van Arst'* by Brent Swancer published on 14th April 2021 on Journal Online:

> *"In August of 1897, a 6-year-old girl named Lillian Carney went missing in the U.S. state of Maine as she was out with her parents picking blueberries. According to the parents, she had vanished right under their noses. A preliminary search of the area would quickly expand to over 200 hundred searchers scouring the area and calling the girl's name, all to no avail. After an extensive search, Lillian was found in the woods in a dazed, trance-like state. When asked what had happened to her, the dazed girl replied that she had been in a place in the forest where the sun had shone the entire time she had been there. This was rather odd considering the weather at the time of her disappearance had been partly cloudy, she had been enveloped by a thick canopy of trees far from any town, and she had been missing overnight, for around 46 hours. What was this continuous "sunlight" she saw, and what significance does it have in Lillian's disappearance? It remains unknown"[92].*

This seemingly trance-like state of confusion or haziness can often come on after someone has experienced being 'pixie led'. That is turned around and made to feel confused or like one has lost their wits. There are several 'Pixie Led' accounts in folklore such as the story of the Reverend Harris as told by author Diarmuid A. MacManus in his book *The Middle Kingdon: The Faerie World of Ireland (1959)*. As the story goes in 1916 the Reverend was on his way to tend to a sick parishioner, this journey door to door was a 7-mile walk and he told his wife he would be back within a few hours. On his usual route, he would take a shortcut across a field, at the other side of this field there was a stile that he would use to cross to the other side where he could pick up the path again. He was quite surprised when he got to this spot as the stile was

---

[91] Ibid.

[92] The Eerie Vanishing and Reappearance of Katherine Van Arst – Article by Brent Swancer on Journal.com April 2021.

nowhere to be found. He had used this style many times before and couldn't figure out where it had gone. The path, the other side of the hedge had also disappeared. At first, he thought he must have simply misjudged the location and so he followed the hedge the whole way around the field, yet he still couldn't locate it. To make matters worse whilst doing this circuit he noticed that he could no longer see the gate that he had used to enter the field in the first place. He continued going around the field in circles, increasingly panicked when after some time things just returned to normal, the gate, the stile, and the path all re-appeared once again exactly where he thought that they should be[93]. There are dozens of historical stories of people being 'Pixie Led' as well as many stories of more modern-day real-life experiences in which people were lucky to not end up in another one of these Missing 411 books!

Going back to the Missing 411 Phenomenon whilst we've discussed the most common of similarities, there are a few other factors that are worth mentioning briefly. Firstly, David noticed that a lot of the people who disappear are wearing brightly coloured clothing, notably the colour red when they disappear. I thought it is worth mentioning as Fae Folk are reported to be attracted to colour. Many accounts of encounters with Fae Folk describe them as wearing most commonly Red. I wonder if the colour Red or the bright colours stand out more and can catch their attention through the veil much better than more muted colours?

Another factor mentioned in a lot of these disappearances is the 'taking' of talented or extremely intelligent individuals. Folk Lore has many tales of Fae Folk taking gifted people, historically it would have been Musicians, Poets, wizards, Bards, and craftsmen. I wonder if their tastes and requirements have matured as our modern world has its own version of 'talented' people. Interestingly, leading on from the abduction of 'talented' people we have the inverse, people being abducted or 'contacted' to give or transfer knowledge. This also ties into our previous chapter on Alien abduction wherein, a person is abducted or 'introduced' to a non-human entity whose purpose for the contact is to impart knowledge. Such as in Bessie Dunlop's case where she claimed Thom Reid gave her knowledge of ointments and medicines or Betty Hill's famous abduction encounter where she was given information about the star system and planets. Certainly, there have been many famous abduction stories, wherein, the abductee is given the knowledge that they allege they did not have previously.

---

[93] Diarmuid A. MacManus - The Middle Kingdon: The Faerie World of Ireland (1959).

In my research, I came across many very interesting subreddits on the Reddit community which led me down many rabbit holes. Down one of these holes, I found a reference (sub-reddits by username 'Trot Trot') to several YouTube mini documentaries by Vikash Pradhan who had investigated the Ban Jhankri[94]. The Ban Jhankri is an entity from Indian mythology. Described as a small humanoid, reddish in colour usually with long matted hair down to the ground and most peculiarly with inverted feet. Which is something I have seen before when looking at the folklore of mythological creatures. Certainly, abnormality of the feet features strongly in mythology. Roman striges who were large monstrous birds had their feet turned backward. The Greek Lamiae were beautiful women with cow or goat feet, sometimes they even had more than two feet! Reports of cloven hoofs are all over folklore whether they are on witches, cyprids, or the very Devil himself. The Ban Jhankri it is said would target young children, it would lure them away from their homes and their villages and into the woods. The now adult abductees recount how the Ban Jhankri could mimic the voices of their friends and relatives in order to lure them away. They also witnessed this entity shapeshifting, from its humanoid form into animals or even into trees or inanimate elements such as earth and rocks.

When being led from their homes they recall being in a trance-like state, not feeling distressed or upset, they recall still feeling as if they were 'at home' for the duration of their experience. This idea of placing subliminal thoughts into the victim's head reminds me of the Mountain Biker experience we looked at earlier. As the children were 'led' through the forest they recall it became very jungle-like, very overgrown with the vegetation getting denser and denser with thick heavy shrubbery. They note that they would not feel pain or endure injury even when pushing through extremely dense rough terrain. They also claim that even though they would have to cross streams and rivers their clothing would never get wet and that they would remain bone dry. They recall being kept in caves and in stories similar to many I've read in mythology and folklore, these caves would lead into large caverns lit by various forms of fire, such as oil lamps and torches and one man even recalls being kept in a cave underwater.

They were fed on bugs, worms, and even sand and earth. They had no concept of time. During this incarceration, they were taught various mantras which they would have to repeat continuously. They were taught how to

[94] Vikash Pradhan YouTube Channel -Abduction: a twist in the tale -
Part 1 of 2: https://www.youtube.com/watch?v=JKDAO-OYHvA
Part 2 of 2: https://www.youtube.com/watch?v=jTU72hNB_Zs

make ointments, how to deal with certain common ailments, and how to fight evil or demonic infestations and possessions. Eventually, the children would be returned to their villages, in some cases, they had been missing for months sometimes years. All would return imbued with this knowledge which they would continue to use into Adulthood eventually reaching Shamon status within their communities.

Pixie Led

According to Folklorist and author Katharine Briggs, being 'Pixie Led' is probably the most common of all the fairy experiences. There are many historic accounts of people being Pixie Led, we've already seen several accounts over the last few chapters of people getting 'turned around', the terrain around them changing instantaneously, the weather changing rapidly and the general vibe feeling odd. This isn't just a historical occurrence, in Steph Young's book *'Stalked in The Woods'* she writes about an account that came directly to her from a gentleman called Luke from the Northern Territory in Australia. Luke has a few strange experiences to relay. The first took place in the Upper Murray area of Northeast Victoria/Southeast New South Wales. When he was in his early twenties, Luke rented some bushland from his uncle and moved into a small shack on this piece of land.

On this land there were two clearings one he called the House Paddock and the other he referred to as the Back Paddock, the paddocks were separated by a very thick bush with a central track in between the two. There was then another track that ran parallel to the western side of the property to a gate that led into the National Park. It was here Luke had his first weird experience after an afternoon of hunting. On his way back home, he headed for the central track rather than the sidetrack as it was a quicker route back to the shack. It's here things took a turn for the bizarre. He describes how all of a sudden there was a vacuum of sound and he suddenly started to feel very nauseous. He noticed that the central track didn't look right. It seemed wider and even more overgrown and somehow even greener than before, so green it almost looked like a jungle. The trees seemed to bend over it giving the illusion of a tunnel, and the tunnel seemed to glow.

He hurried along the track squeezing and pushing himself through the overgrown shrubbery and boughs. Usually, the trip takes 10 minutes from this point to reach the creek. From the creek, he would come across into the House Paddock and back up to the house. This time however he seemed to be pushing his way through this bush for about 2 hours. Finally, he gave up, acknowledging something was terribly wrong when he remembered the advice that his grandmother had given him about fairies when he was little.

So, he took off his shirt, turned it inside out, and fired three shots from his rifle into the air (an SOS sign he and his neighbors had agreed on if either one was in trouble). About five minutes after he turned his shirt inside out, he finally reached the creek. He was relieved, imagining that he would now come out into the House Paddock and see the lights of the house. He didn't, instead, he walked out into a pine plantation which was about 8 kilometers (about 5 miles) from his property. He was dumbfounded, somehow, despite walking south and downhill he'd come out 8km to the West and Uphill! [95].

On the '*Where did the Road Go*' Radio show, David Paulides discusses some similar experiences that people have submitted to him. The first was from two farmers on a ranch in Arkansas, Texas. They said that they were herding cattle, bringing them down a ridgeline on their property, which they'd done a million times before, when suddenly, they didn't know where they were. It was as if the topography had instantly changed around them, and they found themselves somewhere they didn't know. They were understandably shaken and decided to head for a creek that they knew, thinking that they could follow this creek to their property. They said they were walking for hours before they could recognize where they were. It's the strangest experience they've had[96].

The second story involves the disappearance and thankfully reappearance of a young boy. A father and his two sons were chopping wood, the father sends his two sons down to the river to get buckets of water. Each boy has a bucket and the two mosey on down to the river, the first boy fills up his bucket and heads back. The second boy however spills his bucket on his way back, so he turns around and heads back to the river and completely disappears. Thankfully the boy is found safe and well 5 days later and his description of what happened fits our profile here. He said that he walked back to the river and refilled his bucket but when he turned around to walk back, he didn't recognize a thing, the environment around him had completely changed. He said he called out for his brother and then for his father, but no one came back to help or even responded to his calls. Eventually, he began to walk trying to find his way back, and seemingly just carried on walking. He has no idea what happened or where he was or how he even got to his eventual final location[97]. Most bizarre.

The next story comes from a very interesting Reddit post on the Missing 411

---

[95] Young, "Stalked in The Woods".

[96] Where Did The Road Go Radio interview with David Paulides.

[97] Ibid.

subreddit. It's posted by 'RogerDodgerHer' and the poster goes on to relay a story told to him by Larry Kelm during a BFRO (Bigfoot Field Researchers Organization) field trip in Ruidoso, NM. I've copied the text directly from the post as I didn't want to lose any of the context or detail by way of my summarizing his experience:

"In the fall of 1980 I ran a small business as a construction contractor in Eugene, Oregon. During the slow times and in-between jobs I would don my backpack and hiking boots and disappear into the mountains for weeks at a time enjoying the peaceful solitude of long hikes. At that time I was single and didn't answer to anyone so I was free to do what I wanted when I wanted. On the trip in question I decided to hike the old Mollala Indian trail that followed the ridge tops from Saddle Blanket Mountain to Oakridge, one of the Native American's favorite summer camps and trading centers. It was a beautiful August day, two days into the hike (I expected to be gone about two weeks), when literally out of the blue the most terrifying thing that ever happened to me in my life occurred. It would change my perspective of reality forever.

I was walking along the trail enjoying the strong breeze and bright sunshine when, in the middle of a step, everything around me started to turn gray and blurry. The only way I can describe it was as if suddenly I was looking through someone else's prescription sunglasses. I finished the step and started another. Every inch I moved forward the darkness increased and the gray blurring turned into a jumble of shapes that made no sense. I then seemed to pass a barrier and everything started to return back into focus when my foot reached the ground on the second step everything around me had changed. Day had turned into night and there was no wind. All the Douglas Fir and pine trees had been replaced with thick jungle-like growth. The cool thin mountain air was replaced with humid thick air. There were no stars in the sky, but there was a diffused light that let me see everything clearly, however I couldn't tell what the light source was.

As often happens when the human body receives a massive dose of adrenaline the entire incident appeared like it was in slow motion and even though I was only there for a second or two I had time to observe my surroundings. The silence was broken by [a] continuous high pitched keening sound, and I was nearly overwhelmed with a sense of fear and danger. My momentum caused me to take one more step before stopping in my tracks.

It was at this point, I heard a whispered "Gotcha" over my right shoulder. I couldn't tell if I heard it with my ears or inside my head. The word wasn't directed at me but something said the word quietly to itself. I was so terrified I actually felt my heart stop for a moment. That whispered word is what saved me. I opened my mouth and gasped in a huge gush of thick air and recoiled backward in the same footsteps I had entered wherever I was. As I threw myself backward, I looked over my right shoulder. A dark colored hairy right hand and arm was reaching for my throat over my shoulder. The hand had pale ivory spade-shaped fingernails. The nails looked clean and almost had a manicured look to them. The thumb was placed lower (towards the wrist) on the hand than a human's is. Both hand and arm were thin and powerful looking and both were covered with thick coarse black hair.

I got a good look at it because the thumbnail grazed my neck (it did not break the skin) as I moved backwards. As I continued backwards, the hand clutched where my neck had been a split second before and it seemed to fade off into the distance as I returned through the Portal. I took two more steps backwards and everything reversed itself from what had just happened. The world around me became lighter, the fir and pines gradually came back into view and by the third step I was back on Saddle Blanket Mountain.

I continued to move backwards in terror, and as I did, I observed that where I had just come from was a shimmering oval patch of air about the size of a large door. The woods behind it looked like it was under water. By the fifth backward step the shimmering area seemed to just evaporate and everything was back to normal. By then my lungs had nearly burst from the volume of air I had inhaled during the huge gasp I had just taken. My body felt like it was on fire from the adrenaline surge. I spun around and ran back down the trail as fast as my legs could carry me and didn't stop until I reached my truck. I was nearly two days getting to that place and about three hours getting back.
On my way home I was absolutely horrified at the thought of what would happen if I were to drive my truck into something like that. It had been a trap pure and simple. Whatever it was that tried to kill me somehow kept the Portal hidden from me on the way in, and I didn't actually see it until I was back out again. I had terrible nightmares for years and still haven't come to grips with what happened. My fingers are trembling, and the hair is standing up on the nape of my neck as I write this".[98]

The reference to Jungle in the above text I found interesting as its similar in description to Luke from Australias' earlier story, as he had also mentioned his environment resembling Jungle in his description of events. There's a wonderful story in the Jacques Vallee book, *'Passport to Magonia'*, Pages 95 & 96 where a woman in 1950's France encounters a similar unseen attacker whose hairy arms appear from nowhere to grab her. The story is quite long and very detailed so I would do it no justice to summarise it here but certainly check out the story, I'll leave a link in the Notes and Sources section at the

[98] Post on Reddit.com (The Trap by User RogerDodgeHer).

back of the book.

Valleé notes in his book that there was a sub-genre of Fae Folk called 'Lutins' within French folklore, these 'lutins' were also described as being large, hairy, and usually black in colour. They were said to reside in caves and coincidentally had a penchant for scaring young women who had the misfortune to find themselves travelling alone, not unlike North American Sasquatch encounters.

Another story I came across during my deep dive into these personal accounts of possible 'near misses' was through both the *Journal.com* website and Reddit. User 'Rosetta9' posts her account of a strange experience titled *'My very strange and very frightening hiking experience'* on the Missing 411 subreddit.

Her story goes as follows; in July 2016 she was attending a Yoga Retreat in Colorado. She states that she is a seasoned hiker who lives in Colorado so is very familiar with these trails. On the 2nd day of her retreat, she decided to do a solo hike. Only a short time into the hike she comes across a bright sign nailed to a tree that names the National Park she is in, she takes maybe 5 steps off the trail to go read the sign but when she turns back around to return to the trail path, the trail has completely disappeared. Not only that, but she also now seemed to be in a completely different location. She tried not to panic and carefully walked a circle around the area she was in, careful not to go too far but staying in her general vicinity. Oddly the tree with the sign on which she had seen minutes earlier was also now gone. She debated calling her husband or calling 911 for help but she felt very strongly that she shouldn't make that call. Strangely, she felt as if she was being 'led' a certain way but again something inside her was telling her she shouldn't go, and she should try to 'fight' this urge. After a short while, she heard voices, so she tried yelling for help but after a while, she got the strong sense that her voice wasn't being heard. The whole time she had a very uneasy sense that she was being watched by something.

Now fully realizing something was seriously wrong she decided to run. There was a field in front of her, so she just floored it over this field in the direction of the Yoga Center. She said that the topography was weird, like the earlier stories. The grass seemed to get taller and taller as she ran until at points it was taller than her. Despite being a very dry hot day in summer the field she was in felt like a marsh or bog with dips and holes. She felt like she was sinking into it like it was quicksand causing her to trip and badly twist her ankle. Eventually, she got to a trail she recognized just near the facility. Luckily, she was ok, her ankle was injured and weirdly her eyes were red and puffy and hurt for days as if she'd had a chemical reaction to something out there but overall, she came out of the encounter relatively unscathed, if not, a little traumatized[99]. Interestingly, she says that a skier went missing there not long before her experience, he wasn't found by the time of her post. There was also an incident where a foot in a boot was found in that same area. I did find a newspaper article on *The Coloradoan.com* which seems to back up the posters' comments. This Article confirms that the skeletal remains found in a 'snow boot' in the Colorado Ski Resort in 2016 were identified as 83-year-old Ervin Mettler. Authorities say the Denver man appeared to have been camping near Eldora Mountain Resort, but the cause and manner of his death haven't yet been determined. I am not sure if this is the same 'foot' the poster is referring to, but it does seem pretty likely[100].

There is a similar belief in Fae Folk in Eastern Europe, however, in the Eastern versions, they believe this 'Pixie led' phenomenon to be witchcraft and the perpetrators Witches. In her Ethnographic Fieldwork thesis *'Styrian Witches in European Perspective'* Mirjam Mencej (Professor of Folklorists at the University of Ljubljana, Slovenia) describes similar experiences as described above but with the people experiencing this phenomenon attributing it to the work of witches. This experience was similarly called 'Witch Led' or being 'carried by the Witches'. This experience was sometimes related to visual stimuli such as seeing flames, fires, or light anomalies but more often than that there was no preceding event, the person would simply find themselves 'turned about' with no explanation. Similar to the fairy encounters reported, people would be in locations very familiar to them, in a lot of instances their own land or land surrounding their homes which they claim to know every square foot of, and yet still find themselves lost and confused as to where they are. This experience would occur whilst out in the open such as in the forest, or farmland, a lot of incidents seem to occur near a body of water such as a stream, river, pond, or lake. A great number of accounts state the event occurring as it is getting later in the day so afternoon through to dusk and usually lasting until daybreak the next following morning. The core experience is disorientation, confusion, and loss of time. As with fairy encounters people are told to turn clothes inside out to 'break the spell' and stop whatever outside influence is causing the confusion and disorientation.

Below is an excerpt from Mencej's paper detailing a witness's experience which was relayed to her in an interview (Mencej conducted many interviews

---

[99] Post of Reddit.com (My very strange and very frightening hiking experience by User rosetta9).

[100] Skeletal remains found in snow boot at ski resort identified – Article published on The Coloradoan.com.

106

as part of this paper), details of which you can see are similar to the accounts of people who claim to have been 'pixie-led'.

> *But another time (…), another time I went right there on my way home from work, but then I went at 12 o'clock. I walked there many times, many times every day (…) to work and back, you know, but suddenly I can't find my way home, I don't know which is the right path. There was this path and another path, I saw, the paths met, a little way ahead, I saw a house, it was our home, but I couldn't get to it. I was twenty years old.*

The interviewer then asks him '*but how? What did your parents…?* To which the victim responds, '*They told me that the Witches led me*'.

Interestingly, many of the victims of these 'witches' end up in bushes or shrubbery for unknown reasons. Below is another excerpt from an interview:

'Yes, they were saying, even my father said that he once went home from somewhere, and he was not drunk, as they say that this can only happen to drunken people. He went through a wood and came somewhere where he has absolutely never been before. And there were lights around him, you see, shining and surrounding him so that he got confused. Not before the next morning could he come to his senses again. He found himself inside a horrible thicket, that is all he told us, yes'.[101]

Are fairies good or evil? Well, I guess like humans you have both sides of the coin or maybe I'm just imposing our moral and ethical values onto something quite different from ourselves. Do they actively 'hunt' us or do we just fall into their territory, and they decide in the moment what it is that they feel like doing with us? I guess we'll never know, certainly I hope to never get close enough to find out!

The Archetype

So, what is the Green Man Archetype? It is one that can be seen in nearly every religion going back for thousands of years. In terms of timescales, it is hard to place these Archetypes accurately as a lot of these Deities either exist in parallel to each other or are the same but referenced under multiple different names. I've seen them appear at different times, either dying and reappearing much later chronologically or seemingly appearing in different periods depending upon the text being examined. I imagine that religion in some form has existed for as long as mankind has existed, such is our need to believe in something outside of ourselves but tracking its roots becomes

---

[101] Mirjam Mencej - Styrian Witches in European Perspective'.

more and more difficult the further back we try to go. Our history reaches back only so far back before it becomes a myth. Tales of Heroes and Villains, of great triumphs and great adversities told by poets, bards, and philosophers. We do have some accurate accounts as written by the historians of the day which helps us to fill in some of the gaps and to piece together more of the jigsaw but for the purposes of this book and given, I am not a historian (nor do I claim to be) I won't be focusing on the chronology of this Archetype, keeping this more a general look at the Archetype itself.

What was interesting to me in my research is how similar each religion is, how they mirror each other in terms of narrative and archetypes. It does make me scratch my head as to how this can be. How did our early ancestors, people separated by hundreds of thousands of miles, spread all over the world end up with such similar stories? Surely if all these religions and mythologies were organic to each region, to each tribe, and geographical location we'd have a much more diverse account of narratives than we do. Surely, a simple invasion could not account for this, people do not let go of their fundamental beliefs so easily. We've seen this in our recent history with people simply going 'underground' and worshipping in secret re-emerging once the threat has passed, so I cannot imagine all these diverse beliefs would have been so easily eradicated. So, what happened, how did we end up with so many different religions which all share so many commonalities? Well, this is a question that far more educated people than me have been debating for centuries and the truth is we can't say for certain. For me, I believe that at some point there must have been one great 'mother' civilization where the original narrative began and that people from this Civilization were sent to all corners of the earth to 'spread knowledge' to all the different peoples of the world, in a 'Promethean' act of enlightenment. To set in progress the civilization of the entire world.

But how? How could a few people change the existing belief system of many? This is the question that intrigues me. In his thesis the *Origins of Pagan Idolatry*, George Stanley Faber posits that the original great civilization may have been that of Sodom and Gomorrah since the bible says that the people there shared one religion, and all spoke one language[102]. That 'All' came together to build and create these great Cities. That 'All' were instrumental in shaping their civilization and building the great tower of Babel. It is this 'fall' of the tower of Babel that marks the start of the collapse of this great civilization, and this is when the people splintered. That we have a pre-destruction and post-destruction time split. Before the people were all one nation and people,

---

[102] George Stanley Faber B.D - The Origin of Pagan Idolatry (Vol I, II & III) – (London 1816).

shared language and religion then post destruction a civilization fractured, and its people fled to other regions of the world some as far as North Europe accounting for the spreading of the original religious narrative.

This is of course based on biblical texts which are hazy at best on timescales and there is not much consensus by archaeologists, scientists, and Biblical scholars on whether these sister cities even existed, let alone whether or not they were destroyed in the manner described. I do think that the theory is an interesting one though and makes sense if we think of it as a story that tries to explain the ability of a common religion to spread across the entire earth. This is a great hypothesis to springboard off from to discuss where it all began and who the proto archetype derived from.

This is not overlooking nor downplaying the impact that a vast invading force can have on shaping and creating new civilizations. It is very apparent in my research is that each invading force brings with it, its own religious ideology. However, it would appear, that this invading force seems to take elements of the existing native belief system and assimilate it into its own. Rather than simply stamping out or eradicating the existing one. There seems to be an assimilation process that occurs. It would follow that this is the easiest approach given that the 'invading' and 'native' religions do not appear to be radically different. Having enough commonalities already in existence, that an amalgamation is the simplest easiest way to move forward, eventually creating another 'branch' of the existing narrative.

We can trace this 'lather, rinse and repeat' pattern back as far as Ancient Mesopotamia. Unfortunately, however, the further back we go the harder it is to know for certain what is 'fact' and what is 'myth' but I've just had to take a leap of faith here and go with the narrative that makes the most sense to me and with which I feel most comfortable. It's simply my theory based on my interpretation of the information that I have read. It is not my intention to be 'right' or 'wrong' my aim is simply to put forward my conclusion.

The easiest way for me to look at this Archetype is to take it back to the beginning as far as I can chronologically speaking, which brings us to Ancient Mesopotamia, to the Sumerians, and the Akkadians. The Sumerians were, like all ancient pagans, polytheistic, worshipping many Gods. Like the many religions which will follow there are Gods for most things but there is a definite Hierarchical structure in force. There is a 'main' God, the Parent/Father figure who creates and then 'rules' over the other Deities. There is the Great Father's Consort, the mother of all, then finally there is the son. Symbolically the great father is representative of the Sun, the mother, either the Moon or the Earth, and the Son who will eventually supplant the great father to eventually take on the mantle of the Sun ('son') once again. The trinity always exists in some form, sometimes as described above, sometimes a slight variation but it is a staple found in nearly every religious mythology and indeed in much Folk Lore mythology since religion and folklore are good bedfellows.

Let us start with Ancient Mesopotamia, considered the cradle of civilization. According to history, Mesopotamia was created by the various races of people who lived in and migrated to the region, these people would evolve to become the 'Sumerians' and the 'Akkadians'. The origin of the many things we take for granted today were birthed in Mesopotamia. Mesopotamia was populated by two notable races, the Sumerians who settled in Sumer in the South who seem to have settled first and then soon followed by the Akkadians who settled Akkadia in the North (believed to be the Semitic population of the region due to the origin of their language). These races appear to have lived and to have co-existed relatively peacefully in the region for thousands of years. The religion of both appears to have been a shared one as I found many references in my research to both Sumerian names and Akkadian names for essentially the same deities in religious text and artifacts.

Mesopotamia was founded around 7,000 years ago. By 4,000 BC this region had created sophisticated writing systems, art, architecture, horticulture, astronomy, and mathematics. They had concepts of politics and even bureaucracy[103]. The 'origin' of these already civilized Sumerians is an intriguing one. In *The Myth of the Seven Sages* it is said that the native southern population who existed in this region at the time were rough and savage, far from being considered civilized. However, this all changed after the arrival of the original Sumerians who were described as 'Strange Beings' that 'came from the Sea'.[104] So who were these strange people from the sea and how was it that they already had the blueprints for civilization? Coincidently, we have the Mesopotamian mythology of the 'Oannes' from around this time. The Oannes were a race of semi-aquatic beings who were supposedly originated from the Sirius Star System. These semi-aquatic beings were worshipped by the Sumerians and then by their Babylonian successors. The Byzantine Eastern Orthodox Patriarch Photius (820-893) tells us that the beings known as 'Oannes' arrived from the sky in luminous eggs, which were

---

[103] Jean Bottéro - Religion in Ancient Mesopotamia (2001).

[104] Ibid.

put down in the gulf of Persia[105]. The Oannes myth does seem to parallel the story from the Seven Sages.

Linking this to the Oannes mythology even further, we also have the legend of Dagon, the fish God of Sumer, who is supposed to have come from the sea bringing with him knowledge and the precursors to civilization such as language, writing, mathematics, astronomy, architecture, medicine, and civic duty. Dagon was considered a 'Father' God similar to the Mesopotamian God Enlil however I cannot see any reference to him being a fertility or agricultural God, he seems to appear as more of a Promethean figure, providing enlightenment. According to the legend, the city of Sumer seemed to rise up out of nowhere, with no trace of the Sumerian language or culture being found anywhere else in the world[106] from around that same time supporting the argument that they didn't just 'migrate' in from another region. Whilst they have been gone for nearly 4,000 years their impact on the shaping of our history and the influence that they had on civilizations to come cannot be underestimated. Interestingly, the legend of Dagon does also mirror the biblical 'Jonah and the whale story' with Jonah being swallowed and then rather unceremoniously spat out by a great fish ('Dagan) left alive to 'teach' in the Babylonian City of Nineveh.

So as stated above, if Prometheus brought fire to mankind, then did the ancient Sumerians and their 'fish-God' Dagon bring us the concepts required for civilization? If this is true, what great civilization did they come from? One great enough to have already mastered sea travel, had enough people to colonize successfully, and could bring with them their ideas, cultures, religion, and were capable of taming and gentrifying the locals? And one that has managed to conceal its existence leaving no trace of its people, religion, and way of life behind in any other region of the world. It's an intriguing question, that's for sure.

The trinity (or Triad of Gods) in the Mesopotamian Religion comprised of the Father God Anu and his sons the Gods Enki and Enlil. It is the 'Son' God Enlil that interests me concerning the subject at hand as I believe that aspects of our Modern Green Man can be traced back to Enlil. The ancient Mesopotamian religion was nature based with nature worship being front and center of its core belief system. Enlil was considered the God of Agriculture.

---

[105] Allen Greenfield – The Complete Cipher of the Ufonauts (2016 edition).

[106] Ibid.

His name Enlil means Lord of Wind, able to control the element either as a gentle breeze or violent and frightening like a Hurricane. Whilst his father An is sat highest in the pantheon, Enlil is considered to have been even more important where we are concerned as it is Enlil who is considered to have 'birthed' humanity.

The Mesopotamia creation story involves the myth of the Creation of the Hoe[107]. In this myth, it is said that Enlil split the heaven and the earth to make room to sow seeds. He invented the Hoe so that he could break the hard crust of the Earth and then Man sprang forth from the cracks made by the Hoe. Could it be man's ancestors actually came from beneath the ground? Enlil seems to be the 'proto' archetype. Whether he is the first we don't know, his story could be based on an even earlier Archetype that may have existed before him but certainly, Enlil seems to be the 'oldest' of this Archetype I can find. He is the 'Son' (sun), he is directly linked to creation, he is directly linked to fertility and nature and as we'll soon see, he is also directly linked to the 'world in-between' or Underworld. Making him the first Green Man archetype that I can find in the history books. As I mentioned in the Green Man Origin chapter, we know that we have the traditional foliate head 'Green Man' imagery going back as far as Mesopotamian, with one being found at the ruined city of Hatra in Iraq[108]. Evidencing the existence of the Green Man as far back as Mesopotamia.

In another Mesopotamian myth Enlil rapes his Queen Consort Ninlil (the grain goddess), to do this he would shapeshift, taking on different forms to 'surprise' her on 3 separate occasions producing a child with each assault. It should be said that Ninlil loved her husband and followed him to the Underworld when he is banished. The narrative of this particular story seems to be an analogy for the brutality of the changing seasons, the destruction of the earth during winter before fertility can return in the spring. Certainly, we know that the Green Man can shapeshift with his foliate head switching between man and animal face[109]. Enlil was punished for his attacks on his wife by banishment to the Underworld. Indeed, it is said that once his sentence was finished, he chose to stay in the Underworld, to rule and become its King rather than return to the surface. This decision it seems appears to have made him a 'Lucifer' figure in the eyes of several theologians. It does, however, seem that at some point he does return to the Earth after his time below. Symbolically being 'reborn' which is a prerequisite of this

---

[107] 'The Song of The Hoe' – Article published on World History.biz.

[108] Eric Edwards Wordpress.com - The Green Man Phenomenon and Foliate Heads.
[109] Ibid.

Archetype.

Foliate head carving (c. 3rd - 1st Century BCE) in the ruined desert city of al-Hadr (or Hatra),
Iraq

The story appears to have strong symbology representing the destruction and violence of nature and the cycle of life and rebirth after. The Father is death, but he also brings new life, being at once both creator and destroyer. This is a common Pagan theme that we see repeatedly throughout the different iterations of this archetype and the Pagan Religions. In my research on Mesopotamia, I did find the origin story of the first Sumerians to be the most intriguing to me.

It is also worth mentioning that Enlil was not represented anthropomorphically in Mesopotamian iconography. Instead, he was represented by a horned cap, which consisted of up to seven superimposed pairs of ox horns. Interestingly the reference to rams, goats, bulls, and their horns will show up repeatedly when looking at this Archetypal form. He was also succeeded by his nephew Marduk who, coincidentally was described as follows 'He was the Tallest of Gods surpassing in form. His limbs were enormous, he was surpassing at birth'[110]. It's worth mentioning that the offspring of the first Sumerians were referred to as the Anunnaki, which translates to 'Offspring of the Prince' a derivative of the great God An (Anu) and his Queen Consort Ki. It is written in ancient Mesopotamia texts that the Anunnaki were much larger than normal men, giving us a twist on the origin of the first Sumerians. Could they possibly have been extraterrestrial? Biblical scholars also parallel their origin to the Nephilim, the biblical offspring of the fallen 200 angels who defied God and settled on Earth. Could Marduk's description be a nod to either of these narratives?

After Enlil, the next corresponding religious figure I would like to look at is Tammuz. Tammuz was another Mesopotamian God and another nephew of our proto- archetype Enlil. His origins do differ slightly depending on which sources I referred to, but the majority of sources denote him as the son of Enki, brother of Enlil, and grandson of the Father God An so that is what I will also go with. Interestingly Tammuz was referenced in several theses that I read as being worshipped as the 'reincarnation' of the Sun God Nimrod. Nimrod was also a Mesopotamian God who is referenced specifically in biblical texts. Denoted as the son of Cush and the great-grandson of Noah, historians have found it difficult to prove his existence as a King of ancient Mesopotamia given that reference to him only seems to occur in the confines of biblical texts. An interesting character who certainly shares some attributes of our Archetype but not one that I'll be delving into too deeply in the book as I feel he is more of an 'amalgamation' of characters rather than a Green Man archetype specifically.

Tammuz was seen by the ancient Mesopotamians as their Fertility God, in some texts referred to as the Green Man given his ability to create an abundance of plant life and vegetation wherever he wished. He is said to have the power of trees and nature spirits He was worshipped twice a year in rituals that mirror our current Neo-Pagan festivals. One festival falling in early Spring in which his marriage to Inanna was celebrated, symbolizing the fertilization of nature and the prayers for a bountiful harvest for the year to come. The other is held at the end of summer as autumn falls symbolizing the change in seasons, the symbolic death of nature, the death of Tammuz, and the lamenting of his demise at the hands of the demons.[111] This cycle of life, death, and rebirth is intrinsic to the Green Man as he is representative of all three, the simplest yet holiest of all holy trinities.

---

[110] Jean Bottéro - Religion in Ancient Mesopotamia (2001).

[111] Dumuzid – Wikipedia.

As mentioned earlier, in Mythology there is a relationship between the Green Man and his female counterpart. Where he is the male (yin) so 'she' the great goddess is the female (yang) in all iterations of the Green Man archetype there is also his Green Goddess but for the purposes of this book I'll be focusing on the Male aspect but it is impossible to talk about him without acknowledging the Feminine. For Tammuz, we have his relationship with the Mother Goddess Ishtar, who in some texts is referred to as his queen consort, in others she is his Mother. Whatever their relationship we know that Tammuz and Ishtars' story is one of the more romantic and infamous tales in Mythology. It is said that Ishtar betrayed Tammuz after he fails to mourn appropriately whilst she was lost in the Underworld. Hurt by his apparent inaction, Ishtar agrees to let the demons of Hell drag him to the Underworld in her place. Ishtar immediately regrets her betrayal so enters the Underworld to rescue Tammuz. Tammuz however, as common with this archetype does not want to leave but agrees for the love of Ishtar to live in the Underworld for half the year and then spend the other half of the year on earth. Again, strong symbology for the changing of the cycles and the pagan belief in the Horned God ruling for half the year [winter months] with the Mother Goddess ruling for the other half of the year [summer months][112].

The Goddess Ishtar exists in one form or another in every religion. In the Old Testament she is called Ashtorat, in Egypt Isis, Semiramis by the Assyrians, Aphrodite by the Greeks, Venus by the Romans, and simply the Mother Goddess by the Celts and Anglo Saxons. She also exists in elements of the Hunter Goddesses such as Diana or Artemis[113]. Although in my research the original creator deity in most religions does have hermaphroditic qualities, being one entity who singularly births its children before the necessity for gender even comes into play. Certainly, there are aspects of duality with several of the deities I'll mention, Dionysus who we'll look at shortly was born male yet considered to have been raised female and have feminine characteristics.

The cult of Ishtar and Tammuz continued to thrive as late as the 11th Century and even into the 18th century within the Mesopotamian Region. Tammuz was also known by his Sumerian name Dumuzid. The Cult of Dumuzid later spread as far as Greece where he became known by his more recognizable

---

[112] Edwards, "The Green Man Phenomenon".

[113] Hans Holzer - Witches – True Encounters with Wicca, Wizards, Covens, Cults and Magick -(First published by Black Dog & Leventhal Publishers 2002).

Western Semitic name 'Adonis'. Parallel to this, we have the Greek God Dionysus, who shares many commonalities with the 'Adonis' Archetype and is considered by many to be associated with Adonis, Tammuz, and even the Egyptian God Osiris[114]. The link between the Green Man archetype and Greek deities has been explored by many students of the Esoteric, who see him as the spiritual ancestor of these 'death and resurrection' Gods of the Greico-Romans.[115]

Dionysus (also commonly known by his Roman name Bacchus) was the God of Wine, harvest, vegetation, and agriculture encompassing the general fertility of the land. Dionysus's story mirrors that of both Enlil and Tammuz in many aspects. Dionysus is the son of the Father God (Zeus), his mother changes in different tellings of the story, in some it is Persephone, and in others it is Semele. Zeus' wife Hera upon hearing of the pregnancy was so enraged by the affair that she plotted against Zeus' pregnant lover. Telling her that she should ask Zeus to prove his love for her by appearing in his natural form. The poor unfortunate woman did so but Zeus' Godlike form was too much for this mere mortal to behold and she was destroyed by lightning bolts. Zeus rescued his son's unborn fetus and sowed it up his thigh for safe keeping, making Dionysus 'twice born' in mythology. Upon hearing that Dionysus had survived, Hera was furious and commanded the Titans to kill him, they did so by tearing him apart, but legend has it he was bought back to life using his heart which was found unharmed directly after the attack. After this, for his continued protection, he was sent by Zeus to live in Greece with the mountain nymphs[116].

It is said that in his youth he was attended to by Satyrs and Sileni. Sileni is derived from Dionysus' foster father Silenus who was also considered to be the son of the God Pan. Pan, having his roots in Akkadian mythology as the God of Shepherds[117]. His mythos eventually merged with that of the Celtic Horned God to become the 'Half man, half Goat' depiction of more modern times we recognize today. It is said that the main difference between a Satyr and a Sileni is the Sileni has the attributes of a horse rather than a goat. Once again, we have the reference to Goats, which is not surprising given the

---

[114] Dumuzid – Wikipedia.

[115] Fran and Geoff Doel – The Green Man In Britain (2001) Ebook (2013).

[116] Dionysus: Greek God of fertility and wine – Article on Greek Mythology.com.

[117] William Anderson – The Green Man, The Archetype of our Oneness with the Earth (1990).

Akkadian/Sumerian Roots of the Archetype as the Akkadians saw Goats as divine and sacred animals which were worshipped[118]. We'll see the reference and incorporated Goat element repeatedly within the Archetype.

Dionysus himself was closely connected to the Bull, one connection through his wife and lover Ariandne. Ariandne was the daughter of King Minos of Crete. According to the myth, King Minos' son died during a tournament that was organized in Athens. In retribution, the King of Crete attacked Athens and won. He then imposed a heavy burden on the city; he demanded that seven young men and seven young women be sent to Crete every year to be sacrificed, these unfortunates were thrown into the Labyrinth underneath Minos' palace, where the Minotaur dwelt. Theseus, son of King Aegeus of Athens, volunteered to be sent as one of the fourteen sacrifices so that he could kill the Minotaur and thus end the bloodshed for good. When in Crete, Ariadne met and fell in love with Theseus, desperate to save her paramour Ariadne gave Theseus a sword and a ball of string which he could use to defeat and finally slay the beast. After the bull was slain, Ariadne then fled with Theseus for fear of punishment for her betrayal. On route back to Athens they stopped at Naxos to dock for the night. It is here that Ariadne falls asleep on the beach at Islet of Palatia, while Theseus sleeps on board the ship with his crew. It is here Dionysus spies her whilst she sleeps and immediately falls in love with her. There seem to be several versions of what happened next, in one Theseus simply sets sail abandoning her on the beach, and in the other Dionysus appeared to Theseus in a dream and threatens him, forcing him to leave Ariande who is still on the beach. Either way, upon realizing that Theseus has abandoned her she agrees to marry Dionysus[119].

Dionysus himself is linked to the Bull, in some versions of his death by the titans he was in bull form when he was attacked and torn to pieces. In some mythologies, Dionysus was conceived and birthed in an animal form. We have a reference in antiquity to Dionysus being born with horns. His images were often depicted in bull form. On one statue he appears clad in a bull's hide, complete with head and hooves. On one specific vase, he is depicted as a calf-like child sat on his mother's lap. The Bacchanals of Thrace (A cult dedicated to the worship of Bacchus, Dionysus' Roman counterpart) would wear horns to imitate their God. The Bull, it seems is a universally venerated symbol, the bull of Minos celebrated by the Greeks as the Bull of Menu is

---

[118] Sir James Frazer – The Golden Bough (Single Volume Abridged Edition) – published by Penguin 1996.

[119] Naxos and the Gods: The Love Story of Dionysus and Ariadne – Article published on Naxos.gr.

celebrated by the Brahmens or the Bull of Menuis was by the Egyptians. In Thrace, Dionysus was represented as a bull and in Arcadian mythology, it was said that Hermes transformed him into a ram to protect him from the wrath of Hera after his birth[120].

Another animal regularly associated with Dionysus is the Goat. We have already referenced the Satyr and Selini associations to him, but Dionysus was also depicted in Goat form[121]. Indeed, one of his given names was 'The Kid' as with the Bull disguise referenced above, Dionysus often used a goat 'disguise' to evade his potential assassins. In Athens and Hermion he was given the title 'the one of the black goatskin'. In Crete, he was referred to as 'Zagreus' which translates to Wild goat with enormous horns.[122] His roman counterpart Bacchus was also worshipped similarly with goats being ritually sacrificed and eaten in worship of him. The association of Dionysus with these woodland entities cements his 'Lord of the Woods' characterization as similar or corresponding to 'Pan'.

The ability to shapeshift is another commonality within the mythology of this universal Archetype. There are many representations of Dionysus (Roman - Bacchus). It was said by the poet Nonnus that in order to evade the pursuit of the titans he would take the form of a lion or a horse, an old man or young man, and even change gender and appear as more feminine to throw them off his scent[123]. The leaves used within the depictions of the Green Man from around this time are also interesting. The versions that use Vine leaves would appear to directly link our Green Man to Dionysus and Bacchus[124]. The use of Oak leaves in other versions will directly link him to the Celtic versions of this same archetype. The Acanthus leaves often seen in the foliate head depictions represent enduring life and immortality and sacred rebirth. Rebirth being a significant theme for our Archetype.

In Frazer's *The Golden Bough,* he describes how Dionysus was given the title 'Dionysus of the tree' by the Greeks of Boeotia. Whilst the vine itself is most

---

[120] Zan Fraser – The Horned God of Wytches (2007 Emerald City Books).

[121] Frazer, "The Golden Bough".

[122] Fraser, "The Horned God of Wytches".

[123] Frazer, "The Golden Bough".

[124] William Anderson – The Green Man, The Archetype of our Oneness with the Earth (1990).

associated with Dionysus he was also venerated by tree worship. In certain ceremonies, he was represented by an upright post with no arms draped in a mantle with a bearded mask to represent the head and with leafy bough projecting from the head. Yet another reference to a foliate man found in antiquity.

As with Enlil and Tammuz, Dionysus also visited the underworld. In Greek mythology, it is said that Dionysus travelled to the Underworld to bring back his mother. He succeeded in founding his mother, even though he had never met her in life, and faced down Thanatos, the very embodiment of Death, and brought her back to Mount Olympus. This idea of dimensional travel was very prevalent in pagan mythology. It was possible to travel to the Underworld or to travel to the homeland of your Gods and then return back to our reality. The ancient Norse theology believed that all things exist in the 'nine realms' based on the divine meta-physical tree of Yggdrasil. This eternally Green Ash tree (Ash coincidentally factors strongly in Fae Folk and nature worship) stands in the middle of the Earth, each Realm hanging off its own branch off the Yggdrasil. The belief being that if the tree should fall, then it would be the destruction of all of the nine realms. Asgard was the realm of the Gods, Midgard the realm of humans with the other 7 realms being home to other races such as elves, dwarves, and Giants. The ancient Aztecs believed in 13 realms, the Earth itself being made up of 9 realms, each realm being the domain of a different God[125]. In Dante's inferno, there are nine circles of Hell. It is interesting how many of our old religions have a concept of other dimensions, worlds, and planes of existence.

What interests me most about the Character of Dionysus is this 'Promethean' gifting of knowledge. It is said in many myths and stories about Dionysus that he wandered far and wide past Greece into other regions spreading his knowledge, it is said he would show people how to grow vines and make wine. This 'gifting' of knowledge is something that comes up repeatedly, not only in the story of the Archetype that we're looking at but interestingly in the stories of the Fae Encounters and even Alien abduction stories we've already reviewed, where the transfer of knowledge appears to be the motive behind the 'initial contact'.

Dionysus' followers became cult-like, following him far and wide. Spreading and gaining more followers in every place that they came to pass. Unlike the other Olympian Gods, Dionysus was not worshipped at the temple. Rather

---

[125] Mari Silva – Paganism (everything from ancient Hellenic, Norse and Celtic Paganism to Heathenry, Wicca and other Modern Pagan Beliefs and Practices (2021).

his followers would go into the Woods to worship him; bringing our Green Man elements into the myth of Dionysus, or indeed bringing Dionysus' elements into our Green Man story. It was said that Dionysus would be accompanied by wild women, drunk with wine and adorned in fawn skins. These 'Bacchantes' (priestesses of Bacchus) would carry rods tipped with pinecones. In his book *'The Green Man'* Anderson describes them as a fennel stork topped with a pinecone. The stork representing the spinal column which culminates in the pinecone 'pineal gland' through which is transmitted this higher faculty of knowledge and inspiration[126]. Quickly referring back to our previous chapter on colour, Green also has a stimulating effect on the pituitary gland. It causes blood histamine levels to increase dilating blood vessels and aiding in smoother muscle contractions. In short, it is stress relieving and calming[127]. It's also been shown to improve reading ability and creativity, which is an interesting little side note! It is this description of these rods, however, which grabbed my attention as it is not the first time I've come across a reference in mythology to such instruments. As already mentioned in the Fae and Alien encounter stories, rods and wands figure heavily. Indeed, the next Green Man that we'll be discussing is almost always depicted with his staff.

Our next 'Green Man' of Antiquity is Osiris, the Fertility deity of Ancient Egypt. As with Tammuz and Dionysus, Osiris was associated not only with fertility and agriculture but also with the Underworld. Often depicted as being green in colour, Osiris is the Archetypical 'Son' of God character. The Son of the Father God Geb (sometimes seen as Seb or Keb depending on the version of his origin you look at). His mother is referenced as the Sky Goddess Nut. In my reading on the topic, my understanding is that the 'green' depictions of Osiris are meant to reflect him 'post resurrection', after his time spent in the Underworld. The colour Green here symbolizes rebirth and regeneration, he 'dies' in the winter, goes 'under the ground' then re-emerges in the spring, pushing his way through the dirt and the soil, green and full of renewed life force. This is, of course, us interpreting what the ancient Egyptians have implied by the use of the colour, there may be other connotations that we are unaware of and can only speculate about. However, what we do know is that this birth, death, and rebirth are common themes in mythology closely associated with this Green Man Archetype. Interestingly Ivy was closely associated with Osiris and was said to be sacred to him as it

---

[126] Anderson, "The Green Man".

[127] Color, Symbology and Meaning of Green – Article published on Sensational Color.com.

remained always green[128]. Certainly, we have examples of foliate representations involving ivy leaves, possibly a nod to Osiris, as well as Dionysus when used.

As with Dionysus, Osiris was murdered, his brother Set (the Greek Typhon) jealous and power-hungry arranged for his murder. Dismemberment features as the manner of death in both their stories. The imagery of the dead God being torn apart, and these parts of his body being spread across the desired geographical area is again a classic 'Death of a God' narrative and heavy fertility imagery which both Gods allude to[129]. The destruction of the body and its parts spread over the land, symbolic of a return to the earth, feeding it with his body, his blood its libation, death providing sustenance for new life, his body the seeds from which new life will spring forth. Certainly, even in Christianity, we have a version of this narrative with the transubstantiation of the body of Christ, torn apart so that we may feed upon it, his blood shed so that we may drink of it.

Wishing to steal his throne and grab power, Set plotted against his brother these dastardly schemes culminating in a coup d'état. Set had a coffin-like trunk built to Osiris' measurements. One evening at Set's palace, while all were partaking in some drinking and merriment Set showed all those present the coffer and said he would offer it as a gift to whomever the box fit. All took turns trying to fit in this coffer until Osiris took his turn. Once he'd been tricked to get in, Set and his co-conspirators slammed the coffer lid down and nailed it shut. The coffer was thrown into the Nile where Osiris drowned. Isis, Osiris's wife (and sister) after much time searching, eventually found the coffer which had washed up in Byblus. She hid the body but before she could return to reclaim it, Set was able to locate him and in one final act of degradation proceeded to dismember the body, cutting it up into 14 pieces which he then tried to hide. Isis was able to find all but the one body part, she then carefully wrapped what was left of her husband's body in cloth and with her sister Nephthys lamented so long and so hard (in some versions of the story this lamentation is considered to have been an incantation using ritual magick) that the Sun God Ra was so moved that he sent Anubis to Earth to return him to life[130]. Interestingly, this act appears to have made him the first Egyptian to be 'mummified'. The use of magic is another theme that runs alongside the Green Man archetype narrative. Osiris was the ruler of the

---

[128] Frazer, "The Golden Bough".

[129] Ibid.

[130] Ibid.

Underworld, the giver, and taker of life. He could grant life not only to humans but to the wildlife and the land giving him his God of Fertility title. He is said to be responsible for making the Nile flood. Causing destruction and taking life but then leaving the land post-deluge fertile and lush. The cycle of death and life in nature is once more reflected in this Archetype narrative. The celebrations and rituals performed in honour of Osiris naturally tying in with the cycles of nature celebrated in the pagan calendar the same as Dionysus and Tammuz.

Interestingly whilst researching Osiris' mythology I read that there are some Egyptologists who believe Osiris may have been an actual man rather than a mythological God. They postulate that he could have been a former living ruler - possibly a shepherd who lived in Predynastic times in the Nile Delta region, whose beneficial rule led to him being revered as a God. The accoutrements of the shepherd, the crook, and the flail - once insignia of the Delta God Anedjti, with whom Osiris was associated - support this theory[131]. This would also directly link him to the Pan and Dionysus narratives who also have this 'shepherd' element to their stories. The depictions of him with staffs, rods, or wands are many and is another interesting detail that connects him not only to this Shepherd aspect but also with the themes of mysticism and Magick of other notable staff holders such as Moses, Aaron, and Merlin.

Similar to the narrative of Dionysus, Diodorus Siculus (an ancient Greek Historian) gives us another story in which Osiris was described as being an ancient King who taught the Egyptians the arts of civilization, including agriculture, then travelled the world with his sister Isis, various satyrs, and the nine muses, before finally returning to Egypt[132]. This narrative is almost identical to that of Dionysus, the narrative of a king who travelled, gifting the knowledge of civilization and agriculture to those he came into contact with. The satyrs were also identifiable with Dionysus as well as the reference to the nine muses. These could be corresponding to the Bacchantes of the Church of Bacchus.

Indeed, in Plutarch's *Moralia*, On Isis and Osiris, ch. 12 (pg. 97) I came across this interesting text:

"We also have another story told to us by the Egyptians, how that once Atropis, brother

---

[131] Helen Strudwick. The Encyclopaedia of Ancient Egypt. New York: Sterling Publishing Co., Inc. pp. 118–119 (2006).

[132] Osiris – Wikipedia.

to the Sun, fell at variance with Jupiter, entering into an alliance with Osiris and by his means overthrowing his enemy in a pitched battle, afterwards adopted him for his son and gave him the name of Dionysus"[133]

The above text gives us some written confirmation of the correspondence of Osiris with Dionysus. Also, as with Dionysus, we have this association with certain animals, in Osiris's case, he was known as the Ram God. Osiris' soul, also referred to as 'Ba', was occasionally worshipped in its own right, as if it were a separate distinct god, especially in the Delta city of Mendes. Interestingly given the 'feminine' aspect mentioned in respect of the Dionysus narrative, this 'Ba' of Osiris was referred to as Banebdjedet, which is grammatically feminine (also spelled "Banebded" or "Banebdjed"), literally "the ba of the lord of the djed, which roughly means 'the soul of the lord of the pillar of continuity'. Interestingly, as part of Set's dismemberment of Osiris' body, he was castrated, and Isis was unable to find his genitalia (eventually Isis had to 'craft' him genitals) This castration effectively leaves Osiris as genderless for a period of time sharing this 'feminine' aspect as did Dionysus. The djed, a type of pillar, was usually understood as the backbone of Osiris. This is interesting to me as it reminds me of the symbology of the backbone contained within the wands of Dionysus' Bacchantes.

Ba does not strictly mean "soul" as we know it today but instead has to do with power, reputation, and force of character, especially when in reference to a Deity. A soul can have many aspects, the human form just being one expression of this. Since the Ba was associated with power and also happened to be a word for ram in Egyptian, Osiris was often depicted as a ram, or as being ram-headed. A living, sacred ram was kept at Mendes and worshipped as the incarnation of the god, and upon death, the rams were mummified and buried in a ram-specific necropolis. Banebdjed was consequently said to be Horus' father, as Banebdjed was an aspect of Osiris[134]. This association also ties in nicely with the myth of his origin as a shepherd King in the Nile Delta. The same can also be said of Dionysus who was worshipped as the Sun and also venerated in his Goat form. Revered indeed as two distinct deities, although allowed to be 'one' by the old mythologists. This merging or splitting of deities is common within pagan mythology with one deity being split into several or several deities amalgamated into one[135]. This seems to be based on what the particular narrative of the time requires.

---

[133] Plutarch (1874). Plutarch's Moralia, On Isis and Osiris, ch.

[134] Ibid.

[135] George Stanley Faber B.D - The Origin of Pagan Idolatry (Vol I, II & III) – (London 1816).

I've also read in several sources that both Orisis and Dionysus took the form of either a Ram or a Bull. Both were equally worshipped as animals. In Northern Europe, as we'll see later on it is the Stag who starts to take prominence as the sacred animal although reference to Rams, Goats, and Bulls is still very prevalent in Northern European Mythology. Interestingly, when looking at the feminine counterparts, the Celtic Goddess Ceridwen was said to have been attended by three cows and Isis and Io are both depicted with cow horns on their heads or crowns or head adornments featuring cow horns. In Greek mythology, the Goddess Diana is often be depicted as riding a Bull tying in the feminine counterparts to the male symbology described above[136].

In Frazer's' *The Golden Bough* he references the association of Osiris with the Bull Apis of Memphis and the Bull Mnevis of Heliopolis. In the mythology of Osiris' death and resurrection, Isis demanded that an animal be sacrificed at each of Osiri's temples. Each temple had been built on the land where Isis had buried a part of Orisis's dismembered body. The aforementioned sacred bulls were dedicated to Orisis and worshipped as Gods in common with Osiris since these bulls had helped the farmers with sowing corn seed and procuring the benefits of such agriculture. The life and death cycle of corn entwining the Bull and corn with the Mythology of Osiris.

Osiris is also interesting from a biblical perspective, as a lot of the traditional biblical 'Ark' stories seem to originate from the same event within his narrative. Osiris was tricked into getting into a coffin-like casket by his brother Set who then proceeded to trap Osiris within (Cain like fratricide). He then threw this floating ark (similar to the ship the Argha or Theba) into the Nile where Osiris eventually drowned. This drowning, descent into the Underworld, and resurrection is now a common narrative within most Religions. Certainly, many have drawn parallels between Noah's story and Osiris' coffer. The Ark in which Noah was contained, the limbo world contained within where he lived until the deluge dissipated and Noah emerges – reborn safe from his wooden womb.

In his *Origins of Pagan Idolatry* Thesis, Faber posits that the voyage of Noah in his Ark is symbolic of the voyage of the dead to the Underworld. To quote:

> "For in the theology of every ancient Pagan nation we invariably find that the Great Father, who believed to have been preserved during the universal deluge, was either the God of obsequies, or was supposed to have descended into the infernal regions and afterwards to have returned from them, or was imagined to have died and to

---

[136] Ibid.

have been restored to life"[137]

The basis of most religions is the mythology that the world is destined, predetermined even, to be destroyed and renewed many times over. Partly by fire and partly by water, in order to cleanse and purify. Having reviewed quite a few 'flood' mythologies at this point, I would hazard that the great flood appears to the narrative which recycles the greatest number of times across most common religions. Could it be that there is some basis to the mythology, that at one point we did indeed suffer a flood of apocalyptic proportions, which we see as myth and legend today? Take for example the Welsh God Hu whose Oxen drew the great beaver out of the lake thus preventing the repetition of the first deluge proving him to be the Welsh Dionysus or Osirus[138]. Interestingly there were three Oxen, this symbology of the 'three' or the 'trinity' which repeats in mythology and religious scripture once again reflected in a Celtic deluge narrative.

As part of his duties as God of the Underworld, Osiris was the judge of people's souls. This has drawn parallels to the Greek Charon, the infernal ferryman of the river Styx himself. This 'ferrying' of people's souls is something that figures heavily in later narratives with the stories of Odin and his Wild Hunt and of Diana Goddess of the pagans and her nightly exploits riding with the dead. Charon's mythology being identified the same as Cronus or Saturn must also then be identified with Anubis. Anubis (like Charon by association) melts into the same narrative as Osiris. In some versions of Egyptian mythology Anubis is represented as being a version of Osiris and in others, as being the son of Osiris. Certainly, we know that zoomorphic entities such as Anubis and Horus are strongly tied to the Osiris mythology, as Dionysus has his satyrs, so Osiris has these unnatural creatures. I find the connection of this archetype to supernatural beings fascinating, it's a narrative that repeats, lending credence to the theory that whoever the original archetype was, he was zoomorphic and supernatural in origin with the power to influence and create the zoomorphic around him. At some point, the narratives surrounding Anubis do appear to merge with that of Osiris, with Osiris seemingly 'replacing' Anubis as God of the Dead. In this version of the narrative, it's most likely Anubis is seen as an aspect or 'Ba' of Osiris being a separate entity completely. With Osiris absorbing this aspect upon reaching the underworld and then leaving it behind upon his departure. There is also the separation of Horus from Osiris, each of whom, when seen through different aspects are the father and the son respectively. Interestingly, both these aspects of Osiris can be identified with Noah's story,

---

[137] Ibid.

[138] Ibid.

pre- and post-deluge [139]. The commonalities between these deities and their stories are striking. I think that we can clearly posit that the origin of our Green Man lies somewhere here in antiquity most likely predating our Sumerian God Enlil. The Sumerians took their inspiration from somewhere or someone and it's the question of where and who which interests me the most.

As a side note in Valleés *Passport to Magonia* he reports that in 1952 Archeologists discovered a Pyramid on the site of a well-known Mayan city in the Yucatan Region of Mexico. The person for whom this sarcophagus was built is strange as it doesn't match the typical morphology of the time. It appears to have been designed for someone much taller than the average Mayan, measuring nearly 6 feet tall. The sarcophagus was created for a deity the Mayans called 'The Great White God' Kulkulkan[140]. Who was this great White God and where did he come from? It would appear that these larger than normal man, beings appeared across the globe being revered in many different religions.

In the next chapter, I'll be looking at the Green Man mythology in Celtic Europe which is where I feel the heart of our modern Green Man resides.

Diana and The King of The Woods

In the previous chapter, we've looked at the Archetype in antiquity, focusing on the main three - Tammuz, Dionysus, and Osiris. In this chapter we're looking at the Archetype of the Green Man closer to home, crossing the sea from Europe to the Celtic Isles. One of the most impactful imports from the Mediterranean into Celtic Mythology is the Goddess Diana. She is the Goddess who comes up the most when researching the Green Man mythos and the main players involved. Diana (Artemis in Greece) is commonly seen as the Roman Goddess of The Hunt, the Goddess of both wild and domestic animals, and indigenous to woodlands. She has strong ties to fertility which mirror her male counterparts and has, above all other Pagan Gods, remained worshipped and revered even into Modern Day. Diana is often invoked and called upon as the Mother Goddess for most Pagan religions most notably Wicca. Whether she is the same Goddess of the Romans' or whether her name is now more representative of the female aspects she embodies, Diana is one of the few Goddesses actively worshipped today. When looking at her male counterparts the exploration of the feminine element is necessary to

---

[139] Ibid.

[140] Jacque Vallee – Passport to Magonia (Edition - 2014).

understand the broader picture, as the Goddess is the Moon to the God's Sun. One cannot exist without the other and each has a role to play in the cycle of nature and the survival of the human and animal species.

Diana was the daughter of the God Jupiter, who as a side note was often depicted himself as the 'horned' God[141] and certainly shares commonalities with Pan, Dionysus, Osiris, and The Horned God of the Hunt. Jupiter was the devouring God, the great destroyer who aligns with the Celtic Horned God of the Hunt who rules during the Winter Season which sees the end to the abundance of Spring and Summer. Her mother was Latona, the mistress of Jupiter who gave birth to twins, Diana and her brother Apollo. Diana is often depicted as carrying a bow and arrow symbolizing her strength as a hunter, and being accompanied by young maidens, deer, and hounds. As well as being celebrated for her hunting prowess, Diana was also seen as a goddess of fertility, women who were trying to conceive or those who were pregnant but wished for an easy labour and healthy child would pray to her. Diana was also seen as the Moon Goddess, often referred to as Lucina, derived from the moon goddess Luna who Diana eventually displaced[142]. As with Isis and Ishtar, she is also depicted with a crescent moon emblem as part of her headdress, certainly, we can identify Diana with the narrative of Isis and Ishtar they all essentially share aspects of each other. Because of Diana's connection to nature and specifically woodland creatures, hunting, and the Moon she is sometimes depicted with three heads a dog, a boar, and a horse. Indeed, Diana was often considered an aspect of a triple goddess, known as 'Diana triformis': Diana, Luna, and Hecate. According to historian C.M. Green, "these were neither different goddesses nor an amalgamation of different goddesses. They were Diana...Diana as a huntress, Diana as the moon, Diana of the underworld."[143]

It was said that Diana could also be vengeful in her dealings with humans and had a very unpredictable nature. In one myth the hunter Actaeon stumbled across Diana while she was bathing in a river. She was so upset that he had seen her naked (she saw herself as extremely chaste and virtuous) that she turned him into a stag, the scent of which was caught by his own hounds who tore him apart[144]. Interestingly, versions of this myth have been

---

[141] Faber B.D, "The Origin of Pagan Idolatry".

[142] Frazer, "The Golden Bough"

[143] Diana (mythology) – Wikipedia.

[144] Diana – Article published on Greek Gods and Goddesses.net.

referenced as recently as the Scottish Witch Trails. Andro (or Andrew) Man was a self-proclaimed wizard and Cunning Man in 16th Century Scotland who was put on trial for witchcraft. In Andro's story, he recalls that when he was a small boy the fairy queen 'Elphame' came to his mother's house. The fairy queen was pregnant and requested his mothers' assistance during her labour. The young boy made his acquittance with her on this occasion, assisting in fetching water to aid his mother but this wasn't the last time that he would meet this otherworldly queen. When he was grown, I believe in his thirties, she came to visit him again and he said that she seduced him. He claims that from this point onwards they maintained a sexual relationship for some time. He claimed to have fathered many children with her. In return for the children, the fairy queen gifted him with the power of prophecy and healing knowledge.

During one of Andro's interrogations, he spoke of meeting a man who called himself Christonday[145]. Christonday was either Fae Folk or had a strong association with the Fae Folk and at this point seemed to take over from Elphame as Andro's main 'fairy' contact. Judging by his name I think we can assume that there are Christian connotations to Christonday. It is likely Andro under interrogation was trying to distance himself from the pagan aspect, shifting his allegiances to a more 'Christian' character. In one account Andro describes seeing a ritual where he alleges to have seen Christonday come out of the snow in the likeness of a stag, he then saw Queen Elphame riding upon a white hackney along with her companions also emerge and give chase to the 'Christonday' stag as if they were hunting him. This tale of Elphame and Christonday suspiciously mirrors the Diana/Actaeon narrative.

Diana has many commonalities with the Scottish Fairy Queen, both are seen as protectors of women and children, both responsible for helping the dead (specifically dead infants and babies) find their way to the Underworld. Indeed, one of the responsibilities of the Goddess Epona (the Celtic version of the Diana narrative) was to ferry the souls of the dead to the Afterlife. Diana in German folklore was said to undertake nightly journeys riding furiously throughout the night on a bevy of different and fantastical beasts. In these night journeys, she was followed by the souls of the dead, notably the souls of unbaptized children. In his treatise *Daemonologie*, King James I also ties Diana to the fairies:

"The fourth kind of spirits, which by the Gentiles was called Diana, and her wandering

---

[145] Purkiss, "Troublesome Things".

court, and amongst us was called the Phairie (as I told you) or our good neighbours"[146]

Reginald Scott in his *European Demonologist* writes:

> *"You must also understand that after they have delicatlie blanketed with the divell and the ladie of the fairies, and have eaten up a fat oxe, and emptied a butt of malmesie, and a binne of bread at some noble mans house, in the dead of the night, nothing is missed of all this in the morning. For the Lady Sibylla, Minerva or Diana with golden rod striketh the vessel and the binne and they are fully replenished againe"*[146]

The cult of Diana has flourished, spreading to many parts of Europe and today is alive and well all over the globe. Her festival is celebrated from the 13th to the 15th of August and is referred to as Nemoralia or the Festival of Torches. After washing and dressing their hair with flowers, Diana's followers would light their torches and walk around Lake Nemi, the light from their torches reflecting on the surface of the lake (also called 'Diana's Mirror), which must have been quite the magical sight. Dancing was an integral part of her worship; every year young maidens would dance representing tree nymphs (dryads) linking back to the themes of tree worship which is very prevalent in Diana and Green Man mythology. This ceremony was popular through the Peloponnese, bearing such epithets of Limnaea and Limnatis which translate to Lady of the Lake. The Lady of the Lake is instrumental in the romantic Arthurian Legends of the Middle Ages. When looking at Arthurian legend the influence of Diana and the King of the Woods mythology cannot be understated. Indeed, it is very likely that the Anglo-Saxon version of Diana may have had some origin as a local forest entity who then inherited the mythology of her Greek counterpart Artemis[147]. As a side note, I did notice the reference to Diana's golden wand within Scott's *Daemonologist* as we've seen that reference to rods and wands frequently come up in many Fae Folk encounters as discussed already.

Diana has long been connected to the Cult of the Scottish Goddess Nicevenn (Dame Habona) and the female wild hunt mythology. Diana is, of course, the central figurehead of many Wiccan-based religions, as of course is her male counterpart The Green Man. According to Stregheria (Italian roots of Witchcraft) mythos, Diana was the Mother Goddess who created the world

---

[146] King James I – Daemonologie.

[147] Purkiss, "Troublesome Things".

out of her own being, having herself all the seeds of creation within[148]. Diana does appear to be the name given to an amalgamation of many narratives, Roman, Fae, Celtic, and the modern-day Wiccan, Diana being the name given to a more 'general' and symbolic philosophy than to an actual person.

The Golden Bough

According to mythology, Nemi was home to Diana's sacred Grove, there grew a certain tree, a forever green Oak of which no branch could be broken. The exception to this would become the origin of the King of the Wood legend and that of the Golden Bough. The Golden Bough was the large oak branch broken by the chosen one, he who would become Diana's priest and protector of her scared grove and another origin story for our Celtic Green Man.

The Oak was heavily associated with Diana, it is said that not only was her sacred grove at Nemi full of Oak trees but her groves throughout Europe were also made up of Oak. It is said that the ever-burning vestal fire at Nemi was lit with Oakwood. This tree and indeed this grove was always guarded by an appointed Priest whose sole task was to protect the Grove. For this task, he was rewarded with the title of 'King of the Wood' and would live alongside Diana in this sacred Grove and reign as King until another younger, braver, and more capable came to take his throne. This origin of the ritual of the slaying of the in-situ priest at Nemi is described more in depth in Frasers' *The Golden Bough*. Legend has it that only a runaway slave was allowed to try to break it, if he did, he was entitled to fight the Priest in single combat, if he slew the priest, he would take his place and reign in his stead. This narrative has a lot of similarities to the Holy Grail Quest stories which I came across in my reading.

According to mythology, the original Priest or King of the Wood was Virbius[149]. From what I could find it is thought that Virbius is the Roman version of the young Greek hero Hippolytus. Hippolytus was chaste and fair, a fine young man who learned the art of venery from the centaur Chiron, the wisest and most just of all Centaurs. He spent his days with Artemis (Diana's Greek counterpart) hunting and enjoying all the splendors of nature. He caught the eye of Aphrodite who tried to seduce him, but he scorned her advances vowing to remain chaste and virtuous in honour of Artemis. Aphrodite was so angered by this slight that she influenced Hippolytus'

---

[148] Frazer, "The Golden Bough".

[149] Ibid.

stepmother Phaedra to fall in love with him. When he also spurned her advances, Phaedra falsely accused him of trying to seduce her to Theseus his father. Theseus believed her lies and called upon Poseidon to avenge what he perceived to be the insidious act of Hippolytus. So, while Hippolytus was driving in a chariot by the shores of the Saronic Gulf, Poseidon unleashed a fierce bull forth from the crashing waves. This spooked the horses pulling Hippolytus's chariot reared up knocking him from the carriage and dragging him underneath the wheels and to his death. Artemis was so devasted by the death of her favourite human that she convinced Aesculapius, the God of medicine to bring him back to life. Jupiter furious that a mere mortal could escape from the Underworld banished Aesculapius to Hades for his meddling. Fortunately, Hippolytus had already been revived so Artemis was able to hide him from the fury of Jupiter by changing his appearance either by aging him or changing his form into that of a stag and hiding him at the sacred Grove at Nemi[150].

Diana was not the only entity residing at Nemi, Egeria the water nymph also lived in the great lake there. It is said that when Diana (Artemis) hid Hippolytus there, she left him under the care of Egeria and changed his name to Virbius to keep him safe. There, Virbius reigned as King of the Woods and dedicated a precinct to Diana. According to mythology, Virbius begot a son who was also named Virbius who was also a virtuous young man. It is said that he drove a team of fiery steeds to join the Latins in the war against Aeneas and the Trojans. He was worshipped as a deity not only at Nemi but elsewhere. In Compania, we hear of a special priest who was devoted to his service reminiscent of Diana's priests of Nemi. As Faber states in his *Origin of Pagan idolatry* Thesis *"As every ancient Patriarch was at once a king and a priest, so every gentile sovereign was long accounted both as priest and as King"*

As a side note, Saint Hippolytus of the Roman Calendar, who was also dragged to death by horses on 13th August (Diana's day) must surely be the same Greek who, after dying twice over as a heathen was resurrected as a Christian Saint[151]. Here we have another example of the adoption of pagan idols into Christianity, their canonization, and the hijacking of pagan festivals and religious days. What was once pagan, now purified and now considered acceptable for reverence.

Referring back to the idea of Kings and Priesthood as put forth in Faber's thesis, it is said that the Sumerian 'Oannes' people established the idea of an

---

[150] Ibid.

[151] George Stanley Faber B.D - The Origin of Pagan Idolatry (Vol I, II & III) – (London 1816).

'initiatory' priesthood to carry forward their knowledge. These 'Priest' initiates were often descendants of their bloodline, the originator of which is 'Godman' whose sign is fish. Giving us this long history of 'priest-kings' from Sumer right through to Virbius and his successors. This holds similar to the ideas of the Celtic Druids who were priests and also holders of sacred mythological knowledge. The Knights Templar were even supposed to be a part of such a sacred bloodline deriving from the Merovingian bloodline. This famous bloodline comes from the Frankish King, Meroveus who is said to be the son of one of these 'Oannes' semi-aquatic beings[152].

These beliefs in a non-human race of teachers and benefactors were passed down from the Sumerians and Babylonians to the Canaanites, the Phoenicians, and even the Carthaginians before their demise at the hands of the Roman Invading forces. This Oannes 'fish' form shows up again in the story of the prophet Joshua son of Nun (Yeheshuam the fish son), in the story of Jonah and the whale, and even in the story of Jesus, who can walk on water, materialize fish and even takes the fish as his symbol. Let us not forget that Jesus' most loyal disciple was a fisherman, his cousin John the Baptist also contains elements of this narrative within his own story. Interestingly, John the Baptist's feast day is 24th June which coincides with the summer solstice as well as the feast of the Oannes. As a side note, "Oannes" can also be 'translated' as 'John' when decoded using the *cipher of the UFOnauts*. This cipher was dictated to the infamous occultist Aleister Crowley during meditative communications that he had with an ultra-dimensional or interdimensional being called 'Aiwess'. Crowley himself could never decode the Cipher and was never able to use it to access the knowledge he so badly desired. It was later decoded by his successor and then built upon by others some 70 years after Crowley had passed[153]. Coincidentally, Aiwess claimed to be the messenger of Horus, the same Horus that is the son or at very least an aspect of Osiris who we have already looked at in some detail. This detail bemused me given the sheer number of synchronicities that I came across when researching these topics, it certainly does seem that everything leads back to this one Archetype.

The character of Virbius/Hippolytus has a lot of elements of the Dionysus and Osiris' narratives in his story, we could posit that the character of Virbius is simply an aspect or part of the 'Ba' of this Archetype. Diana, herself is also associated with the forest God Silvanus who coincidentally was the adopted

[152] Allen Greenfield – The Complete Cipher of the Ufonauts (2016 edition).

[153] Ibid.

father of Dionysus[154] given her love of sacred groves, of the outdoors, and her association with elementals such as tree nymphs. Connecting Diana to Silvanus, in turn, connects her with Dionysus her connection now morphing into the relationship with the aspect of him which is now Virbius. Sometimes it does feel like 6 degrees of separation researching this topic! Note how the narrative of the Nemi Priest, once he starts to wither and age is slain only to be born anew in the shape of a younger more fertile man. The repeated symbolism of death and regeneration is in keeping with the Archetype narrative, which we'll explore further through our next deity, the Celtic God of the Hunt, the male Diana.

Cernunnos – The Horned God

When researching the Celtic Gods, I found pretty quickly, that the narrative of Cernunnos matched that of our Green Man, King of the Woods Archetype nicely. Cernunnos is the Druidic horned god, as with Dionysus and Osiris he is heavily associated with fertility, nature, fruit, grain, and wealth. In terms of our 'totem' animals, he is associated with horned animals such as the bull, the stag, and the ram-headed serpent. Cernunnos as with all our nature Gods is said to be born at the winter solstice and then symbolically die at the summer solstice giving us our King of the Underworld connection. Many deities are imagined in mythology as rulers of some other extra-dimensional world, be it the Underworld or the Fairy Realm, they always have this connection to this world 'in between' most likely a direct result of their connection both to life and to death. This 'liminal' state is one often connected to the supernatural, where people or places are in stages of transition and often attract a high degree of paranormal activity. Hauntings, poltergeist activity, and just general high strangeness are often aligned with liminal states, take our 'Berry Patches' for example.

There is a head of a Celtic God at the hot springs of Aquae, Sulis in Bath[155] which very much resembles the foliate man visage. Some speculate that is most likely a medusa or a similar male variant of it, however, I think it is most likely a depiction of Cernunnos. The serpents within the foliate image are representative of his time in the underworld, Cernunnos being deeply connected to the imagery of the serpent, often depicted with one, whether investments such as his on his Torq or in physical form. Serpents are representative in Celtic mythology of the underworld since they believed that

---

[154] Frazer, "The Golden Bough".

[155] Celtic Gods, Celtic Goddess – R.J. Stewart (Reprint -Cassell Illustrated – 2006).

souls of the dead could come back in serpent form[156]. In fact, the serpent is so intrinsically tied to Celtic mythology that it is said that the legend of St. Patrick driving the snakes from Ireland is an analogy for the Christian Church driving out the old Pagan Gods. Interestingly, the hieroglyph for Osiris's oldest shrine in Abydos is represented by a coffer or basket with a serpent passing through it, again representing the links to the underworld by use of a serpent motif [157].

Interestingly, in Occultic beliefs and Freemasonry, the serpent represents knowledge, a reptilian source of information, traditionally the image of a serpent on a tree represented wisdom[158]. In many pagan religions, it represents life, death, and rebirth. A symbol of 'transformation'. As with the antlers of our Horned God, the imagery of the serpent has also been perverted by radicalized Christianity, seeing the serpent as another representation of the Devil, ironic since they themselves are the ones who made the Devil up in the first place.

Coincidentally, we also have a link between rods/wands and Serpents, in Exodus 7, Aaron accompanies his brother Moses to speak with the Pharoh to implore him to abide by God's will and to warn him that failing to do so will bring about the Plagues of Egypt. The Pharoh demands to see a 'miracle' as evidence of God's power. Aaron in response throws down his rod which transforms into a great serpent. Shocked at this, the Pharoh's best mages throw down their rods which also transform into serpents; however, Aaron's serpent eats them all before turning back into the Rod. This rod is known as the Rod of Aaron and is considered a sacred artifact in mythology, alongside the Spear of Destiny and the Holy Grail. Osiris himself was often depicted with his staff, which in many versions had 2 serpents wrapping their bodies around it. Again, as with Dionysus' Bacchantes, this represents Kundalini / Uraeus, (Twin Cobras) reaching the top of the staff (Spine), activating the Pineal Gland, symbolized by the (Pine cone), the opening of the Third Eye. The image of this staff originates c. 1224 BC and is housed at the Egyptian Museum in Turin.[159] This image became the foundation for the famous dual snake symbol, often called 'Caduceus' which doctors who take the 'Hippocratic' oath wear. It is also associated with Hermes, the Greek

[156] Ibid.

[157] E.A Wallis Budge - Osiris & The Egyptian Resurrection Vol II (republication, New York, 1973).

[158] Allen Greenfield – The Complete Cipher of the Ufonauts (2016 edition).

[159] Staff of Osiris (Kundalini / Uraeus) – Article published on Mynzahosiris.wordpress.com.

messenger of the Gods, but its origin can be traced as far back as Ancient Sumer (surprise, surprise!).

In trying to research the origin of Cernunnos it was hard to pin down a specific mythology or origin story, in reality, there isn't much that I could find on Cernunnos other than the standard fertility, horned deity narrative. I did stumble across a theory that he is an aspect or derivation of the classic Jupiter Cernunnos which would make logical sense given that Jupiter is often depicted as a 'horned' deity and is also associated with Life and Death, the Creator and the Destroyer so I could see the theoretical argument behind this position.

The imagery of horns and antlers has long been associated with power and masculinity, the great Ram, the majestic Stag, and the strong Bull. This imagery was especially powerful for the Celts, with many Celtic helmets being unearthed bearing horns. This 'horned' form of helmet or headdress has also been seen in Viking, Teutonic, and Samurai warriors. Many deities including those we've already discussed have been depicted with horns or wearing headdresses bearing horns. It was said that the more horns the headdress contained the more powerful the deity and the greater their importance, which can be evidenced by Gods Ashtar and Ishtar being depicted with as many as seven horns confirming their importance in the hierarchy of the Gods[160]. Incidentally, the hanging of stag antlers was also a common feature of Diana's temples and shrines, Plutarch (Plutarch, Roman Questions, 3) noted that the only exception to this was the temple on the Aventine Hill, in which bull horns had been hung up instead.[161] This makes sense given that the King of the Woods narratives which merges with the Cernunnos and Wild Hunt mythos heavily involves Stag imagery.

I think within Cernunnos we have a melting of narratives and character elements from all the Gods we've looked at previously but Cernunnos for me seems to most closely fitted to our modern ideas of who the Green Man is, what he looks like and what he stands for. Certainly, the more romantic themes of the Green Man borne from the Gauls, Britons, Saxons, and Celts are found here in our Horned God of the Hunt. Diana's favourite, her King and symbolic consort. I was surprised when I started to look at this specific deity, how little is known about him and as with The Green Man, his origins seem fuzzy and vague. From the information, I have been able to read I think

---

[160] Fraser, "The Horned God of Wytches".

[161] https://en.wikipedia.org/wiki/Diana_(mythology) (ref Plutarch Roman Questions, 3).

we can trace his mythology back to Diana's King of The Wood. Virbius has all the elements inherited from his spiritual ancestors Dionysus and Osiris to influence this narrative and it makes sense that Cerunnus is the result of several narratives woven into one culminating in our 'Gallic' version of this Archetype.

In one article read on Druidism, Cernunnos was referenced as being born of the Great Goddess Anu (Sumerian) which also ties him back to his spiritual ancestors of Enlil and Tammuz[162]. This isn't to say that his counterpart doesn't exist elsewhere, he certainly does (many have drawn parallels to the Hindu God Shiva) we have examples of our Horned Gods all over the world but for the purposes of our Green Man, I am focusing on this Teutonic European version. According to Gaulish Celtic Mythology, Cernunnos was the God of the forests, often depicted with antlers. Sometimes shown with hair of vegetation akin to our Green Man foliate head imagery. As with The Green Man, Cernunnos was celebrated in Spring and in Summer, his celebrations falling in line with the calendar of most Pagan festivals. In spring he appears as the young son, child of the mother Goddess, budding and growing, greening the world around him. In summer, like the crops he had grown to maturity, vibrant, pulsing with life force, the essence of powerful, positive male energy taking up his mantle as consort to the Green Goddess.

The 'horned one' has a variety of names but his attributes are generally consistent, he is usually depicted wearing stag antlers and/or is accompanied by a stag or sacred ram-horned serpent. It appears that Cernunnos was mostly worshipped in Britain, but other Gallic countries had their equivalents such as Finvarra in Ireland and Arawn or Hu in Wales. Bronze Age rock carvings in Scandinavia and the Italian Alps evidence early man's fascination with these 'horned' men. Other artefacts such as Gundestrups Cauldron, a silver vessel from the Iron Age also show the representation of a horned man, sat holding a serpent surrounded by Stags and other woodland creatures, mostly likely a derivation of Cernunnos.[163]

The name Cernunnos is said to translate roughly to 'The One with Antlers'. Linguists believe that the origin of the name is most likely Latin due to the -os ending which is usually added to masculine nouns. It is assumed then that the Gallic (Gaulish) name would have been Cernunn. The prefixes 'Cer' and 'Her' are interchangeable in Gallic, both being Indo-European roots that

---

[162] Cernnunos - Article by J. M Reinbold published on Druidry.org.

[163] Eric Edwards Wordpress.com - The Green Man Phenomenon and Foliate Heads.

mean 'horn' so Cern may also be written as Hern both being cognate spellings of the same name. The 'Her' element is important here as it links us to some other important characters which are thought to derive from Cernunnos, notably the Anglo-Saxon Herne or Herla as well as other characters which we'll look at shortly[164]. I have also seen Cernunnos written as "Kerntos" with "Kern" being yet another Proto-Indo-European root *Kher(n), meaning "horn, head, "[165]. It is possible that the 'C' and 'K' were interchangeable with the Proto-Indo-European root, alongside the 'H'

The first and I believe only artifact to directly reference Cernunnos as the name of this 'stag head' deity was found during the 18th century by workers during repairs to Notre Dame Cathedral. A four-sided stone alter was uncovered. This alter had been dedicated by sailors to 'Cernunnos' during the reign of Tiberius. Its described as having a man's face bearing both stag ears and stag antlers carved into it and from each antler hangs a Torq (Celtic neck ring). Whilst this may be the only artifact found bearing his name, his symbology is universally recognized as an ancient pagan deity[166]. Cernunnos is sometimes depicted as triple-faced, or representative of tripilism/trinity in other ways. As with the 'holy trinity', Cernunnos can be seen as different aspects, the Father, The Son, and The Spirit of Nature itself. There is a triple-headed statue of Cernunnos holding a ram-headed serpent found in Autun, Saône-et-Loire[167].

Artifacts showing a half-man, half-Stag deity have been found all over the world for at least the last 20,000 years. Les Trois Freres 'Sorcerer' a half man, half-beast figure was found painted on a cavern wall in Ariege, France, and has been dated at around 13,000 BCE placing it within the Paleolithic era[168]. A rock carving from the 7th Century was found in the Camonica Valley which depicts a half man half stag figure and rock art found at Naquane, Italy (dated back to the 7th Century) shows an ithyphallic hunter with a half-man, half-stag figure[169]. In Icklingham, Suffolk, and at Richborough, Kent female

---

[164] Fraser, "The Horned God of Wytches".

[165] The Goddess and The God – Published on Ceisiwrserith.com.

[166] Fraser, "The Horned God of Wytches".

[167] R.J. Stewart - Celtic Gods, Celtic Goddess – (Reprint -Cassell Illustrated – 2006).

[168] Fraser, "The Horned God of Wytches".

[169] Ibid.

deities also depicted with horns have been found. In folklore, horned women were connected to both the Fae Folk and witches. Another Stone age painting found in Four-Neau Du Duable, Dordogne depicts a 'bull man' dancing surrounded by animals[170]. The reference to these half-man half-beast figures either dancing or surrounded by dancing associates is common. In the 17th century chapbook '*Robin Goodfellow; His Mad Pranks and Merry Jests*' shows Robin the Stag-God encircled by celebratory humans.

We'll look at the ritualistic element of dance in the next chapter but it's certainly an interesting element of deity worship. Certainly, this has aspects of the Cult of Dionysus with the half man half bull depictions and the influence of dance within rituals both elements closely connected to Dionysus, but we also see this expressed with Cernunnos, who is referenced as The Lord of the Dance, see below a lovely excerpt from Druidry.com

> "*As Lord of the Dance He is present in the billions and billions of infinitely small movements that make up the seemingly chaotic Dance of Life, the Dance of Making and Unmaking. He is truly the Life that never, never dies, for even as nothingness he is self-originating. He is triple as She is triple. He is Cernnunos: Father, Son, and Wild Spirit.*" [171]

Just within this paragraph, we have reference to the ritual of dance, the cyclical nature of life as well as our theme of the holy triad.

Zoomorphic imagery is found in prehistoric societies all over the world, but it is especially pronounced within the Ancient Celtic World. In her *Dictionary of Celtic Myth and Legend*, Miranda J. Green notes "*There appears to have no rigid division in Celtic perceptions of divinity between human and animal form. Thus, Gods could be depicted with hooves, antlers or horns of bull, goat or ram*"[172]. Animals have long been associated with certain powers, and in turn with certain deities, each God having its own totem animal(s). Indeed, all the Deities we've looked at thus far have been associated with totem animals and Zoomorphic entities.

---

[170] Ibid.

[171] Cernnunos - Article by J. M Reinbold published on Druidry.org.

[172] Miranda J. Green - Dictionary of Celtic Myth and Legend.

Finvarra

When researching Cernunnos you very quickly come across his ties to Celtic Mythology, the Fae Folk, and Magic. A version of the aforementioned 'King of the Woods' legend is that of the Fairy King, a descendant of the old Gods of the Celtic-Teutonic legends. Such a Fairy King is King Finvarra. Finvarra (also Finnbheara or Finnbarr Meadha) was said to be the King of the Daoine Sidhe, a supernatural race of people in Celtic Mythology[173]. Similar to the ancient Gods of fertility which no doubt inspired these legends, Finvarra was said to be benevolent, often ensuring a good harvest and increased fertility. In some accounts, he was the youngest son of the Celtic God Dagda (equivalent to Jupiter) and brother to Oengus mac ind Óg and was one of the Tuatha De Danann (the Celtic Pantheon of Gods). It is said that after the Tuatha De Danann were defeated and driven from Ireland by the Milesians (the human ancestors of the Irish people), a group led by Finvarra decided to stay in Ireland (this group being the afore mentioned Daoine Sidhe). Finvarra was able to negotiate a truce with the Milesians who allowed them to stay, as long as they remained under ground. Finvarra and his people retreated to the forests, Sidha, and built great cities underground within the caves eventually becoming the Fae Folk of Celtic mythology. These Sidha or fairy mounds are circular enclosures surrounded by an earthen or stone bank which were used as farmsteads from about 500 to 1200 A.D. Approximately 40,000 ringforts still dot the Irish countryside[174]. These areas are considered (as mentioned before) to be protected by the Fae Folk and are places of supernatural goings on. Many people still to this day are weary of trespassing into such places.

According to legend, Finvarra had a penchant for mortal women, often kidnapping and romancing them despite his queen consort Oonagh, the Fairy Queen, being by all accounts more beautiful than any mere mortal[175]. Finvarra was described as handsome, often seen dressed in black, in keeping with our description of the men encountered by our ladies of the Witch Trials (our first MIB's). As with the deities which came before Finvarra was also associated with the dead, like Osirus and Cernunnos before him, Finvarra was said to be King of the Underworld, one of his responsibilities like our Goddess Diana was the ferrying of souls to the Underworld. In one story he

---

[173] Finvarra – Article published on en-academia.com.

[174] Faery Mounds – Article published Faery Pool.com.

[175] Fraser, "The Horned God of Wytches".

even appears in a coach drawn by four white horses[176], this element reminiscent of the Fairy Raid Stories which leads us nicely on to the mythology of the 'Wild Hunt' otherwise known as the Fairy Raids or the Furious Ride.

The Wild Hunt

When researching the Celtic Horned God, I was drawn into another aspect of this deity, that of his role as the Leader of the Wild Hunt. The Wild Hunt, Furious Raid, or Fairy Raid is the Teutonic mythology surrounding the nightly procession of the dead. As I mentioned earlier 'Cer' and 'Her' are interchangeable in the Gallic/Gaulic language, so we have many derivations on the Cerunn name, giving us Herunn, Helle or Herla (also Hecla/Hekla), Herne and Herner. All variations of the same name, that is a spin on or aspect of the Horned God but specifically his role as the King of the Underworld. The leaders of these raids originated as Gods but in later versions became famed Hunters, returned from the dead, and all said to lead the Hunt. The most fascinating of these leaders to me is the 'Herle-quin, 'Helle-quin' or as we know it today the Harlequin. There are many accounts of different Wild Hunts all across Northern Europe. There are versions led by the Goddesses such as Diana who is accompanied by a whole band of merry women of the supernatural persuasion, fairies, witches, and the dead, who spend the evenings ferrying the souls of the dead to the Underworld. Whilst the Goddess's nocturnal activities seem to be a more Celtic Mythology, the male version of the Wild Hunt can be seen all over Teutonic Europe.

The Wild Hunt is known by slightly different names all over Europe, sometimes the Savage ride, Furious Horde, Furious Army, and of course The Fairy Raids. This hunting party was said to be a fearsome, deafening mob preceded by a thunderous roar and the howl of the wind followed by the booming sound of pounding hooves and the deafening blasting of horns. In some stories the 'Hunt' can only be heard, this petrifying aural phenomenon filling the unlucky spectator with blood-chilling terror. Others have witnessed the spectral apparitions, lucky enough to stay out of their way and living to tell their bone-chilling tale. The traditional Hunt narrative involves a procession of dead souls astride their large ghost steeds alongside other supernatural elements on a furious ride lead by the King of the Underworld himself. Woe betides any mere mortal who gets in their way, as it is said you may be swept up by it never to be seen again.

---

[176] Katharine M. Briggs (1976) A Dictionary of Fairies.

In some less fatal but no less, terrifying encounters, you may be swept away with them and then dropped at some unknown place far away from home. Or, if you were even less fortunate you would be swept up, carried off, and delivered to the underworld to live as their slave with little chance of rescue. There are stories of men losing their wives to the Raid, their only chance to save them is to be brave enough to face the Raid the following year, stand their ground, and grab their loved one as she passes through. Should they be successful they can pull their wife out, if they fail, she is lost forever[177].

Initially, the Wild Raids or Wild Hunts were led by the Gods and Goddesses, we have Diana leading her nightly multitudes and her consort the Horned God most likely Cernunnos leading his furious pack. Famously Odin led the Norse charge, in the legend of Odin's Hunt, and then his German counterpart Wotan (or Woden) following suit. Eventually, however, the Gods gave way to fearless hunters and intrepid heroes in myths and legends. Such as King Herla's 'Herplapping' translated as Herla's assembly (we discussed Herla in one of our earlier chapters).[178]

To expand upon Herla's story, his Wild Hunt story goes as follows:

King Herla is the King of the early Britons (pre-Saxon invasion) and an avid hunter. One day he and his men are out hunting when all of a sudden, he is approached by what is described as a 'pigmy' due to the small stature of the being. As this small being comes closer, it appears to be sat upon an enormous goat and looked by all descriptions, similar to the Greek deity Pan. He has a large head, a glowing face, and a red beard so long it reached down to his chest. He has a hairy belly, and his legs are not those of a man but rather those of a Goat. He announces himself to King Herla stating that 'He is the King of Many Kings and Chiefs and of a people too numerous to count' so I assume here that he is the 'Fairy King'. He then prophesizes that the King of France will soon offer his daughter in marriage to Herla, Herla in turn shall accept the proposal and that the Pigmy king will attend the ceremony as a guest. In return, Herla must be a guest at his wedding when the Pigmy King himself marries a year to the day later. Amused at the exchange Herla agrees and promptly returns home.

Upon returning home, Herla discovers that the King of France has indeed sent representatives to his Kingdom to propose his marriage to the French Princess. The wedding takes place as predicted and whilst he is sitting at his

---

[177] Katharine M. Briggs – The Vanishing People – (1978 – B.T. Batsford Ltd. London).

[178] Wild Hunt – Wikipedia.

wedding feast the Pigmy King unexpectantly arrives, Herla having forgotten about his strange encounter. He brings with him an entourage so large that the Pigmy King must pitch his own pavilion to accommodate the numbers as there is no more room within the Banquet Hall. The extra tents are thrown up with such an unbelievable speed that onlookers cannot quite believe it, it is as if it were done by magic and from these tents, many servants spring forth with vases made of precious stones and gold and crystal vessels to gift to the wedding. They require nothing from King Herla's court providing their own servants, supplies, and entertainment. Indeed, they prove quite the hit with the wedding guests providing them with unimaginable service and entertainment, winning endless thanks and praise in return. Before dawn breaks and the celebrations end, the Pigmy King addresses King Herla and reminds him that he must keep his end of the agreement and attend his wedding a year hence. With that request, he, his guests, and all his servants and accoutrements simply 'disappear' from sight just before the cock crows.

As promised one year later the Pigmy King reappears to Herla and requests his attendance at the wedding ceremony. Herla, keen to fulfill his obligation and quickly conclude this bizarre covenant follows wherever it is he is being led. He is taken to a cavern on a very lofty cliff, as they go deeper into the cave system they come into a huge well-lit cavern, not lit by the sun but instead by the many lamps of the homes of the Pygmies. This cavern is home to a large and very beautiful ornate city, in which the Pigmy King has his castle. It is at this luxurious castle that the wedding ceremony takes place with Herla and his men as guests. After the wedding ceremony has concluded Herla is free to leave, his obligation now fulfilled. He is given many gifts including Horses, Dogs, and even Hawkes. Upon his departure, the Pigmy King gifts the riding company a small bloodhound with the ominous instruction that the hound should be kept in arms and no rider should dismount their horse until the hound has jumped down from its keepers' arms. Only then will it be safe to dismount.

Herla and his men start their journey home, back out of the cavern and back to the land of Men. On his long journey home, Herla comes upon a Shepherd whom he stops to ask for news of his Queen and his Kingdom. The Shepherd is confused and responds that he did not recognize the name of the Queen given. He also seems to struggle to understand the King, stating that he could hardly understand the language the King spoke saying that he, himself was a Saxon and therefore wasn't familiar with the Briton language the King was speaking. He added that the Britons were all but gone now, having been driven out of England over two hundred years ago. King Herla is perplexed by this response but continues his way home. The group of riders continues for many miles, but they do not recognize their Kingdom and cannot seem to find their way home. Eventually, some of the King's men who are very tired and hungry dismount their horses ignoring the Pigmy King's instructions. The moment their feet touch the ground they instantly turn to dust. Horrified the King and his remaining men hopelessly ride on.

The legend goes that the Dog never leaped from its holders' arms and that the King and his remaining men were doomed to endlessly wander the woods on horseback eventually driven mad. It was said that the march of these poor souls could be witnessed right up until the first year of the Coronation of King Henry II before it is said that they marched themselves into the River Wye at Hereford[179]. The three days of revelry in the Fairy Court it seems, equates to about 200 human years.

It is even said that even King Arthur himself led a Wild Hunt, which is amusing given that his friend and companion Merlin was often known to take the form of a stag, possibly a conflict of interest! In her book *Vanishing People* (1978), Katherine Briggs references the story of Wild Edric and his fairy wife. Eadric (or Edric) was a wealthy and influential Anglo-Saxon who led the resistance against the Norman invasion and has also been named as a possible Hunt Leader. Incidentally, Edric is also identified with the origins of the Robin Hood mythology, being a wealthy and influential landowner who took up arms against invasion.

In England, we also have reference to the Dando Dogs within our Anglo-Saxon hunt stories. These are the mythical black dogs often associated with the Wild Hunt, large fearsome spectral hounds which have also been reported independent of the raids themselves leading to the terms the Devil's Dandy Dogs or Hell Hounds. The myth originates from the tale of Dando, a drunkard priest who liked to hunt. It was said after a day's hunt, Dando and his companions would retire for a drink. Dando having consumed all the alcohol exclaimed that he would go to hell for a drink when a stranger appeared and offered him a drink. Dando took the libation but when the stranger tried to take some game in return for the drink, Dando tried to stop him shouting that he'd follow him to hell to get it back, needless to say, he got his wish and the stranger dragged him to hell. It is said that Dando's hounds tried desperately to follow him but were unable to do. Doomed to roam continuously searching for their master[180].

---

[179] Fraser, "The Horned God of Wytches".

[180] Briggs, "The Vanishing People". Dando's Dogs – Wikipedia.

This idea of a 'mythical' quest or hunt has permeated into our folk lore, tales of the mythical hunt are as much part of our ancestors' legends as the quest for the Holy Grail stories are to us today. In fact, there are contemporaries today who believe that the purpose for the construction of the strange archaeological sites such as the Spiral of Glastonbury, the Torr, or even the stone rings at Stone Henge and Avebury are road maps for these Wild Hunts. Maps that run for literally thousands of miles even reaching the Nazca lines in Peru[181] As well as the appearance of 'The Stag' within these quest narratives we also have the strong symbology of the mighty Steed. It was the mighty Green Knight on his fearsome steed that interrupted Arthur's New Years' Celebrations. It is the spectral horses of the Hunt that are as much a part of the Wild Hunt as the hunters themselves. Horses in mythology are symbolic of war, power, and glory. A white horse is considered divine, celestial in origin, such as Pegasus the winged horse of Perseus given to him by the Gods themselves. Most notably we have the biblical Four Horsemen of the Apocalypse, the Wild Hunt to end all Wild Hunts if you will. Four plagues upon humanity sat upon their mighty steeds ready to hunt us all to the very ends of the earth. Indeed, to witness a 'Hunt' was considered an omen of bad things to come such as war, plague, or famine so this biblical spin on the narrative is not surprising.

Sightings of this Furious Raid span centuries with some of the most recent occurring in the 1940's. These Raids it would seem occur specifically around Yule, Halloween, and New Years important dates in the Pagan calendar, or indeed any calendar. As a result of the Witch Trials, we have testimony of people claiming to have seen such nightmarish sights. A weaver called Giuliano Verdena was tried for witchcraft in 1489. As part of his account, Giuliano confessed that he would gaze into a vase of water (a method of scrying) and he would see the Mistress of the Game who revealed to him "the great properties of herbs and the nature of animals" The Mistress would always be accompanied by a great multitude of people some of whom were on foot, others who were mounted.[182] An account similar to many of the Fae Folk encounters described during the trials.

Jabez Allies in 1846 England writes:

> *"I have been informed by Mr. John Pressdee of Worcester, that the country people used to talk a good deal about the 'Seven Whistlers' when he was a boy, and that he frequently heard his late grandfather, John Pressdee, who lived at*

---

[181] Fraser, "The Horned God of Wytches".

[182] Ibid.

Cuckold's Knoll, in Suckley, say that he oftentimes, at night, when he happened to be upon the hill by his house, heard six out of the 'Seven Whistlers' pass over his head, but that no more than six of them were ever heard by him, or by any one else to whistle at one time, and that should the seven whistle together the world would be at an end."

The Seven Whistlers is a term for the noise that would occur when a Wild Hunt would pass overhead. Sometimes the Hunt itself was not seen, only experienced as an aural phenomenon.

In some versions of the legend, the Wild Hunt only rides when England is threatened with invasion. Edric (Eadric) the Wild and his wife (either called Gondul or Goda) mentioned on the previous page, lead the Wild Hunt towards the foe. Edric and the Hunt have been publicly reported as having ridden in the months before the Crimean War, the First World War, and even as recent as the Second World War.[183] Echoes of this narrative are alive and well today with stories of Ghost Ships, notably the famous portent of doom 'The flying Dutchman'. Said to not only roam the seas but also the skies. In Stan Jones' epic song *'Riders in the Sky'*, he gives us cowboy phantoms, doomed to eternally wrangle a herd of 'red-eyed cows'. As a side note to any Nicholas Cage fans out there, Ghost Rider is the name given to the North American version of the Wild Hunt! The Legend of Sleepy Hollow is another more modern version of the Hunt mythology, a ghostly rider doomed to ride for eternity, head tucked under their arm and supposedly to blame for the otherworldly disappearance of Ichabod Crane. The Headless Horseman, of course, being a mythical figure who has appeared in folklore around the world since the Middle Ages. Indeed, the Green Knight had to pick up his head, tuck it under his arm and carry it away with him after Gawain had separated him from it.

Herne The Hunter

From Elizabethan England, we have the tale of Herne the Hunter, or as he is also known the Keeper of Windsor Forest. As the legend goes Herne was a skilled huntsman and Forester. He was the keeper of Windsor Forest, a job he loved, it was said he knew every inch of the Forest, every tree, plant, and animal. As part of his job, he was also made Master of the Hunt, his proficiency and passion earnt him the respect of the King and for this, he enjoyed much of the King's Favour. The Kingsmen however, jealous of his rising position and influence plotted against him. He was betrayed and

---

[183] The Wild Hunt or Fairy Raed – Article by Geoff Boxell published on Geoff Boxell Tripod.com.

murdered. From this point on an ominous ghostly figure was seen stalking the woods at night, a fearsome, horned rider upon a huge spectral steed. He hunted those who had betrayed him, sending them crazy with fear until they confessed to their part in the plot. The King so furious with their scheming and treachery had each of them hung from the large Oak Tree in the Forest, now known as Herne's Oak. It is said that Herne still roams the Forests at night, leading his own fearsome hunt. Making the ghosts of the men that wronged him ride with him furiously every night never letting up never giving them peace.[184] I also read an alternative version wherein the plot has Herne falsely arrested for poaching and so shamed by this tarnish on his reputation, Herne hung himself from his tree, the rest of the tale remaining the same.

Given his name, I think we can safely deduce that Herne is a derivation of Cernunnos. Although I did also read that the Saxon God Wotan (Germanic Odin) bore the title of Herian, meaning 'Head of the Hunt' so the character of Herne could also have been inspired by the Wotan stories. These legends of Herne and Herla are certainly worthy benefactors of the origin of the Wild Hunt mythology. These stories also greatly remind me of Diana's 'King of the Woods' narrative which these legends most likely borrow heavily from. There are also ritualistic elements to the use of Oak and the 'hanging' symbology again reminiscent of Odin's hanging on the tree of Yggdrasil, Odin himself once being a leader of the Norse Wild Hunt[185]. It would seem that Herne, Cernunnos, and The God of the Wild Hunt are one and the same when seen in this context and I have seen them being used 'interchangeably' throughout several articles and books I've read on the subject.

Herne, as with Edric has also been associated with the legend of Robin Hood or Robin of the Green. He appeared as a character in the 1980s TV series *Robin of Sherwood* as a character who inspired Robin to take up the title of "the Hooded Man." In this TV version, Herne took up a more shamanic role blessing Robin and aiding the Merry Men in their resistance to the Norman Conquest[186] which seems to lean into the Wild Eadric mythology who was also a wealthy nobleman who led the defense against the Normans.

---

[184] Fraser, "The Horned God of Wytches".

[185] Frazer, "The Golden Bough".

[186] Herne The Hunter – Article by Gregory Wright published on Mythopedia.com/ Beware the Ghostly Hunt - Folklore or Fact? Article by David Nash Ford on Berkshire History.com.

Unsurprisingly the great Arthurian wizard Merlin has also had his name thrown into the ring given the multitude of stories of his shapeshifting abilities, often seen taking the form of a stag and being known in a similar King of the Woods role. In Geoffrey of Monmouth's Poem *Vita Merlini*, Merlin becomes Lord of the Animals[187]. Certainly, legend has it that upon his retirement Merlin withdrew to the woods and lived out his day as a recluse, becoming in effect a 'Wild Man' one with nature. The connection between 'Wild Men' and the legends of Merlin, Herne, and Robin is unsurprising. Long have we recounted tales of the Wild Men, Moss Folk, or Wood Wives and husbands. The Green Man as a nature spirit when represented as a 'Wild Man' is hairy, dirty, unkempt, and dressed in leaves and vegetation. Representing the duality of Man, our relationship with nature but also our relationship with our internal animalistic desires. We are nature, we are the animal. In his book *The Green Man*, Anderson likens the mythology of the Wild Man to the stories of the North American Sasquatch. This is not such a big leap for Anderson to make here as one might originally suspect. I, believe Big Foot to most likely be some form of Fae Folk so I can see the link made between Wild Men, Fae Folk, and the infamous cryptid himself.

Horned God of the Wytches

When researching the pagan Horned God, it's not hard to find the association between Wicca and The Horned God. Certainly, within Wicca, we have the Mother Goddess often referred to as 'Diana' and we have her male consort the Horned God of the Hunt. We can infer that this God is also the same Leader of the Wild Hunt, a derivation of Cernunnos and his spiritual ancestors which we have already reviewed in an earlier chapter in our look at The Green Man archetype. This male Wiccan God is seen as embodying positive masculine energy in synchronicity with the female energy, the Ying and the yang, the Sun and the Moon. He is a leader, and a protector, he is death, but he is also life. The Witch has long been associated with the Wild Hunt, but the Female version thereof. The focal point of the female hunt would seem to be the transportation of souls to the afterlife rather than the 'Hunt' aspect which is given over to the male counterpart. Certainly, nocturnal rites or rituals have always been part of Pagan Worship. It's unsurprising then that Diana and her hordes would choose to come out at the witching hour to ferry the souls of the dead to whatever realm lies next. Diana, as mentioned previously, would appear means different things to different people. To some she is a warrior goddess, a protector of the innocent, to others, she is the name given to Mother Earth, to the female

---

[187] Stewart, "Celtic Gods, Celtic Goddess". –

energy and life force, not a God, not a person but an Energy.

In his *Canon Episcopi* of c.900, Regino of Prum the abbot of Treves writes:

> *"Some wicked women, perverted by the devil, seduced by illusions and phantasms of demons, believe and profess themselves, in the hours of the night, to ride upon certain beasts with Diana, the goddess of pagans, and an innumerable multitude of women, and in the silence of the dead to traverse great spaces of the earth, and to obey her commands as of their mistress, and to be summoned to her service on certain nights"*

In her book *Troublesome Things*, Purkiss mentions several witches associated with the Hunt. Madonna Oriente was a Milanese witch who lived around 1380, it was said that she was followed by the living and the dead. People learned herb and healing lore from her, similar to the Fae Folk knowledge exchanges. It was even said that she could revive dead animals. In 1457 two women of the Alpine Tyrol confessed to travelling with Mistress Richella, who claim that she took them somewhere where there was feasting and dancing. In France the mysterious woman went by the name of 'Lady Abundia' and in Morocco, a similar story arose regarding a jinnee (female Jinn) called A'isha. These stories crop up all over Northern and Eastern Europe and even further afield[188].

It was said that witches had the power to call forth the Furious Horde or the Fairy Raid. Suspected witches who were put on trial reported that this 'horde' would comprise of the souls of unbaptized babies, the souls of soldiers who had fallen on the battlefield, and other witches. They said that if you wished to commune with or call forth the Horde, you would need to gather with your coven during the Ember seasons on Thursdays and Saturdays. From what I can make out Ember days are the 2-3 days preceding the change in season, but it may have other meanings that I am unaware of. The Hunt is often associated with the Witch Holda, Holda (also known as Holde, Hulda, or Holle) originates from Germanic and Scandinavian folklore. She was popularized by Jacob Grimm in the 19th century when he referenced her in his fairytale story 'Frau Holle' which appeared in the Gimm Fairytales Stories collection. Grimm seems to have felt that she was at one point a Teutonic Goddess, certainly, in his *Decretum* (1008 to 1012), Burchardt equates the Goddess Diana with the Witch Holda and her wild hordes[189].

---

[188] Purkiss, "Troublesome Things".
[189] Fraser, "The Horned God of Wytches".

Hellequin/Harlequin

England isn't the only country with its Hunter Heroes. In Germany, we have Hecla (or Hekla) leading the Hecla's Hellwain (spectral carriage) or the story of Hackelbernd. Hackelbernd (also seen as Hackelbärend, Hackelberg, or Hackelblock) was a huntsman whose love of hunting caused him to hunt on a Sunday, even though he knew this was sacrilege, for which he was cursed. Doomed after death to ride day and night never knowing peace. Interestingly, Hakolberand is an Old Saxon epithet for Wodan, the Germanic Odin, and the 'hakol' beginning of the name is similar to the Hekla, Helle names associated with the other Hunt Leaders[190].

Probably the most famous of our pack leaders would be the notorious French agent of Chaos, the Harlequinn. Hellequin, when looking at his name, is mostly likely a derivation of the Briton King Herla (also known as King Helle), i.e Herla King or Helle King becoming 'Helle Quin' in the French language. As well as 'Her' and 'Cer' being cognates for the word 'horn', the German word 'Helle' also translates to 'The Underworld'.

According to Zan Fraser's book *The Horned God of The Wytches*, Welsh Courtier Walter Maps' 12th-century account of King Herla roughly coincides timeline-wise with a report of a Wild Hunt led by a 'Harlechin' from Boneval France. There a monk called Ordericus Vitalis (also written as Ordeic Vitalis) reported in his Church History that a priest there had confessed to him that he saw a large spectral procession on New Year's Eve, the priest believed that he even recognized some of the dead as recently deceased parishioners. Vitalis referred to this as *'Doubtless the troop of Harlechin, of which I heard but never believed'*.

The Harlequin soon took on a life of its own, not only being associated with the Wild Hunt but also with being a master of Chaos. Not seen as simply the Hunt Leader anymore, Harlequinn took on qualities more akin to Loki the Norse God of Mischief. He was thought to be a trickster, cunning, and charming but ultimately not to be trusted. This seems to have come about in the Middle Ages which makes sense given the religious climate at the time, given to vilifying pagan heroes and deities. Harlequinn sought to bring chaos wherever he roamed. In the stories of his adventures of mayhem and mishap, he is often accompanied by a carnival of witches and 'hide' covered zoomorphic creatures. These creatures were often referred to as sauvages, selvatici, or homines selvatici – 'Wild Men'. Connecting us even further with the Wild Men, Harlequin himself is associated with a shapeshifting elf, similar

---

[190] Ibid.

in description to Puck, called 'Crokesos'.[191]

In Italy his archetype, Arlecchunio devolves into a more pathetic and comedic figure, his droopy fools hat perverting the once strong horns of the Pagan God into two wilting pathetic appendages, reducing him to an object of ridicule. This is the unfortunate surviving remainder we have today, the correlation with our Harlequin with nothing more than a court jester. He seems to have had more of a resurgence in modern times with Harley Quinn, being the less than docile figure in the DC Universe. It's no surprise that the 'Joker' the ultimate Batman Villain, the pure agent of chaos would have with him, his female counterpart, the ying to his yang in the form of our beautiful Harley Quinn.

Baphomet

When we think of horned deities today, other than the Pagan Horned God, arguably the most recognizable deity in our modern day is Baphomet. Baphomet like Cernunnos seems to have fallen foul of Christian propaganda, seen frequently as being demonic in origin, rather than as an amalgamation of several Pagan Deities. His origin appears to start somewhere around the First Crusades. From what I can find, Baphomet appears to have been the construct of the Knights Templar, basically assimilating the Palestinian God Baal with the Islamic Prophet Mahomet (derivation of Muhammad). This Islamic influence on the Knights Templar isn't surprising given the time they spent in the Holy Land on Crusades, living day to day immersed within the Islamic faith.[192] The sacred writers of the time mention this deity Baal also under the name Berith and he would appear to correspond with our archetype as an Adonis or Osiris figure (or Oswara and Menu).

Baal as with the other Gods we've looked at was considered a God of agriculture and fertility by the Canaanites (Semitic people said to descend from Noah) and was the patron God of the city Zebul. He was also worshipped under the name Muloch. Muloch was sometimes depicted with the head of a Bull, repeating the zoomorphic themes we've seen so much over the previous chapters. [193] Muloch was also said to 'destroy to recreate'

---

[191] The Hellish Harlequin: phantom hordes to Father Christmas – Article on Bone and Sickle.com.

[192] Hans Holzer - Witches – True Encounters with Wicca, Wizards, Covens, Cults and Magick -(First published by Black Dog & Leventhal Publishers 2002).

[193] Faber B.D, "The Origin of Pagan Idolatry".

another aspect that plays a part in this 'nature' narrative and its' cyclical themes. The Cult of Baal did spread out from the Middle East into Europe, in the city of Cilicia which can be found just over the sea from Cyprus coins were unearthed that showed a deity named 'Baal of Tarus' holding an ear of corn in one hand and a bunch of grapes in the other[194]. From what I've read many of the names for these deities seem to be derivative of other spellings or translations for one deity or assimilating another deity with an existing one so following the threads and the different names assigned can become murky, to say the least.

Baal as with Osiris and Dionysus has strong connections to the Underworld, spending time trapped there. The summarized version of the story is a follows; Baal had constructed for himself a beautiful new home, and to celebrate its completion he held a large feast and festivities there. All of importance were invited except for Mot, the God of death and Infertility. Furious by the snub, Mot invited him to dine at his home in the Underworld. When there, he fed Baal a meal of mud (mud being symbolic of death) Baal ate the meal out of politeness but found himself then trapped in the underworld. His wife and sister Anat travelled to the Underworld to rescue him and bring him back to life, echoing the Osiris storyline[195].

In our modern-day Baphomet is frequently seen as an 'Occult' icon and his likeness has been used to depict the Christian Devil in much occultist paraphernalia making an appearance as such in the popular Waite Rider Tarot Card deck. Commonly associated with Witchcraft and Magick, he is also referred to as the 'Sabbatical Goat'. French occultist Éliphas Lévi used the image of Baphomet as a hermaphroditic winged humanoid, with the head and feet of a goat on the front cover of his book *Dogme et Ritual de la Haute Magie* (1861; Transcendental Magic: Its Doctrine and Ritual) and it is this image which has become popularized today.

Interestingly, Baphomet is also used as a hieroglyph or symbol for Alchemy. He represents the turning of crude matter into the Godhead, he is representative of the merging or transmutation of the polarities. The merging of male and female, good and evil, into one singular entity, which represents spiritual Gold. It's almost the anthesis of the usual religious Triad. Instead of one being three, alchemists looked to unify everything spiritually, so the three

---

[194] Frazer, "The Golden Bough".

[195] Baal – on Myths and Legends.com.

inversely become the one[196]. Aleister Crowley, famed Occultist and Author was also a proponent of this thinking, always striving to reach the 'God Head' this spiritual gold where everything becomes one instead of the triads or splits that we have today within religious ideology and spiritual teachings.

Tree Worship, The Druids, and Wicca

The Tree has long been a common focal point of worship whether it's as benign as children dancing around the maypole in celebration or as extreme as the druids hanging their victim's heads from them. Tree worship is believed to be one of the oldest forms of worship and it isn't as medieval as we may think. Forms of Tree Worship exist even today, how many of us still have a wooden crucifix in our houses or some wooden rosary beads, or at the very least, know someone that does? The Tree and its symbology are everywhere, this is especially true of religion, be it pagan or otherwise. The Bible is full of its symbology, Eve plucking the forbidden fruit from the Tree of Knowledge, the trees felled and carved to create Noah's Ark, or even the wooden cross upon which Jesus was executed. The theme of Trees runs heavily throughout religion and Folklore.

Our Green Man, for several authors I've read, is intrinsic to the survival of many occultist theologies and ideas of sacrificial worship. Certainly, Frazer saw links between sacrifice and ensured fertility in many of the Cults and Religions that he studied. Certainly, in our Teutonic Religions, Trees were sacred, and both the Norse and Celtic Gods were heavily connected to them, they were symbols of wisdom and strength. In Odin's story, he hung himself on the Norse Tree Yggdrasil, upside down for nine days to acquire the knowledge and awareness of the runic alphabet to pass this knowledge onto mankind. Similar in gesture to the sacrifice Christ made on the cross. The Goddess Artemis interestingly was also known as 'The Goddess that hangs herself'. I did try to see where the mythology behind the hanging Goddess came from but couldn't find much. There is a correlation between sacrifice and fertility, it was said that effigies would be 'hung' from trees in Artemis's sacred grove as a sacrifice to ensure good health and bountiful harvest. Certainly, the 'killing of the sacred God' is a theme that runs heavily through most religions. The idea of God sacrificing him/herself to nourish his/her people, be it spiritually or indeed physically.

Osiris is also connected to the Tree in his narrative, as mythology tells how Osiris's coffin had drifted ashore at Byblus on the Syrian coast. Where it

---

[196] Sage of Quay Radio - Michael Joseph - 9/11 and Occult Theology (Sept 2017).

landed a fine Erica Tree shot up overnight encasing the coffin within its trunk. The King of Byblus admired this tree greatly and so had it cut down and made into a pillar to stand within his own house. Isis heard of this and went to ask the King for it back, not knowing it housed the entombed body of Osiris he of course returned it to her. Out of this Pillar, Isis carved the body of her dead husband. The wood she cleaved was given back to the King and the Queen of Byblus who stood the wood in the temple of Isis at Byblus as a sign of respect and reverence. Later Firmicus Maternus (Roman Writer) describes a ceremony commemorating this event, where a tree is cut down and hollowed out, from this expunged wood an effigy of Osiris is formed, and then it is encased back within the hollowed-out tree and buried for a year. Once the year is over the tree is dug back up and burnt[197].

Jeanne D'arc (Joan of Arc) frequented a fairy tree known locally in her area as the Tree of Mistresses. The old people said that long ago fairies lived in the tree and that people would lay gifts and offerings at the tree. Young girls would hang flowers and garlands there – similar to the Green Man rituals we've seen during May Day celebrations. Next to the tree was a spring that was said to hold healing properties, like Egeria's Lake at Nemi. Whether Joan of Arc's powers of prophesy and healing were bestowed on her by The Virgin Mary or by the Queen of Fairies is open to interpretation, what is apparent is the similarity of her story to many others who also, unfortunately, died on the pyre of their beliefs[198].

In Celtic Mythology, the realms of the Gods and Goddesses, the spirits of ancestors, and the world of the fairies are blurred. They bleed into each other, mythology and magic irrevocably intertwined. The Oak Tree was particularly significant to the Druids. "Oak" derives from the Anglo-Saxon word, ac, but in Irish, the word is 'Daur' combine this with the Indo-European root 'wid': which means 'to know' and you end up with what most scholars agree to be the likely origin of the title 'Druid'. 'Druid' roughly translated is 'those with knowledge of the oak'. The Sanskrit word, 'Duir', gave rise both to the word for oak and the English word 'door', which suggests that this tree stands as an opening into greater wisdom, or perhaps, an entryway into the otherworld itself[199].

---

[197] Frazer, "The Golden Bough".

[198] Purkiss, "Troublesome Things".

[199] Oak – Article published on Druidry.org.

Their sacred trees were called 'Bile' and were either Oak or Ash, both trees being sacrosanct, especially in Ireland, where once upon a time, being caught doing damage to one was enough to get you executed. The tree was significant due to its positioning, its roots reached deep down into the earth, touching the Underworld, and its branches reached so high up they could touch the stars. Trees were the link between the heavens and the Underworld, a celestial being that could live for thousands of years gaining unimagined knowledge, with roots in all planes of existence. The Earth and the Underworld were extremely important to the Celts and the Tree was a link to both[200].

Druids believed in worship through a spiritual link with nature, based on an awareness of our connection to the world around us. They believed in the 'butterfly effect' the idea that there is a direct causal link between our actions and the knock-on effect they have on the world around us [201]. The Celts believed that their Gods were everywhere. Not on some cloud in the sky or deep in some cave but that their essence was in the earth, the sky, the rivers, and streams, surrounding us with their very being. Druids were an aristocratic priesthood usually divided into three orders, Judges, Prophets, and Poets. Each with its own role to play. People held the Druids to high standards, believing them to be powerful and almost supernatural.

Druidic ceremonies took place in their sacred oak groves, places so steeped in supernatural lore and so eerie and fear-inducing that even some Celts dared not venture there. The Romans created quite the mythos surrounding the Forests and Woods of the Celts that their soldiers would often refuse to enter them so convinced were they of their supernatural origin and malintent[202] There are four main Celtic festivals (Fire festivals) and it is believed that the Celt's festivals were aligned with the constellations as opposed to the seasons. That the November and May fires, mark the setting and rising of the Pleiades star system in the constellation of Taurus[203]. The Pleiades seems to play and important if not obscure part of Celtic Tradition. The main four festivals are:

---

[200] Stewart, "Celtic Gods, Celtic Goddess".

[201] Mari Silva – Paganism (everything from ancient Hellenic, Norse and Celtic Paganism to Heathenry, Wicca and other Modern Pagan Beliefs and Practices (2021).

[202] R.J. Brenda Lewis - Ritual Sacrifice a Concise History (First published 2001 by Sutton Publishing Ltd).

[203] Stewart, "Celtic Gods, Celtic Goddess".

Samhain - Summers' End, often associated with Halloween celebrates the death of the light, the end of summer, and the drawing in of the dark half of the year.

Imbolc – Candlemas, marks the beginning of spring and welcomes back the light and growth.

Beltane – Mayday, the welcoming of Summer, historically this would have been when farmers let the animals into the pastures to eat and roam.

Lughnasadh – The first harvest, the God of this first harvest is our Green Man who sacrifices himself every year to enable a fruitful and bountiful harvest. This is also the start of the shortening of the days, as after the longest day, the shorter days of winter start to come forth.

Interesting going back to the focus on star systems and constellations in the ancient Pagan religions, specifically the Sirius and Pleiades star systems, the Ancient Sumerians and the 'Oannes' people had a ritual for calling down the 'fish-headed' God from Sirius, which mirrors a lot of the Celtic 'Fire' festivals. This ritual involves holding a black mirror to catch the light of the Sirius Star System[204] (reminiscent of Diana's Mirror in her Festival of Lights) at Midsummer (Midsommar). The timing of the rituals is interesting as it ties into our Celtic Fire Festivals, where fires would be lit at this time to signify the astral locations of the Pleiades Star Systems. Here we have two very popular star systems in Extraterrestrial mythology being acknowledged and their movements plotted and celebrated by our ancestors for thousands of years. My mother, who has read far more extensively on Celtic Mythology than I have, tells me that it is believed that one possible origin for the Celtic Tuatha de Danann is extraterrestrial. That these 'fairy people' before they were pushed underground were akin to the Anunnaki of the Sumerians. Indeed, it was the Tuatha de Danann with whom the Druids were able to commune with to obtain knowledge and technology. The link between fairies, aliens, magick, and technology replicated in the ancient Celtic Countries as it was in Mesopotamia, Egypt, and Southern Europe.

In Han Holzer's book *Witches, True Encounters with Wicca, Wizards, Covens, Cults and Magick* he spends much time with various covens and gets to know in depth the rites and rituals of many Wiccan Covens. In the below excerpt, he describes one Coven's practices and theology concerning the Sabbats and their Esbats which I found fascinating and also ties into the lunar movements:

"NEKAM/Phoenix Rising (the Coven) uses the three degree system, observes

---

[204] Greenfield, "The Complete Cipher of the Ufonauts".

*the traditional eight Sabbats and the New and Full Moon Esbats. The sabbats
are celebrated with seasonal rituals, magickal workings, stories and feasting. At
the Full Moon Esbats the Rite of Drawing Down the Moon is performed. The
Coven honors the Goddess in the Great Mother, Creatrix and Destroyer of all
things. She is the Earth Mother, the Lady of the Moon, and the Star Goddess.
In short, the very essence of all life and consciousness; life energy itself. Her God
is her Horned Consort, who is both the Giver of Life and the Lord of Death.
He is that which makes all life fertile and brings the life energy into being. It is
these energies that are the building blocks of all Magickal workings. They believe
and understand that Magick is energy directed through intent. Some form of
Magick is done at every Esbat, and this is also a time when specific magickal
training is given to initiates."*

Ritual Sacrifice and Magick

In his book *The Golden Bough*, Frazer discusses these Fire Festivals and draws
the connection between Fertility and sacrifice. The Gods need to be fed and
appeased therefore sacrifice was required. In terms of importance, the May
and November festivals seem to be the most celebrated, indeed May Day
celebrations in the UK remain strong to this day. As does the tradition of
building fires with Bonfire Night on 5th November here in the UK an annual
event that shows no signs of abating. The Celts would take their time building
their pyres. Only the finest kindling and wood were used, the sacrifices tied
on timber grassy, leafy frames in the center of the pyre. As if the victim was
being entombed in a tree, like Osiris in his tree at Byblus, transforming them
into a tree spirit[205]. It was thought that if the kindling did not spark then the
sacrifice was pure and could be released but I highly doubt this happened
much. As time has worn on, the requirement for physical sacrifice seems
thankfully in most cases to be substituted for symbolic sacrifice. The 'chosen
victim' only having to jump through or over a pyre to satisfy the requirement
rather than being actually burnt upon the pyre.

Another well-known method of burning was in a Giant Effigy, anyone who
has seen the Wicker Man will be familiar with this Pagan concept, it would
appear that the building of these giants is associated with the druids who
would construct massive figures some twenty to thirty foot high made of
Osiers. This 'giant' would be moved utilizing rollers and ropes worked by
men pushing and pulling from within the construct. Often the giant would
be dressed as a Knight, or just made to look like an Ogre[206]. Sometimes it

---

[205] Frazer, "The Golden Bough".

[206] Ibid.

would be accompanied by smaller constructed figures representing the giants' family or associates. I can imagine that this was quite a sight. Of course, we still have the Burning Man festival annually in the Black Rock Desert as well as the Wicker Man festival in Scotland, both of which are a remnant of this form of fire festival. If you believe the stories, the 'Burning of Care' ceremony at Bohemian Grove involves the 'Skull & Bones' initiates burning an effigy with a sacrifice contained within[207]to a giant owl who is supposed to be the ancient God 'Mulach'. I imagine both still provide the God with his sacrifices, many of them accidental of course!! It is interesting to me how many of these large Fire Festivals involve the burning of a 'Giant' could this be symbolic of the destruction of ancient giants by such means as fire? Or an effigy used such as the many Guy Fawkes effigies used on Bonfire night pyres all across the UK. Many latter-day rituals involve symbolic sacrifice with less and less need for animal sacrifice or thankfully human sacrifice.

Even the Gods and Kings must sacrifice, either themselves or their Children for the betterment of Mankind. Odin sacrificed himself on the tree of Yggdrasil, Jesus sacrificed himself on the Cross and the Horned God sacrifices himself every year to seed the earth and yield more crops. In ancient Mesopotamia, the Second Book of the Kings describes how the King of Moab was so desperate that upon finding himself near defeat in battle by the Israelites that he sacrificed his only son and heir, his only way of securing the family dynasty. His son was burnt alive to secure his success which according to the legend it did, as soon after his offering the Israelites withdraw. There are many accounts of people sacrificing their children to the Gods when dire circumstances prevailed. Sacrifices of first-born children were made to Baal by the ancient Phoenicians as did the Canaanites when famine or plague forced their hand [208].

Burning has always been a common form of sacrifice. Burnt offerings symbolized many things, the purification of the act of burning, and making the sacrifice pure during the ritual. There was the art of divination, things could be 'seen' within the flames prophesizing important events to come, or the ashes and the aftermath could also be used for the same purposes. Finally, the drawing of blood or offering of blood, the very life force of the sacrifice is the most potent and efficacious of offerings. Fire sacrifices, however, were seen as fit for the Celestial Gods, not considered suitable for the Earth Gods.

[207] Dark Secrets: Inside Bohemian Grove – Alex Jones documentary (2000) https://www.youtube.com/watch?v=QjTkEyM_aTc.

[208] Lewis, "Ritual Sacrifice a Concise History".

Earth Gods required sacrifices placed on the ground and given to the earth. Often the sacrifice took place out in the open rather than in a temple or on a hill, in a sacred grove, or near or in water of some form. People were thrown into pits and volcanoes or drowned in rivers and lakes. Certainly, offerings to the Teutates' Protector Gods were drowned in various sacrificial rituals.

Indeed, the use of 'water' to cleanse, purify and sanctify exists as a method in all religions, with every main religion having its own version of the 'Deluge' narrative, the great flood that wipes out mankind leaving the chosen few, the prophet saved in his 'wooden' vessel floating in a kind of half death awaiting his rebirth and a second chance at life. In his thesis *The origin of Pagan idolatry*, Faber notes that in Pagan Britain some rituals in commemoration of the Great Deluge where the God Hu's Oxen were used to prevent the second deluge were periodically celebrated around water, near streams and on the borders of lakes. The Celts saw water, river, streams, and lakes as a source of great power. Energy lived in the water, as did the things such as divine beings. It could be seen as a gateway to the underworld. The Romans would often rob the lakes of Gaul as they knew that the Celts would place offerings of treasure and wealth to their water Gods and the Gods of the Underworld.

Burning, however, was not the preferred method of ritualist sacrifice for the Celts. They were renowned Headhunters. To the Celts, the head was the cradle of consciousness, the seat of knowledge, and the most sacred part of the human body. The head is used as both a source of power and a trophy. They would often use the skulls of their victims to drink out of during their ritualist ceremonies. Victims would often be decapitated, and their heads hung from their Sacred Oak. As an aspect of The Green Man and his worship, these 'heads' could be seen to resemble the foliate head, removed from the body, disgorged, and grimacing. In some foliate head imagery, the tongues are extended and swollen sticking out of the mouth in a terrifying death mask similar to the faces of hanging victims[209]. A many number of shrines containing or intended for decapitated heads (or sacred heads) have been found by archeologists examining Celtic Britain and Ireland and even further afield such as the Sanctuary of Roquepertuse where skulls were placed in niches of a French Celtic sacred site[210]. Archeological findings show us the Celts tossed skulls into sacred wells as offerings, combining both the symbolism of the water and the power of the skull in the darkness of this underworld. Representative of a cleanses of one's soul before entering the

---

[209] Eric Edwards Wordpress.com - The Green Man Phenomenon

[210] Ibid.

afterlife[211]. Sacred wells aren't the only place ritualistic skull symbols and heads pop up in Celtic realms. We see carvings of heads used to decorate doorways and hallways of ancient ceremonial grounds and sanctuaries.

When looking at the Celts and tree worship, I feel I do them an injustice with my brevity of explanation, since these were an incredibly complex, nuanced, and intelligent people. The Druids knew many things about the stars, the earth, Magick, and alchemy, a wealth of rich knowledge, unfortunately, lost to us today. However, to find our Green Man amongst these beliefs I'll remain focused on the more relevant points such as Tree worship. The Druidic word for sanctuary seems to be identical in origin and meaning to the Latin word 'nemus' which links us back to Diana's sacred grove in Nemi. It would follow that the Celts held this grove and others like it to be divine places. They would consecrate this holy ground and leave gifts and sacrifices there for their Gods.

Sacrifice has also been a part of ceremonial Magick, going back for thousands of years with this practice being performed all over the world and in every religion. These days we would commonly associate such practices as 'blood magick' with the dark arts, black witchcraft, black masses, and religions such as Voodoo and Santeria but for our ancestors, the act would have been viewed in a much less 'despicable' way. It was a necessity, not only to ensure the continuation of certain ways of life but also for those in the know, a way to unlock great knowledge, access technology, and open doorways to other realms.

May Day

When researching ceremonies and rituals for this book, the most popular of all the festivals in terms of the sheer amount written about the vast array of rituals and practices is that of Beltane or May Day. I knew May Day was popular given that we still celebrate it today in the UK, but I wasn't aware of the sheer number of Rituals and Ceremonies that we use to commemorate it. These tie in nicely with the Green Man rituals and archetype we looked at earlier as many of these rituals involve the covering of individuals in flowers, garlands, and vegetation, turning normal men into literal Green Men by form of transubstantiation.

---

[211] Ancient Cult Of Human Skulls And Communication With The Other World – Article published on Ancient Pages.com.

The most common form of celebration for May Day is the dance around the May Pole. This is a well-regarded fertility ritual in which a Tree is carefully selected, and the men from the community will fell the tree and from its trunk carve the Pole. Pre-made ribbons and adornments will then be attached. The women will prepare the hole in the ground in which the pole will stand and offerings such as milk and honey are given to the earth. As a side note in the Highlands of Scotland tributes such as milk and honey were left for 'The Frid' who were responsible for the fertility of the land[212]. The Children will make garlands from flowers with which to adorn it. The men then 'ceremoniously' march the Pole through the village so that all can see and partake in the blessings it will bring before finally resting it within the hole in the earth where it takes up its residence in one big phallic show. The pole is now ready, and the dancing may begin, people will each take a ribbon and an intricate pattern is danced and weaved into a traditional pattern. The purpose of the ritual is fertility based, raising the energy from the Pole directly into the earth to ensure the fertility of the land[213].

Dancing is integral to Pagan Worship, as we mentioned in our earlier chapter, The Green Man is also referred to as the 'Lord of the Dance' and such movement is integral to his worship, within the *billions of infinitely small movements that make up the seemingly chaotic Dance of Life'*. It is also interesting it is said that the May Pole dancing and also the Morris Dancing (English Folk Dance) are inspired by the Fae Folk who are notably always dancing. The specific steps and movements being 'recreated' from fairy dances as allegedly witnessed by humans. The energy produced from such movement and from the sounds and beats of the music combining to form a trance-like state so high in group energy that it can be manifested in the desired form, whatever is the required outcome of this ritual being performed. As Beltane is the 'mating' season, many of the rituals surround fertility and reproduction. There are many rituals involving the coming together of the King and Queen, of Diana and her Virbius. For example, the King and Queen of May, historically there would be a contest of some kind, the victorious winner would be crowned King and earn the May Queen as his bride, both then adorned in Green and paraded through the village finally crowned in a

212 The Significance of Skulls In Celtic Culture And Art – Article published on Welsh Treasure.com.

213 Briggs, "The Vanishing People".

214 Hans Holzer - Witches – True Encounters with Wicca, Wizards, Covens, Cults and Magick -(First published by Black Dog & Leventhal Publishers 2002).

celebration of fertility[214].

Certainly, in many Teutonic-based religions, this act of coupling is recreated with people from within the tribes. A priest and priestess who come together to simulate the consummation of the Great Goddess with the Horned God. As well as being a celebration of fertility, sex could also be used as a principal in homeopathic or imitative magick. Sex magic has often been used as a way to strengthen energy and manifest results. A similar ritual was performed in respect of Dionysus, every year where he would be married to the Queen or Goddess. The consummation of the divine union as well as the espousals was enacted at this ceremony, whether they used actual people as conduits or an image or an effigy we don't know. I suspect both versions most likely took place. People were far less repressed about sex and sexuality then, than we are now, in many regards the further we travel from nature towards science the more repressed and clinical we become. We know from Aristotle that the ceremony took place in the old 'official' residence of the King, known as the Cattle-Stall, which stood near the prytaneum or town hall on the North-Eastern slope of the Acropolis.

Another interesting May Day ritual is that of George of the Green, a character that we briefly looked at in our earlier chapter. A variation of this 'rain' ritual takes place all over Northern and Eastern Europe. On the eve of St. George's Day, a tree is chosen and felled, then adorned with flowers and garlands. In a procession similar in appearance to the May Pole tradition this tree is then paraded through the streets accompanied by music and festivities. The chief protagonist in this parade is 'Green George', a young athletic male from the village who is chosen to be the 'sacrifice'. This young man is clad in green birch branches and also paraded through the streets. At the close of this ceremony, if he is lucky the boy is substituted for an effigy which is thrown into the water, if not so lucky the boy gets a ducking in the water[215]. I am sure that at some point the required sacrifice was real but fortunately, it appears that an effigy has sufficed the water Gods for some time now. The purpose of the ritual is to ensure rain over the summer months to keep the fields green and crops fresh.

A similar ritual comes from Scotland, however similar versions of this ritual exist all over Northern Europe. This one involves the Burry Man. The Burry Man festival is celebrated in August not May so falls more in line with the First Harvest of Lughnasadh. The unfortunate man picked for the position

---

[215] Frazer, "The Golden Bough".

of Burry Man undertook a bit of an ordeal. Days before the parade, thousands of Burrs (the spikey seeds from the Burdock plant) are collected and dried out. On Burry Day, the gentleman chosen will be dressed in a costume made entirely of these Burrs. They are stuck using their spikey outer casings all over his body. Upon reaching his neck, a balaclava is put over his head topped off by a bowler hat. The burrs are then continued up his neck and all over his face. The costume will cause extreme physical discomfort as the burrs burrow into his clothing spiking and prodding him. Then there is the added inconvenience of not being able to drop his arms fully, close his legs or even sit down. Going to the toilet is impossible so he is not allowed to drink or eat, his only respite being a small sup of whiskey sparingly throughout the day. After an entire day of torment, the Burry Man is returned to his beginnings, his burrs torn off and the man relieved of his duty. A similar festival in Bavarian Whitsuntide ends however with the sacrifice being ducked in water and finally decapitated, symbolically of course! [216].

As a bit of a side note when looking into these Pagan rituals specifically those involving water, I couldn't help but think of a Cult theory that I had stumbled across some years earlier. For those of you who may not be aware, there is a theory floating across the internet that there is a Cult of Killers, often referred to in the Media as The Smiley Face Killers. The theory alleges that there is a group of people who are abducting and murdering College Age men. Men who meet the profile tend to be athletic, good-looking, intelligent, and popular. These men are then (those that are found) disposed of in a body of water, sometimes in the most unusual of poses. I don't wish to get into this theory too much here as there are many good books on the topic if anyone is interested but it is the ritualistic elements that interest me. Certainly, among Teutonic religions, the sacrifice of drowning young men as part of the ritual is common, certainly, we've seen many examples of such rituals like some mentioned above, many of them under Fraser's banner of the 'Killing of the Tree Spirit'. In fact, I did think that as the Smiley Face is the most prolific graffiti tags in the world, then the foliate head is also one of the most prolific images also. I could see the smiley face having some semblance of the foliate head imagery. I speculate of course, but should you go down the 'murderous cult' path with this theory, it wouldn't be a stretch to imagine the tag of the smiley face being used instead of the occultist green man face, which as well as being harder to graffiti might be a little too on the nose for a Pagan Occultist Murder Group! Although the link between pagan ritual sacrifice regarding water and the Green Man shouldn't be overlooked if people wished to explore the occult sacrifice aspect of these deaths.

---

[216] Fran and Geoff Doel – The Green Man In Britain (2001) Ebook Edition (2013).

If indeed there is any merit to the Smiley Face Killers theory, and trust me, much stranger things have already been proven to be true, what would be the motive? Certainly, from my investigation into the theory, we can most definitely say in a select few of the cases there is evidence to suggest third party involvement in their demise. There is clear forensic evidence that some of these men were drugged, held for an indeterminate amount of time, murdered, and then left in a body of water. The police in most of these cases have determined the cause of death as 'accidental drowning'. Each case should be looked at on its individual merits but in some cases, there certainly seems to be some oddities surrounding their deaths and in some cases, the police have been pressured to reopen their investigations.

To understand the motive, it would be helpful to know how much of the killing has a sexual component. If the motive is sexual then I think we could rule out ritual magick, if it is not, if the sexual element could be condensed down to being a simple 'lure' to hook a young man then I think we can speculate that the motive is Ritualistic in nature. What boggles the mind is the sheer scope of the killings, from the outside it appears to be a global phenomenon. What could such a widespread body of people be doing or hope to achieve, do the numbers increase the strength of the ritual and magick produced, or is there another motive? Lay lines are the earth's life force, energy flows at its greatest volume through them, water conducts this energy which is why paranormal activity is always heightened where there is a body of water. It would be interesting to see if there is a correlation between the bodies of water that these men are found in and natural lay lines. Certainly, such a darkening of lay lines would have a negative effect on any people that are near or come into contact with these bodies of water but I digress....

Sidebar - during my many years of true crime binging, I also came across the infamous West Memphis Three case. What I found interesting here was again, similar to the above-mentioned Smiley Face murders is the ritual detail involved in the young children's deaths. These young males were tortured, their bodies left in a body of water and interestingly at an area called 'Robin Hood Hills'. An unintentional nod to our Green Man? I think the satanic panic of the time may have clouded the investigation however I cannot deny the strong ritual elements involved, could this be coincidental? Of course, but it is certainly worth pointing out none the less given the placement or staging of these young men in a body of water.

Having read quite a bit on ritual and sacrifice for this book, sacrifice has been required for a great many things. As a people, we are incredibly ritualistic by nature. We like to partake in ritualistic ceremonies whether we are even conscious of it or not. Something as benign as wearing our lucky socks to take an exam or going to cheer on your favorite football team wearing your lucky shirt is a form of ritual. Communities require ritual, it is something that brings us together, helps to strengthen bonds, and fosters a sense of belonging. It is important to us and it's something that we will continue to partake in, its tradition. The sacrifice of people from poorer, lower-class communities throughout history does also point toward it being used as a tool for social control by those in positions of power.

In this modern day, however, we can remove some of the more base motivations. We no longer need to kill people to ensure that the sun rises, we know through science that this will happen every day. We no longer need to sacrifice for agricultural reasons, although an argument could be made for the continuation of such rituals in 3rd world and economically impoverished areas were reliance on cattle and crops remain as vital as it was hundreds of years ago. So, what could the purpose be for blood sacrifice, in wealthier Western Countries?

My conclusion leads me to ritual Magick, the requirement of a blood sacrifice to manifest something required by the performer. Possibly something as crass as power or money but I think the main purpose is to call something forth to acquire information and technology. Similar to the Druids and their Tuatha De Danann or Crowley and LAM there is a transfer of knowledge during the ritual. Magick ritual has always been in existence. In ancient Greece, the goatherders of Acadia and Thessaly would practice magic and witchcraft in styles similar to the practices of the Celts and the Anglo-Saxons. However, as Han Holzer comments in his book *Witches*, beliefs are shaped by the socio, economic and climatic conditions of their environment. For the Greeks their horned God Pan, is relaxed and playful, spending his day's sun-drenched entertaining with his lute. The Celtic God, given his harsher climate, is colder, harsher less forgiving than his Mediterranean counterpart. *"Gods after all are created in the image of men and not necessarily vice versa"*

Jean Bottero posits much the same in his book *Religion in Ancient Mesopotamia* *"No religion is truly real – identifiable and analyzable – except through and within the individuals who practice it, individuals who, alone, using its mechanisms of the minds and their hearts, hold the secrets of it, even if, they are aware that they do so"*. Never is this so apt, as when talking about Cults, their beliefs, and their rituals.

Cults have existed for thousands of years, Osiris, Dionysus, Diana, and Artemis, all had their cults some existing in some form or another today, and all of them involving either animal or human sacrifice. In Phrygia in West

Central Asia Minor, a cult specializing in the sacrifice of rams centered around the Goddess Cybele and her son Attis (identifiable with Adonis and Dionysus) wherein the members would bath in the blood of the Ram after its sacrifice. Similar sacrifices were performed using Goats and Bulls. Dionysus took both as forms and Frazer theorizes that this ritual was another version of the 'Killing of the Divine King' mythology, the Ram being the God in his animal totem state. The eating and drinking of the animals' blood work very similarly to the transubstantiation of the body and blood of Christ during Mass. The worshippers believe that they are indeed eating the body and flesh of their God. In some versions of this ritual, a human child would be taken from a noble family and given up as the 'goat' sacrifice such as in Chios, Tenedos, and Potniae[217].

The above rituals were part of tradition, and community and answered the requirement of 'feeding' the Gods to ensure prosperity and health for the region. In this day and age, thankfully the requirement for physical sacrifice is rare, with symbolic sacrifice being used when creating and partaking in rituals be it religious or as part of the Craft. As with most things in life, some will take matters a step too far believing that using human victims will manifest their heart's desire, whether its money, power, or knowledge.

For example, in the 1980's a Murderous Cult in Mexico was discovered at the Santa Elena Ranch. The ranch was under investigation for drug trafficking, but police got a lot more than they bargained for when they raided the ranch on suspicion of drug smuggling and found instead the remains of about 15 people. One of those people turned out to be Mark Kilroy, age 21 who had recently gone missing whilst on Spring Break in Mexico. Several members of the cult confessed to the murders, saying that they believed that the sacrifice gave them protection from the Police as well as secured their success in their business activities. Cult leader Adolfo Constanzo was said to be a priest of Palo Mayombe, an Afro-Caribbean religion that involves sacrifice. He was said to also undertake rituals for patrons, his practices gaining him much notoriety and success within the elite criminal world of Mexico[218].

Psychopathic ritualists such as Adolfo Constanzo or Richard Ramirez or Charles Manson commit ritualistic crimes to satisfy their own deluded means. Perpetrators have obsessional or delusional personalities which allow them to twist religious symbolism to meet their specific needs[219]. These types of

[217] Frazer, "The Golden Bough".

[218] The Believers: Cult Murders in Mexico – Article by Guy Garcia published on Rolling Stone.com

[219] Occult Crime: A Law Enforcement Primer.

murders do still occur as serial killers are ritualistic with their process but hopefully quite rare. Taking us back to Hellier and the letter received about the sacrificing of people in the Kentucky forests with knowledge and involvement by officials and people in authority is disturbing but we know such ritualistic practices exist, we only need to look at the recent pedophile rings and the cover-ups of the Catholic Church so see evidence of a great number of people with power, using this authority to corrupt and pervert.

Interestingly, such sacrifice does appear to take place out in the forests, and the location of the ritual does appear to be important. Outside sacrifice is usually performed to connect with the energy or spirit of the location and allegedly in the case of Hellier, there is a specific reference to The Green Man. I know that the Horned God of the Hunt is a deity or energy worshipped in Wicca, but it is interesting that in this specific instance he is referred to by his Green Man motif. It is also interesting the ties to magick as well as to ritual. Whatever (if anything) is occurring within these forests is using magick in ritual as well as a blood sacrifice to try to achieve some end goal. From my research usually it is a 'Crowley-esque' desire to call something forth. To make contact with an entity of some kind. Could it be that they are trying to call forth the spirit of the deity that is the Green Man?

Certainly, if you have picked up this book, I am sure that you are familiar with the speculation around the New World Order, the desire to put everyone and everything under one control. This is nothing new, indeed I would posit that this is not a 'New World Order' at all but simply a desire to recreate the Old-World Order. To emulate that which came before, before Sumar, before the fall of Babel, before we were a fractured, split society. When we had one religion, one language, one master. It would seem that a move towards a 'New World Religion' seems to be in play, the condemnation of monotheistic religions, their bad press, and even worse actions are seen everywhere. Their fall from Grace, beautifully engineered to move us away from such ideologies. The emphasis on 'Green' has once again been thrust into the zeitgeist. We must save our planet, recycle, minimize our carbon footprint, and be more 'Green'. A cleverly orchestrated shift towards nature, towards all things Green, towards a more Earth-centric religion, reminiscent of the old religions, the Pagan religions, let us be once again at one with our Earth. And who might be the figurehead for such a religion? Who, indeed!

The Forests have long been a place of mystery and eerie fascination, they are dark and scary, and many dangers could be lurking within. Fairy Tales have been told to children for thousands of years to keep them from wondering off into the woods never to be seen again. Jacob Grimm, the famous children's author was also interested in the supernatural, writing about such things as The Wild Hunt. This interest permeates his stories, they are dark with a vicious edge, rarely with the happily ever after ending, warning children about the bad things that can happen deep in the woods. Freetown Forest, located within the 'Bridgewater Triangle' in Massachusetts is the focal point of much discussion when talking about ritualistic murder and occult activity. The forest has been the site of quite a few odd murders and there are rumours' of Satanic Cults using the woods to perform their rituals. Reports of strange occurrences, dead pets, and of course murder all abound when looking into Freetown.

In the 1970's a teenage girl called Mary Arruda was kidnapped, taken deep within the forest, tied to a tree, tortured, and left for dead. Another man was found badly beaten there and yet another was stabbed multiple times but managed to stumble to safety. Both men luckily survived their ordeals, and both claimed that it was Satanists that had attacked them. In 1972 in Springfield New Jersey, Jeanette DePalma disappeared. Her body was later found in the woods surrounded by what police though looked to be the outline of a coffin made around her made by an odd array of leaves, sticks, and logs. The police believe that the murder was ritualistic in origin. Dead pets are also frequently found in these same woods and reporters who tried to cover the case and its possible Satanic ties said that the locals appeared scared and were refusing to give up any information that they might have. In fact, the local library said so many books on the Occult were being stolen they had to be kept in a locked cabinet. These woods are said to be haunted with reports of disembodied voices, shadow figures, and even cryptids frequently being made[220].

All over the world we have reports of odd occurrences and suspected Occult Practices within the Woods and Forests. Here in the UK, Epping Forest in Essex is full of tales of suspected occult activity. Its vast dense topography makes it an ideal location for secrecy as well as easy to get rid of unwanted bodies. We have the infamous 'Babes in the Wood' story which took place in Waltham Forest just on the edge of Epping. Two children went missing in the local area only for their bodies to turn up 3 months later. There is a lot of mystery surrounding the finding of the bodies. A reporter, Paul Grant who was writing for a UFO website at the time found himself there whilst investigating the reported lights and UFO activity that had taken place there around the same time the bodies were discovered. He said that the investigation was most bizarre. The police on site were plan clothed, the army was there taking samples and doing investigative work, the families had been

---

[220] Young, "Hunted in The Woods".

told not to speak to anyone and there was a press blackout. Grant thought that the murders were UFO related but many in the area thought that the murders were ritualistic in nature and that the children had been murdered as part of an occult ritual. A known paedophile Ronald Jebsen, confessed to the crime some 30 years later, although many suspect that he had no part in it, taking the blame for killings for benefits unknown.

In 1991 an entire family was arrested for occult practices within Epping Forest, they were arrested after the, then 10-year-old daughter confessed to her grandmother what had been happening, involving the ritual sexual abuse of the children of the families involved and the apparent murder and sacrifice of animals and even babies according to the 10-year-old child. The family was convicted on the abuse charges, but I couldn't find out whether there was any credibility given to the murder charges as the story went cold after the initial arrests[221].

Ritual and Occult Magick has been practiced for thousands of years but had a revival in the 19th century. In trying to research Ritual Magick I found the volume of information so vast and wide-ranging that it was quite difficult to summarize but it seems to fall into two subsets. Natural or sympathetic magick which covers topics such as astrology, alchemy, chemistry, numerology, and botany. On the flip side, we have ceremonial Magick which appears to be the more negative dark side of Magick covering various forms of witchcraft, blood magick, and necromancy. Certainly, there has always been a link between spiritualism, the occult, and magick. Mediums have been used to channel not only the spirits of the dead but entities that were never human, demons and interdimensional beings, even attempting to contact Extraterrestrials. Certainly, as we know Crowley spent much time trying to contact what he considered 'ultra-terrestrials' culminating in his contact with 'Aiwass' his Egyptian messenger of the Gods. Aiwass was not the only entity that Crowley claimed to have made contact with as he also claimed to have made contact with a 'Grey' extraterrestrial whom he called 'Lam'[222].

Occult magick had a resurgence when Éliphas Lévi, occultist and author wrote many successful books about Magick, Alchemy, and Occult practices. Around this time the Spiritualist movement was in full swing on both sides of the Atlantic, with many people being interested and taking part in many Spiritual practices such as seances and mediumship garnering more interest in the occult and the paranormal. At around the same time, the Hermetic Order of the Golden Dawn was founded by three Freemasons, William

221 - Girl tells court of sacrifices in Epping Forest – Article published on Herald Scotland.com.

Wynn Westcott, Samuel Liddell Mathers, and William Robert Woodman. This order was created in 1888, its main purpose being the study and practice of the Occult. The most infamous member of the Hermetic order of the Golden Dawn was Aleister Crowley[223].

Crowley was renowned for being an Occultist who wrote his treatise on Magick creating his system of occult practice. Crowleys' infamy grew due to his reputation for heavy drug use and borderline sadistic sexual practices whilst conducting his rituals. The Golden Order took umbrage with his scandalous practices and growing popularity and refused him entry into the higher echelons of the hierarchy causing a bitter Crowley to leave. Later Crowley would go on to create his own religion called Thelema. Crowley said that during one 'altered state' meditation session he made contact with an entity called Aiwass. Aiwass, Crowley claimed was a messenger of the Egyptian God Horus. As a result of his communications with Aiwass, Crowly was able to come up with the principles of his religion Thelema, which was based on the principal *'Do what thou wilt shall be the whole of the Law. Love is the law, love under will.'* The theology of Thelema postulates that all manifested existence arises from the interaction of two cosmic principles: the Space-Time Continuum; and the Principle of Life and Wisdom. The interplay of these Principles gives rise to the Principle of Consciousness which governs existence. In the Book of the Law, the divine Principles are personified by a trinity of ancient Egyptian Divinities: Nuit, the Goddess of Infinite Space; Hadit, the Winged Serpent of Light; and Ra-Hoor-Khuit (Horus) the Solar, Hawk-Headed Lord of the Cosmos[224] [225]. In his, *The Book of* Law, are contained within certain codes and ciphers dictated to Crowley by Aiwass.

There is no evidence to suggest that Crowley or the Hermetic Order were linked to any form of human sacrifice, and I believe any such practice happening today is most likely confined to small pockets of Cult activity. It does appear that the main focus of this ritualistic behaviour is to summon something from another realm, be it alien, interdimensional being, or demonic in origin. In the case of the alleged activity in Kentucky and the rituals performed to call forth the Green Man, I can only assume that there is some entity that they have a plan to summon that which they believe to be something akin to the archetype that we've been discussing. Something from another dimension, something that's lived in the Underworld, something that's looked into the face of death. Knowledge is the greatest of all power, to have knowledge of things greater than us, to know the mechanisms of how

---

[223] The Last Podcast on the Left Podcast – Episodes 442,443 and 444 on Aleister Crowley.

[224] Hermetic Order of the Golden Dawn – Published on New World Encyclopedia.

[225] Theology and Essential Tenants of Thelema

the other dimensions work, to see beyond the veil. Certainly, in the Hellier documentary series, they reference occult rituals being performed to call forth extraterrestrials as detailed in Greenfield's book *The Secret Cipher of the Ufonauts*.

Certainly, there is a good argument in what we have outlined here to posit that the Green Man is interdimensional or ultra-terrestrial in origin, certainly the prototype if you will for the Deities that we've discussed so far. He is viewed by humanity as 'otherworldly', he is seen to 'die' to go to some otherworld realm but has the power to reappear, to exit this 'other' place, and remain unharmed. The mythology surrounding his narrative does seem to support that his origin is not of this plane of existence. Are there people out there, trying to call him forth, trying to wake him from his slumber, and for what end?

The Book of Giants

In my investigation of the Green Man mythology, I did stumble across another more biblical origin theory which I thought was of great interest, if you will indulge my more theological speculations. As we know the standard bible is made up of 66 books. However, many more books were written but, for reasons we can only speculate about, not included in the final edit. Indeed, about 500 books were written in total which leaves us with about 434 texts that were never included. Indeed, many texts were considered lost, missing, or hidden, however, in 1946 one of the greatest discoveries was made deep within the caves of Qumran in the Judaean desert. Here a Bedouin shepherd stumbled across jars containing lost scrolls deep within the caves whilst looking for a lost animal. These lost texts are often referred to as The Dead Sea Scrolls.

It's within these missing texts, specifically the Book of Giants that I find the information which caught my attention. The book of Giants is thought to be a part of or based on the Book of Enoch as it references Enoch himself multiple times, placing the book within the remit of the 'Enochian' Texts. Interestingly, talking about Enoch and the Enochian language it has been speculated that Enochian is the language of the stars, of the extraterrestrials who settled here long ago. According to George C. Andrews in his book *Extraterrestrial Friends and Foes,* he states *"Enochian is the Linga Franka of the space races, much as Swahili was the lingua franca of the many African languages. Enochian is the correct time-tested traditional way for Earthlings to communicate with Extraterrestrials".* How interesting that the book of Enoch talks about Giants, Watchers, and Nephilim and its language is posited to be of extraterrestrial origin.

I am sure many of you are familiar with the story of the Fallen Angels. According to the bible, there was a group of Angels who saw the daughters of Men and desired them *'the sons of God saw that the daughters of men were beautiful, and they took as wives whomever they chose'* [Genesis 6:2]

These Angels, 200 in total, made a pact between themselves to come to earth and take wives from these women and with that act produce offspring. *"Let us swear an oath, and all bind ourselves by mutual curses so we will not abandon this plant but do this thing"* [Genesis 6:5]. I've also seen references to these fallen Angels as being The Watchers. I've come across references to 'The watchers' in many different mediums, whether its religion, mythology, alien, or fairy folklore, you can find 'The Watchers'. This 'falling of the Angels' occurred antediluvian (pre-flood) era, in an act which greatly angered God. Not because of the lust that the Angels bore towards women, but more than this, he was angered that the Angels would breed with these women effectively altering human DNA, the building blocks of life which God himself had created. It is said that it was the motive of these Angels to corrupt and pervert the genetic code of humans. It was this blasphemy that he could not abide by and this tampering with his genetic coding, his book of life which triggered his need for the great 'reset' otherwise known as 'The Great Flood'.

Within many texts specifically those of the Dead Seas Scrolls we can find more information about the reasoning for the great flood. Within texts which were either left out of or trimmed down for the bible, there are fragments of information. In several texts, there are references to men being described as trees or likened to trees. Now, the bible is nothing if not metaphorical but what if, rather than this being poetic license, what is there was a race of Men who were tree-like in their appearance, like the Ent-like creature witnessed in Yorkshire, England reported in the earlier chapter (The Verdant One), a literal tree man? Mythology referencing such 'tree men' has always existed but what if there is some grain of truth to that description?

In the Book of Giants, a series of fragments from the Dead Sea Scrolls, reference the corruption of the Earth, specifically the perversion of human DNA through crossbreeding with a human woman. These offspring are known as the Nephilim, but I've also seen them (as well as their Fathers) referred to as The Watchers[225]. A cross breed of human women and the celestial Angels. These Nephilim were described as Giants, much bigger in

---

[225] Joseph Lumpkin - The Book of Giants: The Watchers, Nephilim, and The Book of Enoch (Kindle edition 2014).

stature than mankind. However, we should bear in mind that pre-flood, humans were thought to be much bigger, whilst there is not much in the Christian bible about the dimensions of the average human, we do know that they lived incredibly long lives. Enoch is said to have died at 365 years old, his son methuselah died at 969, Methuselah's son Lamech lived to 777 and finally, Lamech's son Noah lived to be 950. We do, however, have other religious texts which do give us some indication of height. In the Quran, Adam is described as being 60 cubits tall, which in our modern measurements would be nearer to 90 ft or 30 meters tall. Certainly, it would appear that humans were much larger than we are now and could live for hundreds of years. So, the thought of women giving birth to Giants takes on new meaning when we realize that these women were not like me today, standing at 5"2 but Amazonian beings, monstrous in size living for hundreds of years. It is said that as punishment for our sins, post-flood, God decided to shorten our lifespan to approximately 120 years. *'Then the LORD said, "My Spirit shall not strive with man forever, because he also is flesh; nevertheless his days shall be one hundred and twenty years."* [Gen. 6:3] This ever-decreasing size of mankind is a result of shortening lifespans, gestation periods, and changes to our environment. Most likely a preventative method on God's part to prevent a possible repeat of what had come before.

Now, of course, this is all speculation and interpretation, I am certainly not positing that the above is a fact, but nevertheless, it is rather interesting. I especially picked up on the various descriptions of these Nephilim, being figuratively described as 'Trees'. Now whether this is due to their enormous height or whether the resemblance is more literal I do not know. The Book of Enoch references the nightmares of several specific Nephilim before the great Flood. One half-breed Giant called Mahway describes a nightmare he had to his brethren. He tells of how he sees a tablet inscribed with many names, the tablet is then submerged in water, and as the tablet emerges from the water only three names remain (another triad). It is thought that these three names may have been Noah and his sons.

Another giant hybrid Ohya has also had a similar nightmare "Then Ohya said to him *'I have been forced to have a dream...the sleep of my eyes vanished so that I could see a vision. [Now I know that on the field of battle we cannot win]... 'I saw a tree uprooted except for three of its roots. While I was as it were watching [some beings] moved all the roots into this garden but not the three"*. In Enoch we have reference to visions wherein trees are upended and destroyed, why the focus on trees and their destruction? Could the trees be symbolic of something else? Someone else? There is another slightly different version of this dream where Oyha says that he dreamt a gardener was watering trees, and he saw 200 of these trees standing in a field, he then proceeds to see these 200 trees uprooted and destroyed by both fire and flood. This dream seems to be a metaphor for the 200 fallen angels and their impending destruction[226].

As mentioned before the Nephilim have been described as Trees previously, in chapter 31 of Ezekiel the Pharoah King of Egypt is compared to an earlier King. This earlier King was the Nephilim King, referred to as 'The Assyrian' or 'The Cedar King' who ruled the antediluvian world and held domain over the corrupted Earth. It is said that he even conquered The Garden of Eden, ruling the Earth from there, making it his Kingdom[227]. Interesting that of all the places he could rule from, he chose to make a garden his home. We can certainly make parallels between the Green Man's woodland retreat, Virbius' sacred grove at Nemi, and the Nephilim Kings' withdrawal to the Garden of Eden.

In Amos 2, the Amorites a race of people ruled by the Nephilim Kings Og and Sihon (sons of the giant Oyha mentioned previously) are compared to Cedar Trees…" *Yet it was I who destroyed the Amorite before them, whose height was like the height of the cedars, and he was as strong as the oaks; yet I destroyed his fruit above and his roots beneath. Also it was I who brought you up from the land of Egypt, and led you forty years through the wilderness, to possess the land of the Amorite"* (Amos 2: 9–10).

While the Amorites are mentioned in the same contexts as other giants a few times, they are specifically described as giants in the Minor Prophets.
Back to Ezekiel, who continues *"behold, the Assyrian was a Cedar in Lebanon with fair branches, and with a shadowing shroud, and high stature […] his height exalted above all the trees of the field, and his boughs were multiplied […] under his shadow dwelt all the great nations"* [Ezekiel 31: 3-6]

Chapter 31 continues *"The Cedars in the Garden of God"* i.e the other Nephilim residing with him within the Garden of Eden *"could not control him and could not hide him so he was cut down"*. *"Thus saith the Lord; In the day when he [Assyrian King] went to the grave I caused a mourning: I covered the deep for him and restrained the floods thereof, and the great waters were stayed: and I caused Lebanon to mourn for his, and all the trees of the field fainted for him"* [Ezekiel 31:15]. Who was this great King, who God himself felt such fondness for that he would let the waters of the great flood be restrained to let the people mourn his loss? Who are the 'Trees in

---

[226] Sage of Quay Radio YouTube Channel - Lost History of Earth Volume 2:1 - #EWARANON (Oct 2021.
[227] Ibid.

the field" who are referred to multiple times? Are they the other Nephilim?

When looking into to Great Flood, as it is one Universal narrative, I was interested to see the number of references to Trees and their destruction within it. What was also of interest to me given what we've already been discussing is the reference to the zoomorphic effects of the breeding Nephilim. As Angels bred with humans, so it is said that the Nephilim were monstrous bloodthirsty beings that corrupted everything, even the animals on the land and the animals of the sea. It is said that as well as defiling humans, they also raped and abused the animals of the earth creating atrocious abominations. This corruption of the DNA created other odd half breeds such as the Babylonian 'Fishmen' and the Dagon Fish God of the ancient Assyrians. This zoomorphic addition is interesting as it now ties the Nephilim into the narrative of ancient mythology with them possibly being the creator of the half-human half-animals seen depicted throughout Mythology. The Saytr that raised Dionysus, the sea nymph in Nemi, Horus the half-bird son of Osiris, the fauns, centaurs, and Minotaurs of myth and legend. Could the origin of all of these creatures be a result of the corrupt DNA?

Now certainly stories still exist post-flood depicting 'Giants' and odd 'Cryptid' creatures. We have the stories of Gilgamesh, the King of Uruk who is considered to be a 'Giant' and the hero of Mesopotamian mythology. Made famous by being the 'hero' of the epic poem The Epic of Gilgamesh, written in Akkadian during the late 2nd millennium BC. We have Goliath, who was a philistine giant, famously slain by David in the book of Samuel and Jack the Giant Slayer from Arthurian legend. The stories of zoomorphic creatures persist even to this day with people claiming to have borne witness to a plethora of cryptids and even half-man, half-animal creatures. According to some legends, some giants did indeed survive the great deluge. Og, the giant was found by Noah clinging to the Ark, Noah showed mercy, and Og was saved. Or some versions say that Og was so tall that the floods only reached his ankles. However, the giants survived, it makes narrative sense that the deluge didn't wipe them all out otherwise we couldn't account for the post-flood stories in which 'giant' men and 'beasts' feature[228].

Not all the children of the angels were said to be bloodthirsty monsters, some were simply spirits considered in biblical terms to be 'demon' creatures that were never incarnate, and then there were those said to great men of renown.

---

[228] Joseph Lumpkin - The Book of Giants: The Watchers, Nephilim, and The Book of Enoch (Kindle edition).

"There were Giants in the earth in those days; and also after that, when the sons of God came in unto the daughters of men, and they bore children to them, the same became mighty men which were old, men of renown"

Interestingly, in some ancient texts, it is said that the offspring of the Sumerians with the local native women were called The Anunnaki, which translates as Offspring of the Prince. The Anunnaki were noted to be giants, much larger than the average man. Could the biblical giants or Nephilim be this same Annunaki? Could it be that the Oannes of ancient Sumeria that we've looked at also be the Annunaki? The same fallen angels referenced in the Bible? Great Men of Renown like Dagon and The Assyrian King, descended to earth, gifting us knowledge and telling us the secrets of the celestials, an act they would be punished severely for.

The mythology of Giants in the British Isles has persisted for thousands of years. It was said that our ancestors were ruled over by Giant Kings and that the bloodline of these giants still runs through the 'ruling elite' and higher echelons of British society. Giants are also described by Geoffrey of Monmouth as the original inhabitants of Britain, who were overwhelmed by human settlers. We have the 'Glastonbury Giant' whose skeletal remains were found in the 12th Century after King Henry II heard that the body of King Arthur was buried in that location. It was said that Arthur was buried beneath the ground between two pyramids in Glastonbury. So here, between two ancient pyramid-shaped pillars said to be engraved with strange markings and symbols, workers set to work digging down to a depth of seven feet where they found a leaden cross with the inscription: *HIC JACET SEPULTUS INCLYTUS REX ARTURUS IN INSULA AVALLONI.* This translates as "Here lies buried the renowned King Arthur in the Isle of Avalon." They continued to dig deeper until they came across a coffin hollowed out of a large oak tree (similar to Osiris and the tree at Byblus) containing two bodies, one a large male measuring nine feet tall, the other body was that of an average size female. It was said that the skull of the male was huge, the eye sockets so large that the male workers could fit their clenched fists easily through them. It's said that the remains were then moved by royal decree to the Abbey that was situated there and there remained interred for the next century. These bones were then moved but the location remains unknown[229].

---

[229] The Higherside Chats YouTube channel - Hugh Newman & Jim Vieira | Giants of Ancient Britain, Geomancy, & Megalithic Sites.

[230] The Glastonbury Giant: Who Did the Mystery Bones of A Nine Foot Skeleton Belong To? – Article by P Robinson published on Ancient Origins.net.

I am unsure if Arthur was ever referred to as being taller than the average man or even being referred to as a giant. I've tried trawling through some of my Arthurian mythology as I hadn't come across that comparison before. The nearest I've come across is references to Arthur as being or belonging to a mythical land one of magical animals, giants, and other wonderful creatures located in the wild parts of the landscape. It is said that the cross itself, bearing the name of Arthur could well have been a hoax concocted by monks at the nearby Benedictine Abbey, in an attempt to reap fame upon the abbey and hopefully secure noble benefactors who would want to support and protect the sacred resting place one of England's greatest ever legends[230].

Despite the uncertainty surrounding the authenticity of the cross and whether the bones found were indeed those of Arthur and the beautiful Guinevere, the actual finding of a giant figure was verified. Respected historian Giraldus Cambrensis personally examined the massive bones in 1194 and he pronounced them genuine. Then hundreds of years later, in 1962-63, archaeologist Dr. Ralegh Radford studied the ancient giant remains following additional excavations of the site and '*confirmed that a prominent personage had indeed been buried there at the period in question.*'

Indeed, we knew that the bones of Giants of similar size or larger have been excavated all over the world. There have even been reports of giant humanoids spotted as recently as the Afghan War with soldiers reportedly having a 'show down' with a red-headed giant within the caves of Afghanistan. Giants are not mythological creatures of folklore and legend but real humanoids which existed thousands of years ago. They may have been our ancestors, or they may have been something else, either way, they shaped our history and their impact on our mythology remains strong today.

Conclusion

I started this book with one clear question, who is the Green Man? The answer, however, is not at all as clear as the question. Indeed, I have more questions now that when I started. It is my interpretation of the information that I've collated that The Green Man is an aspect of the Archetype. As reviewed in our earlier chapters religion and mythology revolve around trilogies. The Father, The Son, The holy Ghost. We see trinities across all religions and in a lot of mythologies. We have ancient Sumeria and its three regions, each deity ruling over one region, Anu the sky, Enlil the Earth, and

Ea the Seas, the three coming together to create 'Life' and being known as the Triad of Gods. The Greeks mirrored this with Zeus of the Sky, Poseidon of the Sea, and Hades God of the Underworld. The Egyptians had similarities with Osiris, Isis, and Horus, Christianity, and Hinduism also share this belief in a Trinity.

Three within numerology is significant and considered by the Ancients as a 'mystical number'. Pythagoras considered it the perfect number. It is associated with knowledge, peace, wisdom, and harmony. Alchemists considered the 'Trinity' as the Tria Prima, the three Primes[230]. These three primes make up the triangle, in which two components come together to produce a third and new component. Paracelsus held the belief that all life consisted of three Primes, for example, the Psyche consists of the Superego, Ego, and Id, and the Existential World is made up of the Spiritual, Mental, and Physical realms. Humans themselves are made up of the body, mind, and Soul.

Mythology is full of examples of the Triad. Cerberus the three-headed dog of Greek mythology, can see past present, and future with each head mirroring the Norse 'The Norns' Goddesses. Three sisters who could also see prophetically, garnering themselves the title 'The Destinies'. For the Greeks, Destiny was controlled by the Three Fates, Clotho who spun the thread of fate, Lachesis who dispensed it, and finally Atropos cut it. How long or short the thread determined the length of the individual's life. Perseus encountered the three witches who all shared one eye and instructed him on how to dispatch the Medusa. Hecate, the three-faced goddess, the goddess of earth, fertility but also of the moon, and witchcraft. The power of three features strongly within Wicca, made famous by the Halliwell sisters in the hit TV show 'Charmed'.

For the Celts, their Gods and Goddesses appear in the Three Worlds, the Stellar World which consists of the constellations, the Solar World which consists of the Sun and Planets, and finally the Lunar World which consists of the Moon and the Earth[231]. Celtic Goddesses are often shown in triple form, either as the Maiden, the Mother, or the Old Crone. The Irish goddess of war and death had three distinctive aspects: Macha, Badhbh, and Morrigu, all unified in one supernatural being. Cernunnos is shown in triplicate on his statue at Atun, Saône-et-Loire, as the father, the son, and the spirit (nature's lifeforce).

---

[231] The Three Primes of Alchemy – Article by Anne Marie Helmenstine, Ph.D published on Thoughtsco.com.

Quest stories are intrinsic to Irish Mythology and in many of these quest tales, there are three opponents, three tasks, or three wishes. Such as in the story of Bricriu's Feast we read about earlier involving our hero Cú Chulainn, who coincidently had his hair tied in triple braids. In early Gaulish and British folklore the mysterious Genius Cucullatus – Hooded Spirit – appeared as a triadic entity concerned with fertility, well-being, and abundance. This triplication is prevalent in Northern Europe, specifically Germany, Gaul, and Britain. Triple-headed deities appear on stonework in such places as Corleck, County Cavan, and on Boa Island, County Fermanagh as well as in the southern reaches of Scotland[232].

Many God and Goddesses have triple forms, one humanoid, one animal (or multiple animals), and one as pure energy or consciousness. Although triplism among humanoid deities usually took the form of three heads or faces, animal gods took on an additional appendage, usually a horn or tusk. Within many of the bull-worshipping cults, a third horn was added to the animal's forehead and probably gave it greater supernatural significance. It might also have symbolized the phallus to combine strength, aggression, and sexual prowess. Figurines of bulls and boars have been found at several grave sites, possibly there to ensure the buried chieftain's continued status in the next world. Most of the triple-horned bull bronzes and clay figures have been found in Gaul although a number have also appeared in Britain. A figurine found at Maiden Castle in Dorset shows the heads of three female deities on its back. It might have been a representation of two Romano-Celtic sculptures, from Paris and Trier, dedicated to the god Mercury, known as Tarvustrigarnus – The Bull with Three Cranes, a stylized bull with three wading birds. Horse cults – particularly those depicted at the shrines dedicated to the goddess Epona – displayed some triplism. In some representations, a three-faced goddess was shown astride a rampaging stallion, in others, a human-looking female figure straddled three horses. The latter may simply be a Roman addition to the cult of the horse.[233]

This aspect of Three as we discovered permeates all religion and mythology and it is these aspects that I believe give us our Green Man. He is simply the 'Father' aspect of our Archetype triad. We have the horned God who represents the Son, fertile and virile, then we have the Spirit, nature itself and

---

[232] Stewart, "Celtic Gods, Celtic Goddess ".

233 Triplism – Article published on Irelands Eye.com.

finally, we have the Father, the old man, wise and knowledgeable retired to his woodland home to live the rest of his days in quiet contemplation. The Green Man is part of the greater narrative, the story of the Hero, the cycles of nature, and even death itself. As in John 5:7 *"For there are three that bear witness in heaven: The Father, the Word, and the Holy Spirit; and these three are one"*.

My search to find out who The Green Man is has taken me down many roads, some religious, some steeped in fact, and others more mythological. It has been a wonderful and eye-opening journey, one which has enlightened me and filled me with awe and wonder at the richness of our history, our mythology, and of who we are as humans, and what we are capable of knowing and becoming. We are truly celestial beings with ancestors so great, so mysterious and so fantastical that we, unfortunately, are only able to know them as myth.

The End

I hope that you enjoyed this book and found the information contained within thought provoking. If you would like to contact me with your own stories which touch on any of the topics discussed I would love to hear from you, if I receive enough experiences I would like to publish a further book exploring peoples real life experiences with these unexplainable phenomena. Please email me at TheGreenMan707@outlook.com

REFERENCES AND SOURCES

Modern Media and Hellier

1- David Paulides 'Missing 411 – The Hunted' (Published 2019)
2- Where Did the Road Go Radio Show - YouTube (David Paulides on Missing 411 Hunters Part 1 August 13, 2016) Link - https://www.youtube.com/watch?v=yDLJtKWVzk0
3- David Maccabee's investigation of his wife's photograph. http://www.brumac.mysite.com/JANs_Phenomenon/JANs_Phenomenon.htm
4- Hellier (TV \Mini |Series) – Planet Weird (aired January 2019) Return of the Kentucky Goblins: New Leads in a Case of Strange Creatures, Crashed UFOs, and the Men in Black article published on WeekinWeird.com 10/03/2015, link below: - http://weekinweird.com/2015/10/03/return-of-the-kentucky-goblins-new-leads-in-a-case-of-strange-creatures-crashed-ufos-and-the-men-in-black/
5- Post on Reddit by Solaris716 'The Shaver Mystery' https://www.reddit.com/r/hellier/comments/emfuro/the_shaver_mystery/
6- The Higher Side Chats Podcast - Hugh Newman & Jim Vieira | Giants of Ancient Britain, Geomancy, & Megalithic Sites (published May 2022) https://www.youtube.com/watch?v=rQqSVOHt07g

The Green Man Origins

7- William Anderson – The Green Man, The Archetype of our Oneness with the Earth (1990)
8- Eric Edwards Collected Works – Wordpress website, link below https://ericwedwards.wordpress.com/?s=green+man
9- The Green Man in Church Architecture (Article by Lady Raglan in Folklore Vol.L published 1939 – pg 45)
10- Carter ROM & HM – The Foliate Head in England – Folklore Society 1967
11- Katherine Basford - The Green Man (First published by Boydell 1978)

The Man with Many Names

12- The Modern Fairy Sighting Podcast – presenter Jo Hickey-Hall (Episode 4 Mysterious Illuminations)

13- Ancient Literature website, Epic of Gilgamesh – Epic Poem Summary – Other Ancient Civilizations – Classical Literature https://www.ancient-literature.com/other_gilgamesh.html

14- Rachel Bromwich - Trioedd Ynys Prydein: The Triads of the Island of Britain. University Of Wales Press (2006)

15- Katharine M. Briggs – The Vanishing People – (1978 – B.T. Batsford Ltd. London)

16- Fran and Geoff Doel – The Green Man In Britain (2001) Ebook Edition (2013)

17- As 15 above

18- The Ring of Kerry website – Puck Fair https://www.theringofkerry.com/puck-fair

Why is the Green Man – Green?

19- Robbins Library Digital Projects - Camelot Project - Sir Gawain and the Green Knight: A Middle-English Arthurian Romance - Sir Gawain and the Green Knight (Jessie Weston – translation) https://d.lib.rochester.edu/camelot/text/weston-sir-gawain-and-the-green-knight

20- Fran and Geoff Doel – The Green Man In Britain (2001) Ebook Edition (2013)

21- John Clark – "Small, Vulnerable Ets: The Green Children of Woolpit", Science Fiction Studies (2006)

22- Diane Purkiss – Troublesome Things; A history of Fairies and Fairy Stories (2000 Penguin)

23- As 22 above

Little Green Men

24- Wikipedia – Little Green Men https://en.wikipedia.org/wiki/Little_green_men#cite_note-10

25- Will the Little Green Men Of Kelly, Kentucky, Return to Watch The Solar Eclipse? Article by Terena Bell on Ozy.com https://www.ozy.com/true-and-stories/will-the-little-green-men-of-kelly-kentucky-return-to-watch-the-solar-eclipse/78627/

26- How the 'Little Green Men' Phenomenon Began on a Kentucky Farm article on History.com by Volker Janssen published Jan 2020.
https://www.history.com/news/little-green-men-origins-aliens-hopkinsville-kelly
Return of the Kentucky Goblins: New Leads in a Case of Strange Creatures, Crashed UFOs, and the Men in Black article by Greg Newkirk published on WeekinWeird.com
http://weekinweird.com/2015/10/03/return-of-the-kentucky-goblins-new-leads-in-a-case-of-strange-creatures-crashed-ufos-and-the-men-in-black/

Fairy Encounters

27- Janet Bord – Fairies Real Encounters with Little People (1997 by Michael O'Mara Books Limited)
28- Walter Wenz - The Fairy Faith in Celtic Countries (2001 Blackmask Online edition)
29- Katharine M. Briggs – The Vanishing People – (1978 – B.T. Batsford Ltd. London)
30- Janet Bord – Fairies Real Encounters with Little People (1997 by Michael O'Mara Books Limited)
31- As 30 above
32- Diane Purkiss – Troublesome Things; A history of Fairies and Fairy Stories (2000 Penguin)
33- As 32 above
34- As 32 above
35- Allen Greenfield – The Complete Secret Cipher of the Ufonauts (2016)
36- Diane Purkiss – Troublesome Things; A history of Fairies and Fairy Stories (2000 Penguin)
37- Sir Malcolm Scott's letters on Demonology and Witchcraft (1884)
38- https://link.springer.com/chapter/10.1007/978-1-137-06954-2_3?noAccess=true
Ann W. Astell - The Virgin Mary and the "Voices" of Joan of Arc (2003) excerpt on Springer.com
39- Diane Purkiss – Troublesome Things; A history of Fairies and Fairy Stories (2000 Penguin)
40- Necronomipod - Podcast Episode titled 'Mothman Part 1' aired 3 February 2019 by Cool Down Media.

41- Janet Bord – Fairies Real Encounters with Little People (1997 by Michael O'Mara Books Limited)
42- Diane Purkiss – Troublesome Things; A history of Fairies and Fairy Stories (2000 Penguin)
43- Janet Bord – Fairies Real Encounters with Little People (1997 by Michael O'Mara Books Limited)
44- Jacque Vallee – Passport to Magonia (Edition – 2014)
45- Walter Wentz - The Fairy–Faith in Celtic Countries (2001 Blackmask Online)
46- Ahmad Jamaludin 'strange Encounters in Lumut' article published October 1981 in Malaysian UFO Bulletin, no. 3.
47- Jacque Vallee – Passport to Magonia (Edition - 2014)

Caves Systems

48- Faery Mounds – on Faerypool.com
http://www.faerypool.com/faery_mounds/
49- Janet Bord – Fairies Real Encounters with Little People (1997 by Michael O'Mara Books Limited)
50- Stranger things: the mystery of the lost children of Hal Saflieni Hypogeum article by Melanie Drury posted on GuideMeMalta.com April 2021.
https://www.guidememalta.com/en/stranger-things-the-mystery-of-the-lost-children-of-hal-saflieni-hypogeum
51- Debunking Urban Legends – The Hypogeum Myths by Warren Bugeja published on Heritage Malta.mt
https://heritagemalta.org/debunking-urban-legends-the-hypogeum-myths/
52- 10 Modern Day Sightings of Reptilian Humanoids by Marcus Lowth published on Listverse.com May 2016
https://listverse.com/2016/05/05/10-modern-day-sightings-of-reptilian-humanoids/
Gregor's experience at Obertrau, Austria 2011 published on Soul Guidance.com
http://www.soul-guidance.com/houseofthesun/ET/reptilians/obertraun.html
53- Devil Creature of Son Doong Cave (photograph) published on Cryptidz Fandom.com
https://cryptidz.fandom.com/wiki/Devil_Creature_of_Son_Doong_Cave

54- Project Red Book published on Angelfire.com
https://www.angelfire.com/ut/branton/redbook1.html

55- Stephen Young – Hunted in The Woods (2015)

56- Where did the Road Go Radio – David Paulides - Missing 411
Interview - 9-22-13 (aired on YouTube 29/09/2013)
https://www.youtube.com/watch?v=sAh02EB7SNI&t=4420s

57- Stephen Young – Hunted in The Woods (2015)

58- As 57 above

59- As 57 above

60- Haunting Ghost Nederland YouTube Channel – Episode titled
S10 E 2 Finding bigfoot in the Netherlands *(creature Holland)*
https://www.youtube.com/watch?v=x-25jRjlrOw

61- Podcasts: -
Expanded Perspectives – The Mysterious Dulce Base (aired 26
Sept 2016)
Hysteria 51 – Episode 121 – Dulce Underground Base: Alien Base
or Absolute BS?
Extraterrestrial – A Parcast Podcast – Episodes 11 & 12 (Dulce
Base P.1: Tin Foil Car and Pt.2 Underground War) aired in April
2019.

62- The Last Podcast on the Left – Episode 187 (aired 12 Aug 2015)
and Episode 188 (aired 19 Aug 2015)

A Fairy Problem – Missing 411

63- Canam Missing Project YouTube Channel - David Paulides
Presents The Stacy Arras Case from Yosemite National Park
https://www.youtube.com/watch?v=uu4okjPUROc

64- Missing Persons Mysteries YouTube Channel - Missing Hikers
who were Found Years Later!
https://www.youtube.com/watch?v=X_OXsGmJREQ

65- David Paulides – Missing 411 Western United States and
California (2012)

66- Pseudiom YouTube Channel - The Impossible Disappearance Of
David Lang | Historia Ephemera – October 2015
https://www.youtube.com/watch?v=drVAv7w-w4A
1880, September 23: The Mystery of David Lang – article posted
on Anomalyinfo.com
http://anomalyinfo.com/Stories/1880-september-23-mystery-
david-lang

67- Disappearances (Paranormal) – Article on Encyclopedia.com
https://www.encyclopedia.com/science/encyclopedias-almanacs-transcripts-and-maps/disappearances-paranormal
Where Did The Road Go Radio YouTube Channel - David Paulides - Missing 411 Interview - 9-22-13
https://www.youtube.com/watch?v=sAh02EB7SNI&list=PLpVjR_HCd9MwCLBOcYWWaTX5qFglWQKss&index=1

68- The unexplained disappearance and death of Mitchell Dale Stehling in Mesa Verde National Park – Article published on Strange Outdoors.com – March 2020.
https://www.strangeoutdoors.com/mysterious-stories-blog/2020/3/15/mitchell-dale-stehling

69- As 68 above

70- A Civilization's Home in the Cliffs – Article published on Visit MesaVerde.com
https://www.visitmesaverde.com/discover/cliff-dwellings/

71- Steph Young – Stalked in The Woods: True Stories of Unexplained Disappearances and Strange Encounters in the Woods (2016)

72- In Iceland, 'respect the elves – or else' – Article by Oliver Wainwright published on The Guardian.com
https://www.theguardian.com/artanddesign/2015/mar/25/iceland-construction-respect-elves-or-else

73- Just Icelandic YouTube Channel – Episode title - True Stories of Elves and Hidden People in Iceland
https://www.youtube.com/watch?v=vO7EB0xnib4

74- American Institute of Physics -- Inside Science News Service. "The secret of a tiger's roar." ScienceDaily. ScienceDaily, 29 December 2000.
https://www.sciencedaily.com/releases/2000/12/001201152406.htm

75- Sasquatch Chronicles YouTube Channel – Episode 57 - Missing people and bigfoot encounters.
https://www.youtube.com/watch?v=hQAyumuc6SQ

76- Marchal S, Bregeras O, Puaux D, Gervais R, Ferry B (2016) Rigorous Training of Dogs Leads to High Accuracy in Human Scent Matching-To-Sample Performance. PLoS ONE 11(2): e0146963. https://doi.org/10.1371/journal.pone.0146963
https://doi.org/10.1371/journal.pone.0146963

https://lostpetresearch.com/2018/11/how-accurate-are-search-dogs-part-2-scent-discrimination-dogs/

77- Where Did The Road Go Radio YouTube Channel - David Paulides - Missing 411: Hunters Parts 1 and 2 (Repost) August 2016
https://www.youtube.com/watch?v=58TclWbcHcw&t=0s

78- The bizarre death of Charles McCullar in Crater Lake – Article Published on Strange Outdoors.com October 2017
https://www.strangeoutdoors.com/mysterious-stories-blog/2017/10/22/charles-mccullar-strange-disappearances-from-us-national-parks

79- Sasquatch Chronicles YouTube channel - SC EP:57 Missing people and bigfoot encounters – 2 December 2018
https://www.youtube.com/watch?v=hQAyumuc6SQ

80- Canam Missing Project YouTube Channel - James McGrogan - Missing 411 - 29 August 2014
https://www.youtube.com/watch?v=-TlGc4slOMo&t=0s

81- LADBible – How to survive a Plan Crash
https://www.youtube.com/watch?v=Z5lcOMvAvIc

82- Weather Fairies – Article published on The Circle.com
https://www.thecircle.com/uk/magazin/psychics/weather-fairies.do
'Tiddy Mun' – Article published on Telling History.co.uk
https://tellinghistory.co.uk/content/1-%E2%80%98tiddy-mun%E2%80%99

83- 'Up Hill and Down Dale' – Pixie Led in the West Country: A Study of Pixie Tricks – Article published on British Fairies Wordpress.com – 5 July 202
https://britishfairies.wordpress.com/tag/weather/

84- Just Icelandic YouTube Channel - True Stories of Elves and Hidden People in Iceland
https://www.youtube.com/watch?v=yO7EB0xnib4

85- Janet Bord – Fairies Real Encounters with Little People (1997 by Michael O'Mara Books Limited)

86- Strange Berry Picker Disappearances – Top Mysteries YouTube Channel published 19/08/2020
https://www.youtube.com/watch?v=Tlz9-j4QzSM

87- 'One tough bird': Woman, 84, asked for a cold beer and a hot tub when rescuers found her in bush – Article by Aidan Geary on CBC news.

https://www.cbc.ca/news/canada/manitoba/missing-woman-piney-found-1.5229628

88- Walter Wenz - The Fairy Faith in Celtic Countries (2001 Blackmask Online edition)

89- P Narváez - Lore and Language, vol. 06, no. 01 (January 1987) https://collections.mun.ca/digital/collection/lorelang/id/3546

90- Strange Berry Picker Disappearances – Top Mysteries YouTube Channel published 19/08/2020 https://www.youtube.com/watch?v=Tlz9-j4QzSM https://www.newspapers.com/clip/3608049/the-pantagraph/

91- Strange Berry Picker Disappearances – Top Mysteries YouTube Channel published 19/08/2020 https://www.youtube.com/watch?v=Tlz9-j4QzSM Story clipped from The Daily Messenger on Newspapers.com https://www.newspapers.com/clip/26721256/the-daily-messenger/

92- The Eerie Vanishing and Reappearance of Katherine Van Arst – Article by Brent Swancer on Journal.com April 2021. https://journal.com.ph/the-eerie-vanishing-and-reappearance-of-katherine-van-arst/

93- Diarmuid A. MacManus - The Middle Kingdon: The Faerie World of Ireland (1959).

94- Vikash Pradhan YouTube Channel -Abduction: a twist in the tale - Part 1 of 2: https://www.youtube.com/watch?v=JKDAO-OYHvA Part 2 of 2: https://www.youtube.com/watch?v=jTU72hNB_Zs

95- Steph Young – Stalked in The Woods: True Stories of Unexplained Disappearances and Strange Encounters in the Woods (2016)

96- Where Did The Road Go Radio interview with David Paulides – Published on their YouTube Channel on 29 September 2013. https://www.youtube.com/watch?v=sAh02EB7SNI&list=PLpVjR_HCd9MwCLBOcYWWaTX5qFglWQKss

97- As 96 above

98- Post on Reddit.com (The Trap by User RogerDodgeHer) https://www.reddit.com/r/Missing411/comments/4rrxau/the_trap/

99- Post of Reddit.com (My very strange and very frightening hiking experience by User rosetta9)

https://www.reddit.com/r/Missing411/comments/51m23e/my_very_strange_and_very_frightening_hiking/

100- Skeletal remains found in snow boot at ski resort identified – Article published on The Coloradoan.com
https://eu.coloradoan.com/story/news/2016/10/19/skeletal-remains-found-snow-boot-ski-resort-identified/92402922/

101- Mirjam Mencej - Styrian Witches in European Perspective'
https://books.google.co.uk/books?id=mVgBDgAAQBAJ&pg=PA367&lpg=PA367&ots=zUTESlmxFs&redir_esc=y#v=onepage&q&f=false

The Archetype

102- George Stanley Faber B.D - The Origin of Pagan Idolatry (Vol I, II & III) – (London 1816)

103- Jean Bottéro - Religion in Ancient Mesopotamia (2001)

104- As 103 above

105- Allen Greenfield – The Complete Cipher of the Ufonauts (2016 edition)

106- As 105 above

107- 'The Song of The Hoe' – Article published on World History.biz
https://www.worldhistory.biz/ancient-history/71849-the-song-of-the-hoe.html

108- Eric Edwards Wordpress.com - The Green Man Phenomenon and Foliate Heads
https://ericwedwards.wordpress.com/?s=green+man

109- As 108 above

110- Jean Bottéro - Religion in Ancient Mesopotamia (2001)

111- Dumuzid - Wikipedia
https://en.wikipedia.org/wiki/Dumuzid

112- Eric Edwards Wordpress.com - The Green Man Phenomenon and Foliate Heads
www.ericwedwards.wordpress.com

113- Hans Holzer - Witches – True Encounters with Wicca, Wizards, Covens, Cults and Magick -(First published by Black Dog & Leventhal Publishers 2002)

114- Dumuzid - Wikipedia
https://en.wikipedia.org/wiki/Dumuzid

115- Fran and Geoff Doel – The Green Man In Britain (2001) Ebook (2013)

116- Dionysus :: Greek God of fertility and wine – Article on Greek Mythology.com
https://www.greekmythology.com/Other_Gods/Dionysus/dionysus.html

117- William Anderson – The Green Man, The Archetype of our Oneness with the Earth (1990)

118- Sir James Frazer – The Golden Bough (Single Volume Abridged Edition) – published by Penguin 1996

119- Naxos and the Gods: The Love Story of Dionysus and Ariadne – Article published on Naxos.gr
https://www.naxos.gr/naxos-and-the-gods-the-love-story-of-dionysus-and-ariadne/?lang=en
Ariadne – Article published on Greek Mythology.com
https://www.greekmythology.com/Myths/Mortals/Ariadne/ariadne.html

120- Zan Fraser – The Horned God of Wytches (2007 Emerald City Books)

121- Sir James Frazer – The Golden Bough (Single Volume Abridged Edition) – published by Penguin 1996

122- Zan Fraser – The Horned God of Wytches (2007 Emerald City Books)

123- Sir James Frazer – The Golden Bough (Single Volume Abridged Edition) – published by Penguin 1996

124- William Anderson – The Green Man, The Archetype of our Oneness with the Earth (1990)

125- Mari Silva – Paganism (everything from ancient Hellenic, Norse and Celtic Paganism to Heathenry, Wicca and other Modern Pagan Beliefs and Practices (2021)
https://skjalden.com/nine-realms-in-norse-mythology/

126- William Anderson – The Green Man, The Archetype of our Oneness with the Earth (1990)

127- Color, Symbology and Meaning of Green – Article published on Sensational Color.com
https://www.sensationalcolor.com/meaning-of-green/

128- Sir James Frazer – The Golden Bough (Single Volume Abridged Edition) – published by Penguin 1996

129- As 128 above

130- As 128 and 129 above

131- Helen Strudwick. The Encyclopaedia of Ancient Egypt. New York: Sterling Publishing Co., Inc. pp. 118–119 (2006).

132- Osiris - Wikipedia
https://en.wikipedia.org/wiki/Osiris#:~:text=Diodorus%20Sicul
us%20gives%20another%20version,before%20finally%20returnin
g%20to%20Egypt.
133- Plutarch (1874). Plutarch's Moralia, On Isis and Osiris, ch. 12
(link below)
https://books.google.com/books?id=VBfgAAAAMAAJ&q=plut
arch+%22queen+of+ethiopia%22+osiris+%22seventy+two%22
&pg=PA76
134- As 132 above
135- George Stanley Faber B.D - The Origin of Pagan Idolatry (Vol I,
II & III) – (London 1816)
136- As 135 above.
137- As 135 & 136 above
138- As 135, 136 and 137 above
139- As 135, 136, 137 and 138 above
140- Jacque Vallee – Passport to Magonia (Edition - 2014)
141- George Stanley Faber B.D - The Origin of Pagan Idolatry (Vol I,
II & III) – (London 1816)
142- Sir James Frazer – The Golden Bough (Single Volume Abridged
Edition) – published by Penguin 1996
143- Diana (mythology) - Wikipedia
https://en.wikipedia.org/wiki/Diana_(mythology)
144- Diana – Article published on Greek Gods and Goddesses.net
https://greekgodsandgoddesses.net/goddesses/diana/
145- Diane Purkiss – Troublesome Things; A history of Fairies and
Fairy Stories (2000 Penguin)
146- King James I – Daemonologie
Pdf version link - https://www.gutenberg.org/files/25929/25929-
pdf.pdf
147- Diane Purkiss – Troublesome Things; A history of Fairies and
Fairy Stories (2000 Penguin)
148- Sir James Frazer – The Golden Bough (Single Volume Abridged
Edition) – published by Penguin 1996
149- As 148 above
150- As 148 and 149 above
151- George Stanley Faber B.D - The Origin of Pagan Idolatry (Vol I,
II & III) – (London 1816)
152- Allen Greenfield – The Complete Cipher of the Ufonauts (2016
edition)

153- As 153 above

154- Sir James Frazer – The Golden Bough (Single Volume Abridged Edition) – published by Penguin 1996

155- Celtic Gods, Celtic Goddess – R.J. Stewart (Reprint -Cassell Illustrated – 2006)

156- AS above

157- E.A Wallis Budge - Osiris & The Egyptian Resurrection Vol II (republication, New York, 1973)

158- Allen Greenfield – The Complete Cipher of the Ufonauts (2016 edition)

159- Staff of Osiris (Kundalini / Uraeus) – Article published on Mynzahosiris.wordpress.com
https://mynzahosiris.wordpress.com/2015/07/10/staff-of-osiris-kundalini-uraeus/

160- Zan Fraser – The Horned God of Wytches (2007 Emerald City Books)

161- https://en.wikipedia.org/wiki/Diana_(mythology) (ref Plutarch Roman Questions, 3)

162- Cernunnos - Article by J. M Reinbold published on Druidry.org
https://druidry.org/resources/cernnunos

163- Eric Edwards Wordpress.com - The Green Man Phenomenon and Foliate Heads
https://ericwedwards.wordpress.com/?s=green+man

164- Zan Fraser – The Horned God of Wytches (2007 Emerald City Books)

165- The Goddess and The God – Published on Ceisiwrserith.com
http://ceisiwrserith.com/BacktotheBeginnings/GoddessandGod.htm

166- Zan Fraser – The Horned God of Wytches (2007 Emerald City Books)

167- R.J. Stewart - Celtic Gods, Celtic Goddess – (Reprint -Cassell Illustrated – 2006)

168- Zan Fraser – The Horned God of Wytches (2007 Emerald City Books)

169- As 169 above

170- As 169 & 170 above

171- Cernunnos - Article by J. M Reinbold published on Druidry.org
https://druidry.org/resources/cernnunos

172- Miranda J. Green - Dictionary of Celtic Myth and Legend

Finvarra

173- Finvarra – Article published on en-academia.com
https://en-academic.com/dic.nsf/enwiki/355132
174- Faery Mounds – Article published Faery Pool.com
http://www.faerypool.com/faery_mounds/
175- Zan Fraser – The Horned God of Wytches (2007 Emerald City Books)
176- Katharine M. Briggs (1976) A Dictionary of Fairies

Wild Hunt

177- Katharine M. Briggs – The Vanishing People – (1978 – B.T. Batsford Ltd. London)
178- Wild Hunt - Wikipedia
https://en.wikipedia.org/wiki/Wild_Hunt
179- Zan Fraser – The Horned God of Wytches (2007 Emerald City Books)
180- Katharine M. Briggs – The Vanishing People – (1978 – B.T. Batsford Ltd. London)
Dando's Dogs - Wikipedia
https://en.wikipedia.org/wiki/Dando%27s_dogs
181- Zan Fraser – The Horned God of Wytches (2007 Emerald City Books)
182- As 181 above
183- The Wild Hunt or Fairy Raed – Article by Geoff Boxell published on Geoff Boxell Tripod.com
https://geoffboxell.tripod.com/hunt.htm

Herne The Hunter

184- Zan Fraser – The Horned God of Wytches (2007 Emerald City Books)
185- Sir James Frazer – The Golden Bough (Single Volume Abridged Edition) – published by Penguin 1996
186- Herne The Hunter – Article by Gregory Wright published on Mythopedia.com
https://mythopedia.com/topics/herne-the-hunter
Beware the Ghostly Hunt - Folklore or Fact? Article by David

Nash Ford on Berkshire History.com
http://www.berkshirehistory.com/legends/herne02.html

Horned God of the Wytches

187- R.J. Stewart - Celtic Gods, Celtic Goddess – (Reprint -Cassell Illustrated – 2006)

188- Diane Purkiss – Troublesome Things; A history of Fairies and Fairy Stories (2000 Penguin)

189- Zan Fraser – The Horned God of Wytches (2007 Emerald City Books)

Hellequin/Harlequin

190- Zan Fraser – The Horned God of Wytches (2007 Emerald City Books)

191- As 189 above

The Hellish Harlequin: phantom hordes to Father Christmas – Article on Bone and Sickle.com
https://www.boneandsickle.com/?s=wild+hunt

Baphomet

192- Hans Holzer - Witches – True Encounters with Wicca, Wizards, Covens, Cults and Magick -(First published by Black Dog & Leventhal Publishers 2002)

193- George Stanley Faber B.D - The Origin of Pagan Idolatry (Vol I, II & III) – (London 1816)

194- Sir James Frazer – The Golden Bough Volume IV Adonis, Attis, Osiris (3rd Edition, London   1927)

195- Baal – on Myths and Legends.com
http://www.mythencyclopedia.com/Ar-Be/Baal.html

196- Sage of Quay Radio - Michael Joseph - 9/11 and Occult Theology (Sept 2017)
https://www.youtube.com/watch?v=DwVNI8OTDZA

Tree Worship

197- Sir James Frazer – The Golden Bough (Single Volume Abridged Edition) – published by Penguin 1996

198- Diane Purkiss – Troublesome Things; A history of Fairies and Fairy Stories (2000 Penguin)

199- Oak – Article published on Druidry.org
https://druidry.org/druid-way/teaching-and-practice/druid-tree-lore/oak

200- R.J. Stewart - Celtic Gods, Celtic Goddess – (Reprint -Cassell Illustrated – 2006)

201- Mari Silva – Paganism (everything from ancient Hellenic, Norse and Celtic Paganism to Heathenry, Wicca and other Modern Pagan Beliefs and Practices (2021)

202- R.J. Brenda Lewis - Ritual Sacrifice A Concise History (First published 2001 by Sutton Publishing Ltd)

203- R.J. Stewart - Celtic Gods, Celtic Goddess – (Reprint -Cassell Illustrated – 2006)

204- Allen Greenfield – The Complete Cipher of the Ufonauts (2016 edition)

Ritual Sacrifice & Magick

205- Sir James Frazer – The Golden Bough (Single Volume Abridged Edition) – published by Penguin 1996

206- As 205 above

207- https://www.youtube.com/watch?v=QjTkEyM_aTc
Dark Secrets: Inside Bohemian Grove – Alex Jones documentary (2000)

208- R.J. Brenda Lewis - Ritual Sacrifice A Concise History (First published 2001 by Sutton Publishing Ltd)

209- Eric Edwards Wordpress.com - The Green Man Phenomenon

210- and Foliate Heads
https://ericwedwards.wordpress.com/?s=green+man

211- Ancient Cult Of Human Skulls And Communication With The Other World – Article published on Ancient Pages.com
https://www.ancientpages.com/2019/03/21/ancient-cult-of-human-skulls-and-communication-with-other-world/

212- The Significance Of Skulls In Celtic Culture And Art – Article published on Welsh Treasure.com
https://www.welshtreasure.com/blogs/news/the-significance-of-skulls-in-celtic-culture-and-art

Mayday

213- Katharine M. Briggs – The Vanishing People – (1978 – B.T. Batsford Ltd. London)

214- Hans Holzer - Witches – True Encounters with Wicca, Wizards, Covens, Cults and Magick -(First published by Black Dog & Leventhal Publishers 2002)

215- Sir James Frazer – The Golden Bough (Single Volume Abridged Edition) – published by Penguin 1996

216- Fran and Geoff Doel – The Green Man In Britain (2001) Ebook Edition (2013)

217- As bove

218- The Believers: Cult Murders in Mexico – Article by Guy Garcia published on Rolling Stone.com
https://www.rollingstone.com/culture/culture-features/the-believers-cult-murders-in-mexico-53577/

219- Occult Crime: A Law Enforcement Primer
https://web.archive.org/web/20170213002447/https://www.ncjrs.gov/pdffiles1/Digitization/124094NCJRS.pdf

220- Stephen Young – Hunted in The Woods (2015)

221- Girl tells court of sacrifices in Epping Forest – Article published on Herald Scotland.com
https://www.heraldscotland.com/news/12549108.girl-tells-court-of-sacrifices-in-epping-forest/

222- The Last Podcast on the Left Podcast – Episodes 442,443 and 444 on Aleister Crowley

223- Hermetic Order of the Golden Dawn – Published on New World Encyclopedia
https://www.newworldencyclopedia.org/entry/Hermetic_Order_of_the_Golden_Dawn
https://branchcollective.org/?ps_articles=dennis-denisoff-the-hermetic-order-of-the-golden-dawn-1888-1901

224- Theology and Essential Tenets of Thelema
http://web.mit.edu/jrising/groups/esg/pagan/thelema.txt

The Book of Giants

225- Joseph Lumpkin - The Book of Giants: The Watchers, Nephilim, and The Book of Enoch (Kindle edition 2014)

226- Sage of Quay Radio YouTube Channel - Lost History Of Earth Volume 2:1 - #EWARANON (Oct 2021 - 90 Minutes)

https://www.youtube.com/watch?v=fNsorMrCOl0&list=PLjYSj
nO1TwG6zCP-v6qO8vqWV7KtomRrQ&index=1

227- As 226 above

228- Joseph Lumpkin - The Book of Giants: The Watchers, Nephilim,
and The Book of Enoch (Kindle edition 2014)

229- The Higherside Chats YouTube channel - Hugh Newman & Jim
Vieira | Giants of Ancient Britain, Geomancy, & Megalithic Sites
https://www.youtube.com/watch?v=rQqSVOHt07g&t=4094s

230- The Glastonbury Giant: Who Did the Mystery Bones of A Nine
Foot Skeleton Belong To? – Article by P Robinson published on
Ancient Origins.net
https://www.ancient-origins.net/artifacts-other-
artifacts/glastonbury-giant-0011444

Conclusion

231- The Three Primes of Alchemy – Article by Anne Marie
Helmenstine, Ph.D published on Thoughtsco.com
https://www.thoughtco.com/tria-prima-three-primes-of-
alchemy-603699

232- R.J. Stewart - Celtic Gods, Celtic Goddess – (Reprint -Cassell
Illustrated – 2006)

233- Triplism – Article published on Irelands Eye.com
http://www.irelandseye.com/aarticles/culture/talk/complete_celt
ic_mythology/spirits_earth_air_03.htm

Printed in Great Britain
by Amazon

42530865R00109